B I B L I C   L I A

(SACRA SCRIPTURA ANTIQUITATIBUS ORIENTALIBUS ILLUSTRATA)

44

D1707785

biblica et orientalia - 44

F. W. DOBBS-ALLSOPP

Weep, O Daughter of Zion: A Study of the City-Lament Genre in the Hebrew Bible

EDITRICE PONTIFICIO ISTITUTO BIBLICO — ROMA 1993

ISBN 88-7653-346-X

EDITRICE PONTIFICIO ISTITUTO BIBLICO
Piazza della Pilotta, 35 – 00187 Roma, Italia

To Leslie
and
in memory of my dad
Fred W. Allsopp
(Jan 11, 1934 - May 31, 1988)
and
in celebration of the birth of my son
William Charles Dobbs-Allsopp
(Feb 7, 1992)

Acknowledgements

This monograph represents a slightly revised version of my Ph.D. dissertation submitted to the Department of Near Eastern Studies of The Johns Hopkins University (1992).

In the preparation of the dissertation and throughout my graduate studies I have been fortunate to have had many good and inspiring teachers who have patiently encouraged and nurtured me. It is a great pleasure to thank them here. Foremost is Delbert R. Hillers, who served as my dissertation adviser with his usual rigor, erudition, precision, and concision, reading tirelessly through every draft and commenting perceptively and judiciously on its every aspect. His teaching and scholarship will always serve as the model for my own work. Jerrold S. Cooper served as the other main reader of the dissertation and teacher of all things Mesopotamian. His comments, particularly concerning the logic of the argument, always proved insightful, and his camaraderie has always been appreciated. Both men greatly improved my prose as well. P. Kyle McCarter, Jr., from whom I have learned much, also read portions of the dissertation and made helpful observations. I wish to express my gratitude to the remainder of the Near Eastern Studies faculty at Johns Hopkins, Betsy M. Bryan, Hans Goedicke, Samuel Iwry, Georg Krotkoff, Glenn M. Schwartz, and Raymond Westbrook, who taught me much through courses and informal conversations. I wish to also acknowledge my indebtedness to the Old Testament faculty at Princeton Theological Seminary, most especially Patrick D. Miller, Jr., J. J. M. Roberts, Katharine Doob Sakenfeld, C. Leong Seow, and Richard E. Whitaker, who first introduced me to the field of biblical and ancient Near Eastern studies, and who have continued to influence my thinking through their writings and our occasional meetings. Much of what is good in this monograph is due to all of these people.

I also want to thank Fr. James Swetnam, S.J., for his willingness to include my work in the series *Biblica et Orientalia*, and for his and his colleagues' helpful comments and suggestions. I am indebted as well to Jim Higginbotham, who kindly read through the whole manuscript, checking for grammatical and other errors.

I owe a special debt of gratitude to Dr. Anita N. Griffiths, who many years ago taught a dyslexic little boy how to use his mind. Without a doubt this remains one of the most precious gifts I have ever received. While no words can adequately express my gratefulness to Dr. Griffiths, perhaps the words in this monograph, which form coherent and meaningful sentences, paragraphs, and chapters, may serve as a partial thank you and pay tribute to her work.

Lastly, I wish to thank my family, especially my mom, who impressed upon me the value of education from a very early age, and who has continued to encourage and support my educational pursuits. She and her husband Ernest Smith, who is a welcome addition to our family, through their generous financial support have made it possible for this monograph to see the light of publication sooner rather than later. My wife Leslie is my lover and best friend, a constant source of spiritual and physical support. Nothing I do can be separated from her; she is that which makes me whole. In love and appreciation I dedicate this volume to her.

Contents

Abbreviations

The abbreviations used in this work are essentially those found in the *Journal of Biblical Literature's* "Instructions for Contributors" or *The Chicago Assyrian Dictionary*. In addition, the following abbreviations are used:

*	unattested form
✓	root
Ar.	Arabic
ASJ	*Acta Sumerologica*
c	common
C	Causative
CA	"Curse of Agade"
CLAM	*The Canonical Lamentations of Ancient Mesopotamia*, M. E. Cohen
D	Piel
Dp	D-passive (Pual)
EA	*Die El-Amarna-Tafeln*, J. A. Knudtzon
ES	Emesal
f	feminine
FM	first millennium
G	Qal (or *Grundstamm*)
Gp	G-passive
H	Hiphil
Hp	H-passive (Hophal)
HUCAS	Hebrew Union College Annual Supplements
imperf.	imperfective
impv.	imperative
K	*ketib*
KTU	*Keilalphabetischen Texte aus Ugarit*, eds. M. Dietrich, O. Loretz, and J. Sanmartin

LE	"Eridu Lament"
LN	"Nippur Lament"
ln(s).	line(s)
LSUr	"Lamentation over the Destruction of Sumer and Ur"
LU	"Lamentation over the Destruction of Ur"
LW	"Uruk Lament"
m	masculine
N	Niphil
NJV	*New Jewish Version*
NRSV	*New Revised Standard Version*
OAN	"Oracles Against the Nations"
OTM	Old Testament Message
p	plural
part.	participle
perf.	perfective
Q	*qere*
s	singular
SANE	Sources from the Ancient Near East
Syr.	Syriac (Peshitta)
Targ.	Targum
UBL	Ugaritisch-Biblische Literatur
Ug.	Ugaritic
Vulg.	Vulgate
WOC	*An Introduction to Biblical Hebrew Syntax*, B. Waltke and M. O'Connor
WS	West Semitic
YNER	Yale Near Eastern Researches

1

The Problem, History of Research, and Methodology

1. Introduction

"Alas, my city! Alas, my house!" runs the repeated plaint of Ningal in the "Lamentation over the Destruction of Ur." The "Lamentation over the Destruction of Ur" is the best known and perhaps prototypical member of a long-lived genre of laments from Mesopotamia known as city laments. These city laments vividly depict and mournfully lament the destruction of the most important cities in Mesopotamia and their chief shrines. During the past fifty years scholars have periodically recognized resemblances between this Mesopotamian genre and the biblical book of Lamentations. The significance of these resemblances, however, has been debated. Recently it has been observed that the kinds of parallels scholars have noted between Lamentations and the Mesopotamian city laments occur outside of Lamentations as well, especially in the prophetic "oracles against the nations" (=OAN). If this observation proves correct, then one might legitimately posit the existence of a native Israelite city-lament genre comparable to the one in Mesopotamia. The existence of such a genre in Israel could alter how the relationship between Lamentations and the Mesopotamian city laments is conceived.

The present study seeks to explore this possibility. Its primary goal is to establish that a native city-lament genre can be found in the Hebrew Bible. As such, the task is fairly straightforward: to call attention to a literary genre whose existence in the Hebrew Bible, until recently, has gone largely unnoticed, or at least, not fully appreciated. Proof of the city lament's presence in the Hebrew Bible is sought primarily through comparison with the Mesopotamian city laments. The methodology, therefore, is comparative in nature, and makes use of concepts from genre theory.

The study contributes to the field of biblical studies in at least three areas. By framing the question in the broader context of how the Israelite city laments relate to their Mesopotamian counterparts, it contributes to the ongoing debate over the nature of Mesopotamian influence on Lamentations. It identifies and substantiates the existence of a new genre, which has significance in its own right. Genre-recognition, literary critics argue, plays a fundamental role in the interpretation of literary texts. The process of identifying a new genre also brings with it the prospect of discovering new interpretations of passages, or at least, making the imagery in these passages more comprehensible. Thus, by uncovering evidence of a city-lament genre in Lamentations, the prophetic literature, and some of the communal laments of the Psalter, the study contributes more generally to the interpretation and exegesis of this material.

2. History of Research

S. N. Kramer is perhaps the most prominent of those scholars who positively assess the resemblances between Lamentations and the Mesopotamian laments, proposing that the city laments were the forerunners of Lamentations.[1] He has been followed in this observation by the C. J. Gadd and H.-J. Kraus, and more recently by H. L. J. Vanstiphout, Norman K. Gottwald, and Claus Westermann.[2] While Gadd

---

[1] *Sumerian Mythology* (Rev. ed. Reprint. 1961. Philadelphia: University of Pennsylvania, 1972) 14; cf. "Sumerian Literature and the Bible," in *Studia Biblica et Orientalia 3: Oriens Antiquus* (Analecta Biblica 12; Rome: Pontificio Istituto Biblico 1959) 201, n. 1; "Lamentation over the Destruction of Nippur," *EI* 9 (1969) 89.

[2] C. J. Gadd, "The Second Lamentation for Ur," in *Hebrew and Semitic Studies Presented to Godfrey Rolles Driver* (eds. D. W. Thomas and W. D. McHardy; Oxford: Clarendon, 1963) 61; H.-J. Kraus, *Klagelieder* (Threni; BKAT. 3d ed.; Neukirchen-Vluyn: Neukirchener, 1968) 9-11; H. L. J. Vanstiphout, "Een sumerische Stadsklacht uit de oudbabylonische Periode: Turmenuna of de Nippurklacht," in *Schrijvend Verleden* (ed. K. R. Veenhof; Leiden: Ex Oriente Lux, 1983) 330-41; Norman K. Gottwald, "Lamentations," in *Harper's Bible Commentary* (ed. James L. Mays; San

points out a few parallels between the "Lamentation over the Destruction of Sumer and Ur" and Lamentations, it is Kraus who puts together the most comprehensive list of parallel motifs. With regard to content and style, Vanstiphout observes that Lamentations bears some affinity with the city laments. In fact he presages the type of investigation to be conducted here when he writes, "It would be extremely interesting to investigate the history and the different formats of this genre [i.e. the city-lament genre] typologically and, maybe even, genetically in world literature."[3] Gottwald expresses some support for this notion.[4]

Westermann also argues in favor of a relationship between Lamentations and the city laments.[5] Impressed by the number of parallels between the two bodies of literature, he queries how so many commentators of Lamentations could have failed to note them. In an effort to account for these parallels, he suggests that the early experiences of the destruction of the great cities made such an impression that they began to be thought of as reflecting humanity's earliest experiences.

Among those who dispute this position, arguing that no connection exists between Lamentations and the Mesopotamian laments, are Thorkild Jacobsen, W. Rudolph, A. Weiser, O. Eissfeldt, and most especially Thomas F. McDaniel.[6] Jacobsen denies that Lamentations stands in a Sumerian literary tradition from which it derives literary patterns and phraseology. He argues that one has to first prove that the

---

Francisco: Harper & Row, 1988) 647; Claus Westermann, *Die Klagelieder* (Neukirchen-Vluyn: Neukirchener, 1990).

[3] Vanstiphout, "Stadtsklacht," 341. This writer wishes to express his gratitude to Jan Verbruggen, who kindly translated from the Dutch original of this article. The English translation is his.

[4] "Lamentations," 647.

[5] *Klagelieder*, esp. 22-31

[6] Thorkild Jacobsen, Review of *The Sumerians* by Samuel Noah Kramer, *JNES* 1 (1946) 147, n. 32; W. Rudolph, *Das Buch Ruth, Das Hohe Leid, Die Klagelieder* (KAT 17; 2d ed; Gütersloh: Mohn, 1962) 9; A. Weiser, *Klagelieder* (ATD 16; Göttingen: Vandenhoeck & Ruprecht, 1962), O. Eissfeldt, *The Old Testament: An Introduction* (trans. P. R. Ackroyd; New York: Harper & Row, 1976) 504; Thomas F. McDaniel, "The Alleged Sumerian Influence upon Lamentations," *VT* 18 (1968) 198-209.

"similarities go beyond what similar subject matter and similar situations will naturally suggest to any good poet."[7] Rudolph, Weiser, and Eissfeldt follow this lead.

In his seminal article McDaniel presents and analyzes fourteen of the closest parallel motifs (most of which are cited by either Gadd or Kraus) between Lamentations and the Sumerian city laments. For almost all of the parallels he concludes that they either result from common subject matter, are attested otherwise in biblical literature, or have a prototype in the literary motifs current in Syria-Palestine.[8] He also notes that some of the dominant themes found in the Sumerian laments, such as the "evil storm," are not found in Lamentations.[9] And finally, he argues that the geographical and chronological "gap" which separates the Sumerian city laments and the biblical book is too great to support the supposition of literary influence or dependence.[10]

Hillers in the first version of his Anchor Bible commentary on Lamentations is also skeptical about a connection with the Mesopotamian laments.[11] Nevertheless, he does point out "genuine parallels" throughout the commentary.

The inability of this group of scholars to reach a consensus[12] on the significance of the Mesopotamian data can be attributed to at least three factors. First, they cite only individual parallels and provide little extended discussion of them (McDaniel is an exception to the latter point). Second, they collect parallels from a limited number of Mesopotamian sources, mainly from the "Lamentation over the Destruction of Ur," "Lamentation over the Destruction of Sumer and Ur," and "Curse of Agade." Finally, they pose the question of Lamentations' connection to the Mesopotamian city laments too narrowly in terms of direct literary

---

[7] Review of *Sumerians*, 147, n. 32.

[8] McDaniel, "Sumerian Influence," 207.

[9] Ibid.

[10] Ibid., 209.

[11] *Lamentations* (AB 7a; Garden City: Doubleday, 1972) xxix.

[12] Cf. Norman K. Gottwald, *The Hebrew Bible -- A Socio-Literary Introduction*, (Philadelphia: Fortress, 1985) 543.

influence or dependence (esp. McDaniel). This latter preoccupation is especially regrettable.

For the most part, scholars seem to have framed this question principally in terms of *how* a single sixth century work from Israel could be influenced by a foreign literary genre. To begin with, the very assumption of literary dependence rejects the possibility of polygenesis, wherein a genre may originate independently in two different literatures,[13] and it also underestimates the notorious difficulties involved in establishing that a relationship of literary dependence exists.[14]

A hypothesis proposed by Simon Parker to explain the existence of similar speech types in a variety of distinct literary traditions may be applicable to this problem. He suggests that the common elements of a genre that transcend cultural bounds may result because "institutions and situations common to the societies in question produced similar forms of expression for similar purposes."[15] That is, a generic relationship may be posited for texts from different literary traditions without necessarily implying the literary dependence of one on the other.

However, even assuming the fact of some type of literary influence, the idea that text A must be the direct source of text B is somewhat simplistic.[16] Often the "emitter" and "receiver" of literary influence are not directly linked, but are connected by "intermediaries."[17] This supports Kramer's idea that Sumerian influence probably "penetrated the Bible through Canaanite, Hurrian, Hittite, and Akkadian literature."[18] Contrary to McDaniel, the city-lament genre continued in

---

[13] Alastair Fowler, *Kinds of Literature: An Introduction to the Theory of Genres and Modes* (Cambridge: Harvard University, 1982) 154.

[14] Tremper Longman III, *Fictional Akkadian Autobiography: A Generic and Comparative Study* (Winona Lake: Eisenbrauns, 1991) 33.

[15] Simon Parker, *The Pre-Biblical Narrative Tradition* (SBLSBS 24; Atlanta: Scholars, 1989) 62.

[16] See Parker's lucid discussion ("Some Methodological Principles in Ugaritic Philology," *MAARAV* 2/1 [1979] 16).

[17] Ulrich Weisstein, *Comparative Literature and Literary Theory* (Bloomington: Indiana University, 1973) 30.

[18] *The Sumerians: Their History, Culture, and Character* (Chicago: University of Chicago, 1963) 291.

Akkadian literature.[19] Still, one cannot rule out the possibility of more direct influence, since the city-lament genre continued in the form of Sumero-Akkadian bilinguals into the Seleucid era.[20]

Moreover, given the geographical proximity of cultural areas within the ancient Near East, one cannot discount the possibility that these Mesopotamian traditions entered the Hebrew Bible orally,[21] or that the connection between the two traditions was ongoing and mutually influential, not limited to a single place, date, or direction of borrowing.

Finally, that one cannot fix the precise avenues of literary transmission does not *a priori* invalidate the comparison with the Mesopotamian literature, as McDaniel and others seem to suggest. William W. Hallo perceptively writes:

> Modern literary criticism properly investigates literary parallels without necessarily or invariably finding the exact route by which a given idea passed from one author to another. And given the fragmentary nature of the ancient record, the answers cannot always be forthcoming.[22]

All of which stresses that past approaches have been too simplistic and perhaps a little misguided.

---

[19] McDaniel, "Sumerian Influence," 208. Cf. Jeffrey H. Tigay, Review of *Lamentations* by Delbert R. Hillers, *JNES* 35 (1976) 140; Leland E. Wilshire, "Jerusalem as the 'Servant City' in Isaiah 40-66: Reflections in the Light of Further Study of the Cuneiform Tradition," in *The Bible in the Light of Cuneiform Literature* (eds. W. W. Hallo, B. W. Jones, and G. L. Mattingly; Lewiston: Edwin Mellen, 1991) 243-47.

[20] W. C. Gwaltney, Jr., "The Biblical Book of Lamentations in the Context of Near Eastern Lament Literature," in *Scripture in Context II: More Essays on the Comparative Method* (eds. W. W. Hallo, J. C. Moyer, and L. G. Perdue; Winona Lake: Eisenbrauns, 1983) 191-211.

[21] W. G. Lambert, "A New Look at the Babylonian Background of Genesis," *JTS* n.s. 16 (1965) 300.

[22] "Compare and Contrast: The Contextual Approach to Biblical Literature," in *The Bible in the Light of Cuneiform Literature* (eds. W. W. Hallo, B. W. Jones, and G. L. Mattingly; Lewiston: Edwin Mellen, 1990) 6.

The works of W. C. Gwaltney, Jr. and Hillers address these caveats.[23] Gwaltney points out that "lineal liturgical descendants" of the city laments, the *balag* and *eršemma*, were used into the Seleucid era. Therefore, he concludes, one can no longer claim a chronological "gap" between the Mesopotamian laments and Lamentations.[24] He suggests that exile, whether in Assyria or Babylonia, provided the opportunity for Israelites to encounter the laments.[25] In addition to parallel motifs, Gwaltney cites similarities in ritual occasions, form/structure, poetic techniques, and theology.[26]

In the revised version of his commentary, Hillers fully embraces the notion of a connection between Lamentations and the Mesopotamian laments.[27] In the introduction to that work, Hillers proposes the existence of a native Israelite city-lament genre, about which he writes the following:

> A "city-lament" genre would be an abstraction made, for the sake of discussion, to refer to a common theme: the destruction of city and sanctuary, with identifiable imagery specific to this theme, and common sub-topics and poetic devices.[28]

In support of this hypothesis, he presents evidence that parallels to the Mesopotamian lament genre occur in the prophetic literature. For example, he cites passages like Amos 5:2 and Jer 48:17-18 which use *qînāh* meter, personify the nation or city as a female mourning figure, and/or contain other motifs characteristic of Mesopotamian city laments.

Gwaltney and Hillers provide a basis from which a better treatment of the question can proceed. Gwaltney greatly expands the comparative material by calling attention to the relevancy of the *balag*s and *eršemma*s, and he correctly sees the need to make comparisons

---

[23] Gwaltney, 191-211; Delbert R. Hillers, *Lamentations* (AB 7a. 2d rev. ed.; Garden City: Doubleday, 1992) 32-39.

[24] Gwaltney, 210.

[25] Ibid.; cf. Gadd, 61.

[26] Gwaltney, 205-10.

[27] *Lamentations* (2d), 35.

[28] Ibid., 36.

beyond individual motifs. However, he still continues to conceive of the connection between Lamentations and the Mesopotamian laments in terms of uni-directional cultural borrowing.

Hillers shows the way out of this dilemma. His positing of a native Israelite city-lament genre and furnishing of initial support for it raises the possibility that Lamentations and the Mesopotamian laments may be generically related. That is, if one can show that Lamentations has identifiable generic resemblances to the Mesopotamian laments and that in the Hebrew Bible these features are not unique to Lamentations, then one might legitimately suggest that both the Israelite and Mesopotamian literary traditions contained city-lament genres.

The attractiveness of this hypothesis lies in its potential to correct past scholarship's narrow focus on and simplistic understanding of literary influence and dependence, and to account for the noted resemblances and differences between Lamentations and the Mesopotamian laments. The resemblance would result primarily from the Mesopotamian and Israelite texts' generic relationship, a relationship which may have originated through any one or more of the processes outlined above. Yet assuming the existence of an Israelite city-lament genre for an extended period of time, one could reasonably suppose that other Israelite religious and literary traditions, as well as traditional Israelite imagery in general, would make their imprint on an Israelite city lament. Thus, one could expect some genuine differences with the Mesopotamian laments as well. Consequently, the biblical and Syro-Palestinian prototypes, like those cited by McDaniel, become relevant. The existence of such prototypes in and of themselves do not argue against a connection with Mesopotamia. Rather, they provide positive evidence for the existence of a native Israelite genre which over time was molded and developed in light of its own traditional stock of literary imagery.

A final word remains to be said about Hedwig Jahnow's classic study of the *Totenklage* or funeral dirge.[29] Jahnow's study remains relevant today. In this study she brings together a wealth of comparative

---

[29] *Das hebräische Leichenlied im Rahmen der Völkerdichtung* (BZAW 36; Giessen: A. Topelmann, 1923).

material to show that the funeral lament or dirge is common throughout the world. She is able to locate forms and primary motifs. She then turns to discuss the biblical exemplars of this *Gattung*. While Jahnow does not treat the Mesopotamian texts herein under review, there is no doubt that much in them bears clear resemblances to funeral dirges. For example, the characterization of the lamenting gods and goddesses, which are so prominent in the laments, owes much to the prototypical person in mourning as discussed by Jahnow. Nevertheless, it remains equally clear that the Mesopotamian laments are examples of a particular genre apart from the *Totenklage*, however much they make use of themes, motifs, etc. which may have developed in the original life situation of the *Totenklage*.

This study treats some of the same texts that Jahnow studied in her investigation. Some of the results differ fundamentally from hers, while others are more complementary. Jahnow, herself, notes that only two good examples of the *Totenklage* exist in the Hebrew Bible, Jer 38:22 and 2 Sam 3:33-34.[30] The rest reflect literary and poetic transformations of the original *Gattung*. Under the influence of Gunkel, Jahnow understands these transformations as the degeneration of a once pure form.[31] Needless to say, Gunkel's assumption that an original *Gattung* must necessarily be short and pure is no longer tenable. More to the point, however, the types of transformations adduced by Jahnow, especially the mourning of the ruination of a political entity and the personification of the city or state,[32] have forerunners already in the Mesopotamian laments. Eissfeldt, Westermann, and Hillers put forward additional reasons to doubt the usefulness of understanding Lamentations solely in terms of the funeral dirge.[33] The present study suggests that a better understanding of Lamentations and the other texts herein surveyed results from their primary classification as city laments, a genre which clearly shares or incorporates some of the motifs and themes common

---

[30] Ibid., 124-31; cf. Westermann, *Klagelieder*, 15.

[31] Jahnow, 172, etc.

[32] Ibid., 164.

[33] Eissfeldt, 501-2; Westermann, *Klagelieder*, 15-22; Hillers, *Lamentations* (2d), 32-33.

to the funeral dirge, and which may even prove to have developed from the funeral dirge.

3. Comparative Methodology

The comparative study of the Hebrew Bible in light of its broader Near Eastern background has become an accepted research practice.[34] The historian must return, as best he or she can, to the historical and cultural milieu of the artifact being studied. This writer understands the broader cultural and historical milieu of biblical literature to include "the entire Near Eastern literary milieu to the extent that it can be argued to have had any conceivable impact on the biblical formulation."[35]

In this study a detailed comparison is made with the Mesopotamian city-lament genre. By comparing the repertoire of features in the established Mesopotamian genre with similar features in various biblical materials, it can be shown whether a city-lament genre existed in Israel. That is, the Mesopotamian laments provide concrete examples of the kinds of motifs (topoi), configuration of themes, and types of structural elements one might expect to find in an Israelite city-lament genre.

Recently, Tremper Longman has conducted an investigation similar to the one envisioned here, only on a somewhat smaller scale. In the midst of his study of *Fictional Akkadian Autobiography*, Longman argues that the so-called Akkadian prophecies should more accurately be

---

[34] E.g. Shemaryahu Talmon, "The 'Comparative Method' in Biblical Interpretation -- Principles and Problems," in *Göttigen Congress Volume* (Supplements to *VT* no. 29; Leiden: E. J. Brill, 1978) 320-56; Daniel Harrington, *Interpreting the Old Testament* (Wilmington: Michael Glazier, 1981) 45-49; J. J. M. Roberts, "The Ancient Near Eastern Environment," in *The Hebrew Bible and Its Modern Interpreters* (eds. D. A. Knight and G. M. Tucker; Chico: Scholars, 1985) 75-121; "The Bible and the Literature of Antiquity: The Ancient Near East," in *Harper's Bible Commentary* (ed. James L. Mays; San Francisco: Harper & Row, 1988) 33-41; Longman, *Fictional Akkadian*, 23-36.

[35] William W. Hallo, "Biblical History in Its Near Eastern Setting: The Contextual Approach," in *Scripture in Context: Essays on the Comparative Method* (eds. C. D. Evans, W. W. Hallo, and J. B. White; Pittsburgh: Pickwick, 1980) 2; cf. Talmon, 326.

classified as apocalypses.[36] He arrives at this conclusion by comparing the generic features commonly attributed to the biblical apocalypses with those of the Akkadian prophecies. This study moves in the opposite direction, using the Mesopotamian laments as the standard for comparison.[37]

4. Survey of the Mesopotamian Laments[38]

---

[36] Longman, *Fictional Akkadian*, 163-90.

[37] While this study notes how the biblical texts under discussion compare as well as contrast with the Mesopotamian laments, the emphasis falls decidedly on the comparative aspect of the endeavor. In other words, the study presupposes that noticeable differences exist between the biblical and Mesopotamian laments. These are obvious to anyone who has read through both bodies of literature, and therefore space is not taken up with detailing every area of contrast which might exist between these texts.

Moreover, the comparison undertaken in this study has a specific goal: to establish the existence of a new genre in the Hebrew Bible. Accordingly, comparison is made with a single Mesopotamian genre, the city-lament genre. It goes without saying that some of the biblical passages treated in this study may be further enlightened by consideration of other Mesopotamian texts. In and of itself this would not invalidate the results of this study. Nevertheless, these results may need modification in light of a broader study of the relevance of the Mesopotamian literary tradition for understanding the Hebrew Bible, an endeavor which obviously cannot be undertaken here.

[38] Unless otherwise noted, this study uses the version of the Sumerian text of a given city lament as found in the standard scholarly editions: LU (Samuel N. Kramer, *Lamentation over the Destruction of Ur* [AS 12; Chicago: University of Chicago, 1940]), LSUr (Piotr Michalowski, *The Lamentation over the Destruction of Sumer and Ur* [Winona Lake: Eisenbrauns, 1989]), LE (Margaret W. Green, "The Eridu Lament," *JCS* 30 [1078] 127-67), LW (Margaret W. Green, "The Uruk Lament," *JAOS* 104 [1984] 253-79), LN (Samuel N. Kramer, "Lamentation over the Destruction of Nippur," *ASJ* 13 [1991] 1-26), and CA (Jerrold S. Cooper, *The Curse of Agade* [Baltimore: Johns Hopkins University, 1983]). All the *balags* except one have been collected by Mark E. Cohen in his two volume work *The Canonical Lamentations of Ancient Mesopotamia* (Potomac: Capital Decisions Limited, 1988), and the edition of the texts found in this work has been used here. For convenience, however, this study refers to the *balags* numerically according to their order in the Neo-Assyrian catalogue published by Sir Henry Rawlinson (*The Cuneiform Inscriptions of Western Asia* [2d ed.; 5 vols; London: British Museum, 1861-1909]; cf. Mark E. Cohen, *Sumerian*

Fortunately, others have adequately surveyed the Mesopotamian lament genre which forms the comparative basis for this study, so only a sketch of this genre is offered here.[39] The Mesopotamian city-lament

---

Hymnology: The Eršemma [HUCAS 2; Cincinnati: KTAV, 1981] 42-47; Jeremy A. Black follows a similar practice ["A-še-er Gi₆-ta, a Balag of Inana" *ASJ* 7 (1985) 11-87]). For example, *balag* 13 refers to am-e bara₂-an-na-ra "For the Bull on the Lofty Dais." A list of correspondences between the NA catalogue and Cohen (*CLAM*) has been provided in Appendix 1. This study uses Joachim Krecher's edition of é-e še àm-ša₄ (=*balag* 57 in the NA catalogue; *Sumerische Kultlyrik* [Wiesbaden: Otto Harrassowitz, 1966]). lugal dim-me-er-an-ki-a "King, God of Heaven and Earth," which does not occur in the NA catalogue, has been labeled *balag* 58 for the purposes of this study. In addition the works of Raphael Kutscher (*Oh Angry Sea (a-ab-ba hu-luh-ha): The History of a Sumerian Congregational Lament* [YNER 6; New Haven: Yale University, 1975]; *balag* 16), Black (*balag* 50), and K. Volk (*Die Balag-Komposition ÚRU ÀM-MA-IR-RA-BI* [Stuttgart: Franz Steiner, 1985]; *balag* 42) have also been consulted. For the text of the *eršemma*s, this study uses the editions in Cohen's *Sumerian Hymnology*.

　　　Furthermore, it should be made clear from the outset that the writer does not in any way consider himself a Sumerologist. The writer has been trained primarily in the fields of Biblical and Northwest Semitic studies -- it is to these fields which this study seeks to make a contribution. Sumerian was learned so that the writer could read through this material and become more sensitive to the kinds of problems one encounters when reading Sumerian texts. The translations used in this study are original, but they intentionally remain close to the broad interpretive guidelines established by the Sumerologists who have treated these texts. Since this study's primary task is to use the Mesopotamian laments as a means for establishing an Israelite lament genre, idiosyncratic interpretations of any given passage have been studiously avoided, and problematic passages have not been utilized for the purpose of comparison with the biblical material.

[39] Mark E. Cohen, *An Analysis of the Balag-Compositions to the God Enlil Copied in Babylon During the Seleucid Period* (Ann Arbor: University Microfilms, 1970) 40-55; balag-*Compositions: Sumerian Lamentation Liturgies of the Second and First Millennium B. C.* (*SANE* 1/2; Malibu: Undena, 1974) 5-15; *Sumerian Hymnology*, 1-28; *CLAM*, 11-44; Margaret W. Green, "Eridu in Sumerian Literature" (Ph. D. dissertation, University of Chicago, 1975) 277-325; Kutscher, 1-7; Cooper, *Agade*, 20-26; Gwaltney, 194-205; Vanstiphout, "Some Thoughts on Genre in Mesopotamian Literature," in *Keilschriftliche Literaturen. Ausgewählte Vorträge der XXXII. Rencontre Assyriologique Internationale. Münster, 8.-12.7.1985* (eds. K. Hecker and W. Sommerfeld; Berlin: D. Reimer, 1986) 1-11; Michalowski, *Lamentation*, 4-9.

genre consists of three distinct but related types of laments: the city lament, *balag*, and *eršemma*.[40] Most scholars employ the term "city lament" to refer to the five literary laments which describe the destruction of Sumer at the end of the Ur III period and more local calamities in the following early Isin period: the "Lament over the Destruction of Ur" (=LU), "Lament over the Destruction of Sumer and Ur" (=LSUr), "Nippur Lament" (=LN), "Eridu Lament" (=LE), and "Uruk Lament" (=LW).

These historical city laments describe the destruction of particular cities and their important shrines. They attribute the cause of this destruction to the capricious decision of the divine assembly. Once the decision is made, it is irrevocable. After the chief gods and goddesses abandon their cities and shrines, the poems narrate the onslaught of Enlil's storm, a metaphor for the military attack of the enemy. Another typical characteristic of these laments consists of the portrait of the weeping goddess who bewails the destruction of her city. No copies of these laments have been found which date later than the Old Babylonian period. Scholars usually place the *terminus ante quem* for these city laments at ca. 1925 B.C.E.[41]

The earliest examples of the *balags* and *eršemmas* date from the Old Babylonian period, and they are used continuously down into the Seleucid era. These liturgical laments retain much of the generic repertoire found in the historical city laments, but present them in a mechanical, often boring, repetitive, and unimaginative way. The various elements of the generic repertoire become generalized, often framed in

---

[40] The terminology employed in this study to refer to the city-lament genre may be somewhat confusing at first. This situation arises because the term "city lament" is both the traditional designation of the classic or literary city laments (i.e. LU, LSUr, LE, LW, and LN) and the generic designation of the entire city-lament genre (i.e. city laments, *balags*, and *eršemmas*). The writer has been unable to avoid using "city lament" with both of these senses. However, as a partial help to the reader, other distinct terms have also been used throughout the study. The classic city laments are frequently referred to as the "Sumerian city laments" or "historical city laments," whereas the city-lament genre as a whole is regularly designated by the locution "Mesopotamian laments."

[41] Cohen, *balag*, 9.

set pieces, and therefore become easily adaptable to different cities, occasions, and times. On the basis of structure, content, opportunity for development, and ritual use, Cohen demonstrates that a connection between the *balag*s and city laments is highly probable.[42] Jacobsen and Kramer also find much similarity between the city laments proper and the *balag*s.[43]

Many of the *balag*s and *eršemma*s exist in Sumero-Akkadian bilingual versions. They address an individual god. The *balag* consists of three principle elements: praise of the deity; narrative describing the destruction of the land, city, and population and the reactions of the weeping goddess; and entreaties to halt the destruction and assuage the god's anger.

The Old Babylonian *eršemma*s consist of one single literary unit. One can distinguish three kinds of subject matter in these *eršemma*s: mythological narratives, wails over catastrophes, and hymns of praise. The first millennium-*eršemma*s, while retaining the same subject matter (except for the mythological narratives which are lacking), contain as many as three separate literary units. The last of these units almost always contains near or at the end "a heart-pacification unit" in which assorted deities are enlisted to calm the angry god.[44] By the first millennium the *eršemma*s became so closely identified with the *balag*s that every *balag* was provided with a concluding *eršemma*. In this way a composite lament was formed.

Scholars believe that the Mesopotamians normally used the city laments in cultic ceremonies during the razing of the old sanctuaries, just prior to their restoration. No such single cultic setting, however, seems to adequately characterize the use of the *balag*s in the first millennium. In addition to sanctuary-razing ceremonies, they were used in *namburbi* or *namburbi*-like rituals to avert portended evil and recited regularly on fixed days of each month and during the *akītu*-festival.

---

[42] *balag*, 9-11; *CLAM*, 34-39.

[43] Jacobsen, Review of *Lamentation*, 223; and Kramer, "Nippur," 90.

[44] For details, see Cohen, *Sumerian Hymnology*, 21-22.

The cultic use of the *eršemma* in the Old Babylonian period is not well known.[45] In the first millennium it was used in conjunction with the *balag*s. In addition it seems to have been used independently of the *balag*s as a part of a fixed liturgy for certain days of the month.

5. Genre[46]

In conjunction with a comparative methodology, Hallo, Parker, John Barton, Vanstiphout, and Longman advocate a more sophisticated appreciation of the role of genre in ancient Near Eastern and biblical literature.[47] Hallo writes that "perhaps the most fruitful literary comparisons and contrasts can be drawn on the level of genre."[48] Recent work in genre theory has clarified the concept of genre and the processes which form and transform genres.[49]

---

[45] A *gala*-priest may refer to an *eršemma* in an OB Mari ritual, see Cohen, *Sumerian Hymnology*, 40-41.

[46] The discussion of genre that follows is not intended to be an exhaustive treatment of modern genre theory. Rather, it means to present an approach to genre that is well represented in the literature and apply it to ancient biblical (and Mesopotamian) literature. The discussion draws from a variety of works on genre. Fowler, Heather Dubrow (*Genre* [London: Methuen, 1984]), and Adena Rosmarin (*The Power of Genre* [Minneapolis: University of Minnesota, 1985]) contain excellent bibliographies of studies of genre not specifically cited below. Alastair Fowler's work was found to be especially helpful. For the sake of clarity and succinctness, the study often uses his terminology.

[47] William W. Hallo, "Individual Prayer in Sumerian: The Continuity of a Tradition," *JAOS* 88 (1968) 71-89; "New Moons and Sabbaths: A Case Study in the Contrastive Approach," *HUCA* 48 (1977) 1-181; "Biblical History," 1-26; "Contextual Approach," 1-30; Parker, "Principles," 7-41; John Barton, *Reading the Old Testament* (Philadelphia: Westminster, 1984); Vanstiphout, "Genre," 1-11; Tremper Longman III, "Form Criticism, Recent Developments in Genre Theory, and the Evangelical," *WTJ* 47 (1985) 46-67; *Literary Approaches to Biblical Interpretation* (Grand Rapids: Academic Books, 1987); *Fictional Akkadian*.

[48] "Contextual Approach," 8.

[49] The understanding of genre presented here is compatible with both oral and written literatures. The topic is discussed, however, in terms of written literature because the study deals explicitly with written texts. If any of the texts under discussion in this study should at some point prove to be orally transmitted or

Alastair Fowler writes that "in literature there is no creation *ex nihilo*."[50] That is, in the sense that a writer[51] draws on previously known literary conventions of one type or another, he or she does not compose a work which is completely *sui generis*. The work that avoids recourse to literary convention cannot communicate to the reader. In order for any communicative process to proceed successfully, both parties involved must share a common set of conventions or codes. Ludwig Wittgenstein likens this set of conventions to "the rules of a game" which one needs to know in order to play the game properly.[52] E. D. Hirsch, Jr. refers to it in terms of the "principle of shareability," and H. P. Grice calls it "conversational implicatures."[53] This set of regularly clustering conventions is what is meant by "genre" in literary circles.[54]

Genre comprises the set of codes and conventions which form a tacit contract between writer and reader and make literary communication possible. The writer begins with a specific genre in mind. He or she

---

originate from oral prototypes, the concept of genre as developed here would remain valid.

[50] Fowler, 156; cf. Tzvetan Todorov, *Genres in Discourse* (Cambridge: Cambridge University, 1990) 15.

[51] While the notion of writer or author or poet has changed some since antiquity -- in the ancient Near East authors were mostly anonymous figures who leaned heavily upon literary traditions and conventions (see Piotr Michalowski's observations in "Sailing to Babylon, Reading the Dark Side of the Moon," to be published in the proceedings of the 1991 William Foxwell Albright Centennial Conference) -- it does not impact significantly on the concept of genre presented in this study. That is, both modern and ancient authors depended to some extent on established generic conventions.

[52] Ludwig Wittgenstein, *Philosophical Investigations* (trans. G. E. M. Anscombe; New York: Macmillan, 1953) secs. 53-54.

[53] E. D. Hirsch, Jr., *Validity in Interpretation* (New Haven: Yale University, 1967) 31; H. P. Grice, "Logic and Conversation," in *Syntax and Semantics: Speech Acts* (Vol. 3; eds. P. Cole and J. L. Morgan; New York: Academic Books, 1975) 41-58.

[54] Cf. René Welleck and Austen Warren, *Theory of Literature* (3d ed.; New York: Harcourt, Brace, & World, 1963) 226-37; Hirsch, 68-126; Paul Hernadi, *Beyond Genre* (Ithaca: Cornell University 1972); Fowler, 20-24; Todorov, *Genres*, 13-26; M. H. Abrams, *A Glossary of Literary Terms* (5th ed.; New York: Holt, Rinehart and Winston, 1988) 72-74; Robert Alter, *The Art of Biblical Narrative* (New York: Basic Books, 1981) 47-49; Longman, *Literary Approaches*, 76-83.

may work through its generic conventions, transform or add to them, or even explode them. In other words, these conventions both constrain the writer and are constrained by him or her. Genre provides an initial frame of reference for the reader, a guide post by which the reader can begin to extract meaning from what he or she is reading. Genre establishes certain expectations on the reader's part, some of which may be satisfied, while others may not.

Knowledge of the relevant generic conventions is also crucial for the interpreter of literary texts. Hirsch makes this point quite forcibly,[55] as does Fowler, who writes, "Understanding of old literature depends on at least some knowledge of the relevant genres."[56] Closer to home, Parker, Barton, Hallo, and Longman make the same point.[57] Thus, the elucidation of the specific genres and the generic conventions which may have informed the biblical writers comprises an important and necessary research goal for biblical scholars.

Genre is typically imagined as a fixed and immutable category whose members share a certain minimum number of characteristic traits. However, upon observation genres turn out to be anything but fixed and immutable. Rosalie Colie, in her study of Renaissance genre-theory, stresses that genres, or kinds as she prefers to call them, are metastable, and that mixed forms permeate literary works.[58] The system of genres is not rigid, but rather more like "a body of almost unexpressed assumptions ... which took for granted certain basic rules of expression."[59] Elsewhere she compares genres to the "craftsman's tools" by which the craftsman creates conventional as well as more innovative works. She concludes, "Significant pieces of literature are worth more

---

[55] Hirsch, esp. 89-102; cf. Dubrow, 35-36; Fowler, 256-76; Rosmarin; John R. Shawcross, "Literary Revisionism and a Case for Genre," *Genre* 18 (1985) 413-34.

[56] Fowler, 162.

[57] Parker, "Principles," 24, 34; Barton; Hallo, "Contextual Approach," 8-9; Longman, *Fictional Akkadian*, 15-17.

[58] Rosalie L. Colie, *The Resources of Kind: Genre Theory in the Renaissance* (ed. Barbara K. Lewalski; Berkeley: University of California, 1973) 30, 76-102.

[59] Ibid., 115.

than their kind, but they are what they are in part by their inevitable kind-ness."[60]

Hirsch and Fowler appropriate Wittgenstein's ideas of "family resemblance" and "fuzzy boundaries" to describe what Fowler calls "a looser concept of genre."[61] "Family resemblance" entails the idea that members of a genre may be related to one another without all members having any characteristics in common that define the genre. That is, their relatedness and commonality is better compared to "the various resemblances between members of a family" whose "build, features, colour of eyes, gait, temperament, etc., etc., overlap and criss-cross in the same way."[62]

By extension, then, genres have degrees of membership and no clear boundaries, what Wittgenstein calls "fuzzy boundaries." Genres can be extended indefinitely presuming that the new members resemble some other members in appropriate ways. One may also establish artificial boundaries for particular purposes. The more peripheral members of a genre may concomitantly have membership in other genres.[63] This concept of fuzziness also stresses the mutual relations among genres. As Fowler observes, genres relate to one another through processes such as inclusion, mixture, antigenre inversion, and contrast.[64]

One can appropriate another concept from Wittgenstein which has relevance for understanding genres, the idea that categories have members, called prototypes, which are better examples of the category, and therefore, more or less central to it.[65] Thus, readers and critics alike judge certain members of a particular genre as constituting a better example of that genre than other members.

---

[60] Ibid., 127-28.

[61] Hirsch, 70ff.; Fowler, 40-44.

[62] Wittgenstein, sec. 67.

[63] Cf. Tzvetan Todorov, *The Fantastic: A Structural Approach to a Literary Genre* (Ithaca: Cornell University, 1973) 22.

[64] Fowler, 216, 251-55.

[65] Cf. the discussions by George Lakoff (*Women, Fire, and Dangerous Things* [Chicago: University of Chicago, 1987] 12ff.) and John R. Taylor (*Linguistic Categorization: Prototypes in Linguistic Theory* [Oxford: Clarendon, 1989] 59ff.).

Fowler conveniently explains the various operations of genre systems in general and thereby provides a helpful vocabulary or terminology for discussing them. Although no minimal list of generic characteristics suffices for determining generic membership, nevertheless, some such list of characteristic traits is necessary to speak tangibly about which works comprise a certain genre. Fowler terms such a list the "generic repertoire." "The repertoire is the whole range of potential points of resemblance that a genre may exhibit.... Every genre has a unique repertoire, from which its representatives select characteristics."[66] These characteristic features may be formal or substantive. They include themes, motifs, structure, meter, size, scale, values, mood, occasions, *mise-en-scène*, character, action, style, etc. Fowler further insists "that almost any feature, however minor, however elusive, may become genre-linked."[67]

The mode is an extension of a genre. It always has "an incomplete repertoire, a selection of the corresponding kind's features."[68] It usually lacks overall structure. Modes of one kind or genre are used to modify another genre, to provide "various effects, from overall tones to touches of local color."[69] Fowler calls this "generic modulation." He argues that generic mixture need not always involve the combination of two or more genres with their full repertoires. Rather the more common method of mixture consists of modulation. "In this way, 'the poetic convention of one style,' or genre becomes quite literally 'the poetic resource of all styles.'"[70]

Vanstiphout discusses the Mesopotamian laments in terms of these advances in genre theory.[71] He depends especially on Fowler's understanding of the life and death of a genre.[72] Vanstiphout suggests that LSUr best reflects the primary phase of the lament genre's historical

---

[66] Fowler, 55.
[67] Ibid., 72.
[68] Ibid., 107.
[69] Ibid., 191.
[70] Ibid., 191; cf. Colie, 67; Shawcross, 429-30.
[71] "Genre," 7-9.
[72] Cf. Fowler, 149-69.

development, when the generic repertoire is in the process of being assembled. The city-lament genre finds its "definitive form," he argues, in LU. Here one might more usefully speak about LU as the prototypical city lament.

According to Vanstiphout, the secondary or classical phase consists of the LE, LW, and LN. The laments of this phase supposedly were composed according to the norms established by the laments of the primary phase. However, the secondary phase may make generic contributions of its own as well.[73]

The tertiary phase, or final phase in a genre's life, "usually consists of a more or less radically new use of the formal features of the type," but at times, may even entail the death of the genre.[74] Vanstiphout argues that the historical city lament ceased with LN, but that the lament genre itself lived on in the radically new form of the "liturgical laments," the *balag*s and *eršemma*s.

While Vanstiphout's sketch of the city-lament genre accounts for the genre as it is presently known, the actual historical reality may nevertheless be more complex. The "Curse of Agade" (see below) pre-dates all the known historical city laments and already contains much of the genre's generic repertoire, suggesting that other early exemplars of the city-lament genre may have existed but have not survived into modern times.[75] Furthermore, it is not clear whether or not the historical city laments circulated contemporaneously with the *balag*s and *eršemma*s. Nonetheless, Vanstiphout's analysis has developmental significance and effectively demonstrates the advantages of analyzing the Mesopotamian laments according to recent genre theory. It explains the laments' family resemblances as well as their heterogeneity,[76] accounts for the prototypical form of LU, and provides a plausible explanation of how the *balag*s and *eršemma*s relate to the historical city laments.[77]

---

[73] Cf. Fowler, 161.

[74] Vanstiphout, "Genre," 8.

[75] The so-called "Lagash Lament" (*FAOS* 5/1: 334-37) by Uruinimgina may constitute an early 24th-century precursor of these city laments.

[76] Cf. Michalowski, *Lamentation*, 5.

[77] This last point nicely supplements Cohen's arguments; see above.

One can further illustrate how attention to genre and the way genre systems operate may potentially lead to a more meaningful understanding of individual literary texts by considering the generic affiliation of the Sumerian composition the "Curse of Agade" (=CA). Scholars have not yet precisely defined the genre to which CA belongs.[78] CA often appears in discussions of the Mesopotamian city laments, but it is not a city lament *per se*.[79] From the above discussion of genre, two alternative explanations of how CA relates to the city-lament genre suggest themselves. For the sake of convenience, the discussion draws specifically on suggestions made by Jerrold S. Cooper and Piotr Michalowski.[80]

Cooper compares and contrasts CA with the city laments and other Sumerian literary-historical texts. He believes CA shares characteristics from both of these genres. One could suggest that CA is a hybrid which has resulted from the mixing of two generic repertoires.[81] Or, perhaps more realistically, one of the contributing genres should be identified as a mode. For example, one might suppose that the author uses the literary-historical mode to modify the more dominant city-lament genre. According to this scenario, the author employs various elements taken from the city laments' generic repertoire, especially the contrast motif, and thereby signals to the audience that he intends to address the fall of Agade. By infusing his composition with a literary-historical mode, however, the author significantly alters the conventional makeup of the city lament: Agade will never again be rebuilt.

In comparing LSUr to CA, Michalowski observes that the author of LSUr uses much of the structure of CA, but reshapes it for his own purposes. He switches the accent "from guilty to innocent protagonist, from curse upon the destroyed city to a curse upon those who fulfilled the destiny pronounced by the gods and who took part in the destruction of Sumer."[82] If Michalowski is correct, then this represents an example

---

[78] See Cooper, *Agade*, 7-8.

[79] Cf. Green, "Eridu," 279-80; Kutscher, 1; Cooper, *Agade*, 20.

[80] Cooper, *Agade*, 20-28; Michalowski, *Lamentation*, 8-9.

[81] See Fowler, 183-88.

[82] Michalowski, *Lamentation*, 9.

of what Fowler describes as counterstatement or countergenre.[83] Counterstatement involves "antithetic relations within a genre."[84] Counterstatement may go beyond the limits of a single genre and eventually give rise to a countergenre or antigenre, which constitutes the antithesis of the existing genre. Fowler notes that "this contrast may take the form of rhetorical inversion, whereby dispraise is modeled on inverted praise, malediction on valediction, and so forth."[85] This seems very close to the type of "reshaping" envisioned by Michalowski.

Obviously more work would be required to prove either case, if they can be proved at all. However, their hypothetical nature notwithstanding, both examples indicate possible ways in which CA could belong peripherally to the city-lament genre and illustrate the importance of generic categories for the interpretive process.

6. A Greek Lament Genre

Margaret Alexiou identifies what she calls a "historical lament for the fall or destruction of cities" in the Greek tradition.[86] The evidence for this lament type in the classical period, unfortunately, is fragmentary. It mostly consists of formulaic structures repeating the question *where?* (e.g. "Where is your much-admired beauty, Dorian Corinth? / where is your crown of towers, where is your possessions of old?"[87]). "Nevertheless," concludes Alexiou, "the fact that this type of lament is known to have existed in several different literary forms, with some degree of similarity in formulaic structure, suggests that it may have had some kind of common basis."[88]

---

[83] Fowler, 174-79.

[84] Ibid., 174.

[85] Ibid., 175.

[86] *The Ritual Lament in Greek Tradition* (Cambridge: Cambridge University, 1974) 83-101.

[87] Ibid., 85.

[88] Ibid., 85.

The lament for cities survived into the Byzantine and modern periods. Niketas Choniatës records a lament for the destruction of Constantinople in 1453 C.E., a part of which reads as follows:

> O prolific City, once garbed in royal silk and purple and now filthy and squalid and heir to many evils, having need of true children! O City, formerly enthroned on high, striding far and wide, magnificent in comeliness and more becoming in stature; now thy luxurious garments and elegant royal veils are rent and torn; thy flashing eye has grown dark, and thou art like unto an aged furnace woman all covered with soot, and thy formerly glistening and delightful countenance is now furrowed by loose wrinkles.[89]

Another lament for Constantinople portrays Aphrodite weeping for the "fine young men" and "beautiful girls."[90] A lament over Rethymnon in 1646 C.E. presents the personified city as tearing her cheeks, beating her breasts, and pulling her hair.[91] An 1881 lament over Chios personifies the city as a female mourning figure.[92]

The relevance of these Greek laments for cities does not lie in their affinity to the biblical or Mesopotamian city laments, although this piques one's curiosity, but rather in how they relate to other Greek laments. In addition to laments for cities, Alexiou studies the ritual lament for individuals and gods and heroes in Greek tradition.[93] She concludes that all three kinds of laments share common structures, conventions, themes, formulae, etc.[94] In other words, one could say that the lament genre in Greek tradition has at least three subgenres: (1) the ritual lament for individuals, (2) the ritual lament for gods and heroes, and (3) the historical lament for fallen cities. Fowler writes that subgenres "have the common features of the kind -- external forms and all -- and, over and above these, add special substantive features."[95]

---

[89] Harry J. Magoulias (trans.), *O City of Byzantium, Annals of Niketas Choniatës* (Detroit: Wayne State University, 1984) 317.

[90] Alexiou, 89.

[91] Ibid., 91.

[92] Jahnow, 178.

[93] Alexiou, 3-51, 55-82.

[94] Ibid., 131-205.

[95] Fowler, 112.

Hence, they are formed in the opposite way of modes. In the case of the subgenres of the Greek lament, however, one cannot construe the concept of subgenre quite as narrowly as does Fowler. Nevertheless, the application of this concept remains valid because these subgenres do bear a certain family resemblance to one another, at least according to Alexiou's investigation.

The possible existence of a wider kinship relationship among the members of the Greek lament tradition holds heuristic value for the present study. The supposition that a similar relationship exists among the various kinds of laments in the Mesopotamian and Israelite traditions might claim some *a priori* plausibility. In Mesopotamia, a certain amount of overlap exists between divine laments and city laments, e.g. the portrayal of ritualistic mourning practices[96] and the motif of the weeping goddess.[97] This might also explain why the Dumuzi tradition appears frequently in some *balag*s (e.g. 42, 48, 49) and *eršemma*s (e.g. 60, 88, 97, 165) and is mixed in with city-lament imagery in an Akkadian lament.[98]

Some ritual laments for individuals (or funeral dirges) do exist in Mesopotamian literature, e.g. *Two Elegies* and *The Death of Ur-Nammu* in Sumerian[99] and Gilgamesh's lament in Akkadian.[100] Moreover, both the acts of self-demolition depicted in divine and city laments and the plaints, like "Oh, my child!" and "Oh, my father!", that appear

---

[96] Bendt Alster, "The Mythology of Mourning," *ASJ* 5 (1983) 1-16.

[97] Samuel N. Kramer, "Lisin, the Weeping Mother Goddess: A New Sumerian Lament," in *Zikir Sumim: Assyriological Studies Presented to F. R. Kraus* (eds. G. van Driel, Th. J. H. Krispun, M. Stol, and K. R. Veenhof; Leiden: E. J. Brill, 1982) 133-38; "The Weeping Goddess: Sumerian Prototypes of the Mater Dolorosa," *BA* 46 (1983) 69-80.

[98] W. G. Lambert, "A Neo-Babylonian Tammuz Lament," in *Studies in Literature from the Ancient Near East... Dedicated to Samuel Noah Kramer* (ed. Jack M. Sasson; New Haven: American Oriental Society, 1984) 211-15.

[99] Samuel N. Kramer, *Two Elegies on a Pushkin Museum Tablet: A New Sumerian Literary Genre* (Moscow: Oriental Literature Publishing House, 1960); "The Death of Ur-Nammu and his Descent to the Netherworld," *JCS* 21 (1967) 104-22.

[100] Hans-Peter Müller, "Gilgameschs Trauergesang um Enkidu und die Gattung der Totenklage," *ZA* 68 (1978) 233-50.

frequently in city laments (e.g. *balag* 10:a+113, 116) are characteristic features of funeral dirges in general.[101] Thus, the ancient Mesopotamians had some familiarity with the types of funeral dirges better known from other parts of the ancient world.

In addition to the city laments presently under discussion, the Hebrew Bible contains communal and individual laments, funeral dirges, and divine laments.[102] The communal and individual laments are related in some obvious ways, e.g. the invocation of Yahweh, motives for the lament, expressions of confidence in Yahweh's ability to help, etc. Jahnow observes that the divine lament involves the same mourning customs as the funeral dirge for individuals.[103] Parker illustrates this point quite emphatically.[104] He shows that the deaths of Baal (*KTU* 1.5.VI.8-6.I.18), Aqht (*KTU* 1.19.II.27-IV.22), and Abner (2 Sam 3) trigger a common pattern of mourning customs: lament and acts of grief, retrieval and burial of the remains, cursing of those held responsible, and additional mourning. Hillers supposes that the city-lament genre was related to, but separate from the dirges over dead individuals.[105] Thus, one might legitimately propose the existence in Israel of an overarching lamentation genre which contains the variety of subgenres identified above. The generic repertoire of this superordinate genre might consist of, among other elements, the general appearance of lamentation and wailing, the use of the contrast motif, and the repeated asking of *how long?*. Each of the subgenres, of course, would contain "special substantive features" which would distinguish them from the other subgenres. As with the Mesopotamian subgenres, however, these "special substantive features" seem more constitutive than their generic similarities.

---

[101] Cf. Jahnow, 11ff., 94ff.

[102] See Jahnow, 108-24; Burke O. Long, "The Divine Funeral Lament," *JBL* 75 (1966) 85-86; Mark E. Smith, "Jeremiah IX 9-- A Divine Lament," *VT* 37 (1987) 97-99; "Death in Jeremiah, IX, 20," *UF* 19 (1987) 289-93.

[103] Jahnow, 111.

[104] *Pre-Biblical*, 122-34.

[105] Hillers, *Lamentations* (2d), 36.

The conclusions reached in the present study are not predicated upon the actual existence of this broader lamentation genre in Mesopotamia or Israel. The hypothesis offers a heuristic model which helps to explain some of the resemblances observed among the various kinds of laments in Israel and Mesopotamia. This could be especially important for the understanding of Israelite lamentations, where the existence of a wider generic kinship might explain why scholars in the past have usually attributed city-lament features to the better known lament genres in the Hebrew Bible, e.g. the laments from the Psalter or the funeral dirge. But the model may, nevertheless, have to be modified or even discarded in light of subsequent research.

7. The Parameters and Structure of the Study

The following investigation is conducted chiefly at the generic level. That is, it focuses explicitly on the generic conventions themselves. At times the biblical writers implement a city-lament theme or motif according to its generic conventions (as established by the Mesopotamian laments), while at other times they may subvert the specific convention or use it for other purposes. While the individual poet's manipulation of these conventions is of interest and on occasion is commented upon, it is secondary to the main task of identifying and establishing the genre in question. In other words, this study aspires to be chiefly descriptive in nature, leaving the more substantive discussion of poetic artifice to another project.

Genre is understood as operating at specifically two levels of classification. At the most basic level, genre calls attention to resemblances, etc. between texts in a single literary tradition. At a more general level, genre can refer to the resemblances between texts from separate literary traditions. That is, different literary traditions may contain the same genre, and thus these genres may be said to be generically related to one another. Consider Longman's treatment of biblical and Akkadian apocalypses. If his analysis is correct, there is an apocalyptic genre in the Israelite literary tradition and an apocalyptic genre in the Akkadian literary tradition. Moreover, these genres are generically related in that they share a number of traits commonly attributed to apocalypses. Likewise, this study addresses the distinctive Israelite and Mesopotamian city-lament genres as well as these genres' generic relationship.

This study does not distinguish sharply between "literary tradition" and the individual writer, poet, or prophet. At a distance of more than two thousand years, it is often hard to determine precisely to what extent an individual poet was aware of the generic source of his materials. That is, a poet could have known what motifs and imagery to use when writing about the fall of a city without realizing their origin and function in city laments. To borrow an analogy from linguistics, this would amount to the difference between linguistic performance and linguistic competence. A native speaker of a language will be able to successfully use the language without necessarily knowing all the morphological or syntactic rules which govern it. Thus, this study does not hope to specify the nature of the Israelite poets' knowledge of the city-lament genre. Rather, its more modest goal is to determine only whether certain texts exhibit evidence of the genre, whatever level of knowledge this may represent.

A final matter of definition concerns the terms theme and motif. These are employed flexibly. Motif is roughly understood as "the frequent repetition of a significant phrase, or set description, or complex of images" that recur frequently in a work or body of literature.[106] By contrast, theme refers to a general idea which may recur in a variety of guises. Thus, the motifs of the weeping goddess, divine warrior, and Day of Yahweh are called motifs because they involve a repetition of a more or less set complex of images. On the other hand, divine abandonment and the return of the gods are labeled as themes because their presentation does not always involve a set complex of images. That is, for example, a god's abandonment of his or her temple may be reported in a variety of ways. Nonetheless, it should be stressed that this distinction between motif and theme is not meant to be rigid and is not

---

[106] Abrams, 110.

crucial to the argument of the study. Rather, it is simply intended to make clear the writer's choice of terms.[107]

The investigation that follows progresses in two principal movements. The first, consists primarily of a comparison between Lamentations and the Mesopotamian laments (Chapter Two), while the second identifies use of the Israelite city-lament mode in the Prophets and Psalms (Chapter Three). Chapter Two is designed chiefly to set out the generic repertoire of the Israelite city-lament genre, a taxonomy of the genre's most characteristic features. This is achieved by comparing and contrasting the repertoire of features commonly associated with the Mesopotamian laments with similar features found in Lamentations. To this end, the chapter is structured according to the major motifs, themes, and structural devices found in the Mesopotamian laments.[108]

The rationale for initially defining the generic repertoire only in terms of Lamentations is twofold. First, it allows one to gather a comprehensive[109] list of features common to both Lamentations and the Mesopotamian laments. Such a collection seems desirable since hitherto, scholars raised the question of the influence of the Mesopotamian laments solely in connection with the study of Lamentations. Secondly, and more importantly, Lamentations provides the best (and perhaps only) exemplar of a Israelite city lament in the Hebrew Bible. That is, if the analysis below proves convincing, one of the major streams of tradition which helped to shape the poems in Lamentations is that of an Israelite city-lament genre. Other literary genres doubtlessly helped to give Lamentations its unique character, but the city-lament genre is dominant among them. Consequently, Lamentations preserves the most complete repertoire of city-lament features in the Hebrew Bible.

---

[107] The use of motif for the "contrast motif" (and by extension the "reversal motif") simply follows the German phraseology.

[108] Cf. Green, "Eridu," 283-310; Vanstiphout, "Genre," 8; Gwaltney; John H. Walton, *Ancient Israelite Literature in its Cultural Context* (Grand Rapids: Zondervan, 1989) 162-63.

[109] The citation of Mesopotamian data, especially passages from the *balag*s and *eršemma*s, is not meant to be exhaustive, but rather comprehensive and illustrative. As a rule, however, the writer has tried to be more complete when citing close parallels.

Having established the basic shape of the generic repertoire in Chapter Two, Chapter Three proceeds in a more exegetical fashion. This chapter identifies passages in the Prophets and Psalms which contain city-lament features. The concept of generic modulation becomes relevant in this chapter. For the most part, the poets responsible for the laments in the prophetic literature and Psalter did not make use of the full generic repertoire as known from Lamentations. Instead, they used the city-lament mode to mold and shape other literary forms or types.

The final chapter summarizes the study's results and the conclusions drawn from them.[110]

---

[110] The exegetical treatment of individual biblical passages in this study is not meant to be comprehensive in nature. Rather, it is meant to address only those issues which are pertinent to the study's main thesis. To that end, the writer has consulted the major commentaries on a given text and tried to situate his discussion in light of the leading canons of interpretation.

2
The City-Lament Genre:
Lamentations and the Mesopotamian Laments

In this chapter nine major generic features attributed to the Mesopotamian city-lament genre are examined and shown to occur in Lamentations.[1] The preponderance of these features in the biblical book both substantiates the thesis that it is to be classified generically as a city lament, and goes far towards establishing the existence of such a genre in ancient Israel. At the same time, this comparison provides an initial description of the Israelite genre's generic repertoire. The following features are analyzed: subject and mood, structure and poetic technique, divine abandonment, assignment of responsibility, the divine agent of destruction, destruction, the weeping goddess, lamentation, and restoration of the city and return of the gods. To decide whether Lamentations represents an Israelite city lament similar to the Mesopotamian ones requires consideration of the generic repertoire as a whole. That is, the analysis offered in any one of the sections below may not be fully convincing when taken in isolation. What persuades, however, is the cumulative force of all nine features. In other words, the probability of classifying Lamentations as a city lament increases with the increasing number of features it shares with the Mesopotamian city laments.[2]

It should be noted that elements of the generic repertoire do not appear throughout the whole of Lamentations. Most noticeably, much of

---

[1] For identification of the Mesopotamian features, see Krecher, *Kultlyrik*, 45-51; Green, "Eridu," 277-325; Cooper, *Agade*, 20-26; Vanstiphout, "Stadtsklacht," 330-32, 338-39;"Genre," 1-11; Gwaltney, 194-205; *CLAM*, 11-44; Michalowski, *Lamentation*, 4-9.

[2] Cf. Hirsch, 179; 174.

the third chapter of Lamentations lacks any kind of city-lament features. Only the fragmentary communal lament in vv. 42-47 and the first person address in vv. 48-51 manifest evidence of the types of city-lament features noted throughout the rest of the book. This confirms what scholars have observed since Gunkel, namely that Lam 3 differs formally and substantively from the rest of the book.[3] The first person address poses no problems when understood as an address by the poet (see 2.2a below). And the presence of city-lament overtones in the fragmentary communal lament in vv. 42-47 makes sense in light of a similar use of the city-lament mode in some communal laments of the Psalter (see 3.3a-b below) and in Lam 5.[4]

1. Subject and Mood

Fowler lists subject and mood among the features which commonly become genre-linked.[5] The Mesopotamian laments and Lamentations treat a common subject matter, the destruction of cities, and their mood is generally mournful and somber. These two features by themselves are not sufficient to provide evidence for a city-lament genre.[6] However, in conjunction with other generic features, they

---

[3] For a convenient survey of scholarly opinion on the question, see Westermann, *Klagelieder*, 65-71.

[4] For the understanding of Lam 5 as a communal lament, see Hillers, *Lamentations*, 102; Westermann, *Klagelieder*, 60; see 2.2a below.

If the existence of a superordinate lamentation genre in the Hebrew Bible should prove correct, then the inclusion of an individual lament in Lamentations is not so problematic. While closer inspection reveals a lack of specific city-lament imagery in most of Lam 3, the individual lament, as a member of the superordinate lament genre, would be generically related to city laments, and thus would be considered appropriate in this context (note the positive assessment of Lam 3 by more recent commentators, e.g. Hillers, *Lamentations*, 61-64; Westermann, *Klagelieder*, 66). Moreover, the structural flexibility of city laments in general and the use of multiple points of view (see 2.2a below) allow for relatively easy incorporation of distinct forms in them.

[5] Fowler, 64-66, 67.

[6] See the comments by Jacobsen (Review of *Sumerians*, 147, n. 32) and McDaniel ("Sumerian Influence," 200-1).

become important, genre-linked features, whose presence may be incorporated into the whole picture as part of the cumulative evidence. In fact, without specific reference to the sad destruction of a city, one would probably not guess that a given text could be a city lament. Therefore, these two features are highly significant despite their more general nature.

2. Structure and Poetic Technique

Each of the Mesopotamian laments is a unique composition; no single overarching structure typifies all of them. However, they all share some characteristic structural devices and poetic techniques. Similarities between Lamentations and the Mesopotamian laments involving some of these devices and techniques has been pointed out by Gwaltney.[7] Additional evidence is presented here.

a. **Authorial Point of View**

Gwaltney notes that, like the Mesopotamian city laments,[8] Lamentations contains an interchange of speakers involving first, second, and third persons.[9] This interchange of speakers concomitantly entails a change in the authorial point of view. This ability to shift points of view gives the city laments depth, an ability to express a variety of views and feelings without seeming contradictory. It also results in a certain amount of repetition. For example, the destruction of the city is often retold from two or more points of view. The use of multiple points of view is certainly not unique to the city-lament genre. Most literary

---

[7] Gwaltney, 209.

[8] See Green, "Eridu," 288.

[9] Gwaltney, 209; cf. William F. Lanahan, "The Speaking Voice in the Book of Lamentations," *JBL* 93 (1974) 41-49; Daniel Grossberg, *Centripetal and Centrifugal Structures in Biblical Poetry* (SBL Monograph Series no. 39; Atlanta: Scholars, 1989) 88-94.

compositions make some use of this technique.[10] The generic significance lies rather in how several of the viewpoints in the Mesopotamian
laments coincide with those in Lamentations.

The poet normally assumes the role of the impartial narrator or
reporter in the Mesopotamian laments. This is evident from even the
most cursory review of the city laments, *balags*, and *eršemmas*. In the
Sumerian city laments, he narrates in third person Sumerian. The role of
reporter also constitutes the poet's primary function in Lamentations (e.g.
1:1-11b; 2:1-10; 4:1-16). In both the Mesopotamian laments and
Lamentations, the narrator is omniscient and reliable. For example, in
LW he knows what happens in the divine assembly (first *kirugu*); and
in CA 151 he knows that Enlil will destroy Agade out of revenge.[11] In
Lamentations the poet knows that Yahweh's destruction of Jerusalem is
punishment for Zion's transgressions (e.g. Lam 1:5). He reports
Yahweh's intentions (e.g. Lam 2:17) and feelings of anger (e.g. Lam 2:1-
4). The poet knows what the Daughter of Zion "remembers" (Lam 1:7a,
9a).

The poet often abandons his role as impartial narrator and stands
rather as a privileged, internal observer, who nonetheless is not actually
involved in the action; he speaks from his own "spatial level."[12] In this
role the poet directly addresses the city god/goddess (e.g. *kirugu* 8 of
LU; 5 of LN; 7 of LE (?); *balags* 4:1-14, 108-27, 171-76; 5:f+225-65,
266-77; 6:30-95; 7:b+73-85; 10:a+45-46, 49-51; 12:62-74 (FM);
25:f+109-34).[13] In the *balags* and *eršemmas* this stance becomes even
more prevalent, since, unlike the Sumerian city laments, these compositions are directed at a specific god or goddess.

In Lam 2:13-19 the poet addresses the Daughter of Zion,
describing anew the destruction. Although this speech is somewhat
comparable to the eighth *kirugu* of LU, the tenor of the two passages
differs. In LU the poet describes the city's vast ruination and asks the

---

[10] See Adele Berlin, *Poetics and Interpretation of Biblical Narrative* (Sheffield:
Almond, 1983) 43-82.

[11] See Cooper's comments (*Agade*, 248-49).

[12] See Berlin, 56, 58.

[13] Cf. Gwaltney, 209.

goddess Ningal how long she will remain away from the city. He tries to cajole her back. Most of his address embodies a variation on the divine abandonment theme. Naturally the divine abandonment theme in Lamentations focuses on Yahweh, not the Daughter of Zion. The personified city in Lamentations is the sufferer because she is abandoned by Yahweh, who is both city and national god. In LU Ningal, the city goddess, is the sufferer because she is made to abandon her city by the national gods (see 2.3 and 2.7 below).

The passages also differ because the goddess and city are distinct entities in LU, whereas the figure of personified Zion combines both goddess and city imagery in Lamentations (see 2.7 below). Thus, when the poet describes the Daughter of Zion's sad condition, he is also describing the city's plight. Although city and goddess are distinguished in LU, the city's devastation nevertheless implies the sadness of the goddess.

The poet of Lamentations ends his address to personified Zion by exhorting her to begin lamenting:

> Cry out[14] from the heart[15] to the Lord,[16]
> O wall[17] of Daughter of Zion! ·
> Cause tears to flow like a torrent
>   day and night.
> Do not give yourself relief!
>   Do not still your eyes!

---

[14] Emend MT *ṣāᶜaq* to *saᶜăqî* (G Impv. 2fs) with most commentators; see Artur Weiser, *Klagelieder* (ATD 16; Göttingen: Vandenhoeck & Ruprecht, 1962) 60; Hans-Joachim Kraus, *Klagelieder* (Threni) (BKAT; 3d ed.; Neukirchen-Vluyn: Neukirchener, 1968) 38; Wilhelm Rudolph, *Das Buch Ruth, Das Hohe Leid, Die Klagelieder* (KAT 17; 2d ed.; Gütersloh: Mohn, 1962) 220; Bertil Albrektson, *Studies in the Text and Theology of the Book of Lamentations* (Lund: CWK Gleerup, 1963) 116; Thomas F. McDaniel, "Philological Studies in Lamentations, II," *Biblica* 49 (1968) 203-4; Hillers, *Lamentations*, 39-40; Westermann, *Klagelieder*, 124.

[15] Following McDaniel ("Studies II," 203-4), the *mem* of *libbām* is understood adverbially "from the heart."

[16] See LU 145-46, 155-56 in which Ningal cries out to An and Enlil.

[17] Contrary to most commentators, MT is retained here. For a full discussion of 2:18, see pp. 89-90 below.

Start crying[18] at night,
>   at the beginning of each watch.
Pour out your heart like water
>   before the face of the Lord.
Lift up your hands to him
>   for the lives of your children.   (Lam 2:18-19)[19]

This instruction proposes to gain Yahweh's attention that he might have compassion on the city (cf. Lam 3:49-50). In this, the poet's address to the Daughter of Zion is not so very different from its counterpart in LU *kirugu* eight (and elsewhere in the Mesopotamian laments).

Speaking to the Daughter of Zion, the poet highlights the utter hopelessness of her situation. He asks:

To what may I liken[20], to what compare you,
>   O[21] Daughter of Jerusalem?
To what can I compare you, that I may comfort you,

---

[18] Here *qûmî* may be an aspectual verb indicating inceptive or ingressive action, "start crying." This interpretation is made likely by the temporal adverbial *lĕrōʾš ʾašmūrôt* lit. "at the head of watches," i.e., "at the beginning of each watch." The use of finite (or serial) complementation (where both the aspectual and main verb appear in identical finite forms) -- as opposed to non-finite complementation (where the main verb appears as an infinitive following the finite aspectual verb) -- is common in BH. However, the physical act of getting up from bed is also possible, in which case, the more traditional translation "Arise" would be preferred.

[19] All translations are the writer's unless otherwise noted.

[20] Reading *ʾeʿĕrōk* with Vulg. (*cui comparabo te*) for MT *ʾāʿîdēk* "testify," see Hillers (*Lamentations*, 39) with additional literature. Westermann aptly cites Isa 40:18 as a close parallel (*Klagelieder*, 126).

[21] The definite article in BH is often used as a vocative marker (cf. WOC 13.5.2c). But if the vocative is a function of definiteness, then one wonders why the definite article is necessary. By the normal rules of Hebrew grammar, *bat* would be considered definite without the article. Perhaps this is a hypercorrection of sorts (?). GKC lists other passages in which the definite article appears to be redundant (though most do not involve vocatives; cf. GKC 127f). Two of these passages involve titles like *bat* GN (see 2.7 below): *hāʾēl bêt-ʾēl* (Gen 31:13) and *hammelek ʾaššûr* (Isa 36:16). The LXX reads a simple vocative without a definite article: *thygater Ierousalēm*. This either gives witness to a textual tradition lacking the article or simply represents an interpretation of MT.

> Maiden, Daughter of Zion?
> For your ruin is vast as the sea --
> who can heal you?   (Lam 2:13)

This type of rhetorical question also occurs periodically in the Mesopotamian laments. In *balag* 42 the poet asks the following about the goddess Inanna:

> Who has experienced anything like what was done to the heart of the lady of
> heaven?   (c+280-81 [FM])

A similar question is put to the god Enki in LE 7:1-2. In *balag* 48 Inanna herself asks an analogous set of questions:

> As for me, the lady, who has ever been treated as I have?...
> Who has ever [experienced] bitterness as I have?...   (18-19 [FM])

Compare the latter passage to the words of the Daughter of Zion in Lam 1:12b: "Is there any pain like my pain?..."

The shift from narrator's point of view to that of the city god or goddess gives these poems a real sense of pathos. This role is filled prototypically by the city goddess (especially in the *balag*s and *eršemma*s, but note that, at least to some extent, the gods Nanna in LSUr and Enki in LE fill this same role). The shift to direct speech by the goddess usually involves a change in dialect to Emesal.[22] She protests the divine assembly's decision (e.g. Ningal in LU, *kirugu* 4, esp. lns. 145-46, 155-56); she expresses anger and outrage, sorrow and hurt through her laments (see 2.7 below); she may even address the chief god Enlil directly (*kirugu* 4 of LU) or the city god (Enki in LE, *kirugu*s 5-6; cf. *balag*s 1:60-63; 7:1-25; 8:b+58-82 [OB]; 26:38-59; 43:g+335-61; 39:a+71-89; *eršemma*s 79:29-32; 32:36-48; 171:30-38). In Lamentations personified Jerusalem occupies this role.[23] Note especially her speeches

---

[22] Cf, Green, "Eridu," 288. The *balag*s and *eršemma*s are written predominantly in Emesal. For a more extensive discussion of this dialect, see Krecher, *Kultlyrik*, 12-14; Cohen, *balag*, 32; Green, "Eridu," 288-89.

[23] Gwaltney, 209.

in Lam 1:11c-22 and 2:20-22. In the latter, a response to the poet's plea, the Daughter of Zion addresses Yahweh directly.

Occasionally, even Enlil, the chief antagonist throughout many of the Mesopotamian city laments, is given a voice (e.g. LSUr 360-70, 460-69; LW 3:2ff.; *balags* 12:d+117-30 [OB]; VAS 2 16 rev. col. v:1-15[24]; *eršemma* 171:40-45), as are other male deities who fulfill Enlil's role in the *balags* and *eršemmas* addressed to them (e.g. *balags* 3:f+187-89 [Enki]; 29:d+153-63 [Nabû]; 31:a+136-61 [Nergal]; *eršemma* 185:33-36 [Iškur]). Lamentations, however, lacks direct speech by Yahweh.

In addition Lamentations employs a point of view not as common in the Mesopotamian laments, that of the community, embodied in speeches in the first person plural (Lam 3:42-51; 4:17-20; 5) -- although the communal lament is not totally unparalleled in the Mesopotamian laments, e.g. LSUr 227-42,[25] 396-402, *balags* 12:e+161-71 (OB), 15:a+177-87.[26] However, despite the difference in point of view, Lam 5 bears certain formal resemblances to the *balags*, especially to those addressed to male deities. Both address a single deity, praise that deity, contain a narrative or complaint about the present devastation of the temple, city, or country, and make pleas to halt the destruction and assuage the god's anger.[27]

balags 5, 6, and 16 [FM] contain the basic elements common to many *balags*.

a) They each address Enlil
b) They praise Enlil (e.g. 5:1-52 [Enlil's word]; 6:1-18; 16:a+51-73, 74-98)

---

[24] *CLAM*, 266-67.

[25] This part of the text is broken and difficult to understand, but note the consistent use of the 1 cp pronominal suffix (/-enden/) throughout this section.

[26] Cf. Kraus, *Klagelieder*, 10.

[27] Cf. Cohen, *balag*, 7; Gwaltney, 206. Hallo ("Prayer," 74-75) and Roberts ("Environment," 90) recognize the *balags*' potential relevance for interpretation of the communal laments in the Psalter (see 3.3b below) and Lamentations. Neither scholar, however, is specific about what they have in mind.

  c) They describe the devastation (e.g. 5:54-100, d+165-201; 6:19-
   23, 30-42, b+214-46; 16:1-a+39).
  d) They raise up laments, e.g. *until when, how long?* (6:24-29
   [Sum. èn-šè = Akk. *adi mati*], a+107-19 [Sum.
   me-na = Akk. *mati*], c+247-57 [Sum. me-na-šè = Akk.
   adi mati]; 16:a+2 [Sum. èn-šè], 28-30 [Sum. me-na-šè],
   99-111 [Sum. me-na-šè]) and *why?* (16:c+188-95 [Sum.
   te = Akk. *minu*]).
  e) They offer a variety of pleas to Enlil, e.g. they beseech Enlil
   to look upon the destruction (5:18-19; 6:b+121-
   32) and change his mind (16:b+112-25); implore a host
   of deities to offer prayers to Enlil in order to calm his
   heart (5:f+225-65; 6:43-83, b+139-78; 16:b+126-c+57);
   and ask that Enlil not abandon the land (5:f+266-74;
   6:84-92; b+179-88; 16:c+158-66).

Lam 5 contains similar elements: a) an address to Yahweh (5:1); b)
praise of Yahweh (5:19; this section is usually prolonged in other
communal laments); c) description of destruction (5:2-18; this section is
fairly extensive for biblical laments;[28] d) lament (5:20); and e) pleas for
Yahweh to look on the destruction (5:1) and restore his people (5:21).

  But differences exist as well between the *balag*s and Lam 5. The
*balag*s are usually longer and more repetitive than biblical communal
laments. The *balag*s also contain numerous references to other deities,
especially to the lamenting city goddesses.[29]

b. **Contrast and Reversal**

  Both the Mesopotamian laments and Lamentations frequently
utilize two poetic techniques for depicting the destruction of the city. In

---

[28] See Hillers, *Lamentations*, 102.

[29] Note also that Lam 5 differs from the rest of Lamentations in that it is not an
alphabetic acrostic (see 2.2d below), does not utilize *qînāh* meter so pervasively (see
2.2d below), and conforms closely to the formal pattern of the communal lament, cf.
Hillers, *Lamentations*, 102; Westermann, *Klagelieder*, 173-74.

one, the so-called contrast motif (*Kontrastmotiv*), the poet compares the glorious past to the desolate present.[30] This technique is common to funeral dirges and laments alike.[31] Consider the following examples from the city laments:

> The house which at one time had cried like a bull was silenced.
>
>   (LSUr 315)

> The sacred box which no one had ever seen, the enemy saw.   (LSUr 442)

> The city (with) the purest *mes* -- its *mes* were changed.
> (Whose) rites were the best *mes* -- its *mes* were altered.   (LE 1:16-17)

> In the city where daylight used to shine forth -- the day darkened.
> In Eridu where the daylight used to shine forth -- the day darkened.
>
>   (LE: 1:22-23)

> Uruk, the good place, (was now) ... with dust.[32]   (LW 5:16)

> May your aristocrats,[33] who eat fine food, lie down in hunger.[34]   (CA 249)

In each of these passages, the poet explicitly compares the past with the present (also see LU 116-17, 122-23, 133, LSUr 304, 312, 313; LN 31, 32-33, 103). The contrast motif appears in Lam 1:1, 2:1b, 4:1-10,[35] and especially 4:5, "Those who ate delicacies, perish in the streets, / those who were brought up in purple, cling to trash heaps" which nicely parallels CA 249. In addition Kraus calls attention to the presence of

---

[30] Kraus, *Klagelieder*, 10-11.

[31] See Jahnow, 98-99; Kraus, *Klagelieder*, 10; Hillers, *Lamentations*, 18; Westermann, *Klagelieder*, 16.

[32] The verb is missing here but the contrast is clear: the good place (Sum. ki-du$_{10}$), Uruk, is now characterized pejoratively with the Sumerian word sahar "dust."

[33] For this translation of Sum. dumu-gi$_7$, see Cooper (*Agade*, 240) and the relevant literature cited there.

[34] For this understanding of Sum. ú-šim-e ... nú, see Cooper, *Agade*, 255; Michalowski, *Lamentation*, 96.

[35] Jahnow, 179; Westermann, *Klagelieder*, 165-66.

this motif in Lam 2:6b, 15 and 4:20.[36] Note, however, that in these verses the contrast is more implicit than explicit; the image of the glorified past (i.e. when festivals and the sabbath were observed faithfully, Jerusalem was a prestigious city, and the king signified protection) stands in contrast to present reality.

The contrast motif has a broader structural function in several of the city laments. Cooper observes that the first 54 lines of CA, which describe Agade's prosperity, contrast with the picture of destruction contained in the curse of the last 71 lines.[37] Thus, the contrast motif is employed quite literally. In LN, however, the motif seems to be employed in a reverse fashion. That is, the present state of desolation (constituting the first *kirugu* of LN) contrasts with a future state of prosperity (contained in LN *kirugu* 6-12). Obviously, these latter *kirugu* also entail an embellishment of the restoration theme found in the Mesopotamian laments (see 2.9 below).[38] Finally, Michalowski calls attention to how Ur, under threat of destruction in line 259 ("Ur, like a great triumphant bull, [bowed][39] its neck to the ground"), contrasts with the image of the once proud city in line 52 ("Ur is a great triumphant wild bull, proud of itself"), structurally indicating the extent to which the destructive storm had progressed.[40]

The second technique relates to the first. In the motif of reversal, the destruction of the city is described via a succession of literary representations depicting the reverse of the normal order of things. In this way a contrast is implicitly made with the past. That is, in presenting a description of the city's desolation, the poet assumes that his audience can supply the more normative picture with which he wants to contrast it (in some ways, the reverse of the examples brought forth by Kraus). For example, in Lam 5:8 slaves rule the people; in CA 166-67 criminals man the watch and brigands occupy the highways; and in

---

[36] *Klagelieder*, 10-11; cf. Jahnow, 179.

[37] *Agade*, 37-40.

[38] Of course the themes of divine abandonment and return of the gods are two sides of the same coin. The second is the culmination of the first.

[39] For this restoration, see the parallels cited in Cooper (*Agade*, 23).

[40] *Lamentation*, 14. Cf. LN 62, 75, and 252.

balag 42:27 (OB) a slave wields a weapon. These portraits are nonsensi-
cal unless one supplies the more normative images of life to which they
must be compared: slaves do not normally rule or wield weapons, and
criminals usually do not protect the public's well-being.

The breakdown of the family is a common reversal-image. The
father abandons his son and the mother her daughter; the husband
deserts his wife and the wife her child; the brother does not recognize
his brother or sister (LU 233-35; LSUr 12-16, 95-96; CA 216-18; LN
42, 212; *balags* 5:97-101; 6:31-33, b+133-38; 10:a+112-21; 13:f+203-15;
43:c+212-23). Other reversal-imagery includes: people no longer
fulfilling their assigned tasks (LU 361-66; LSUr 42-46, 293, 335-37,
351; LW 2:14'-16'; LN 107; *balag* 43:a+44-45); the transportation
system is not functioning normally (LU 367-68; LSUr 38-39, 323, 327-
28; CA 162, 264-65)[41]; song and singing are turned into weeping and
lamentation (LU 359-60; LN 69, 118-21; see LSUr 436-37 and compare
Lam 5:15b ["our dancing has turned to mourning."[42] Also, much of the
curse section of CA (210-81) consists of this type of imagery, and
additional but very idiosyncratic reversal imagery occur elsewhere
throughout the laments.

The reversal motif is used in Lam 1:4a-b,[43] throughout 5:8-14,
and in 5:15b.

---

[41] See Cooper, *Agade*, 26.

[42] Cf. McDaniel, "Sumerian Influence," 206; Delbert R. Hillers, *Treaty-Curses and
the Old Testament Prophets* (BibOr 16; Rome: Pontifical Biblical Institute, 1964) 57-
58.

[43] McDaniel compares this verse to LU 213-16 and concludes that the references
to gates and roads are not really parallel ("Sumerian Influence," 202). This may be so;
a connection nevertheless does exist between these texts. As McDaniel notes, in the
LU passage the poet "contrasts what used to happen in those places with what had
happened in defeat and destruction" (ibid.). Similarly, in Lam 1:4a-b the mourning
roads and languishing gates are implicitly contrasted with an earlier time when these
same roads and gates would have been filled with celebratory festival-goers.
Furthermore, both passages are concerned with the disruption of cultic functions.

c. **Focus**

A final element relevant for structural considerations in both the Mesopotamian laments and Lamentations involves focus. To account for the division between the "*balag*s of Enlil" and the "*balag*s of Inanna" in the Neo-Assyrian catalogue, Jeremy Black suggests that the "*balag*s of Enlil" "stress the destructive power of the deity or deities held responsible," while the "*balag*s of Inanna" "focus ... on the destruction wrought, especially the temple and its patron goddess."[44] This observation may apply to the Sumerian city laments as well. One notes that whenever the deity or deities held responsible for the destruction of the city (usually Enlil) come into focus, stress falls on their destructive power (e.g. *kirugu* 4 of LU; LSUr 22-26, 58-64, 72-80, 164-66; the monster in LW; LN 79-96; CA 149ff., 210ff.). On the other hand, when the poet focuses on the goddess (or the city god fulfilling this role[45]), attention turns to the destruction wrought (e.g. LU 208-51; LSUr 340-56; LN 53-78, 118-40).

This distinction also characterizes structural units in Lamentations. The focus of Lam 1:1-11b and 11c-22 falls on the Daughter of Zion. Concomitantly, these sections depict the ruination of the city: the people are exiled (1:5c, 18c), religious festivals are disrupted (1:4), the temple is profaned (1:10), and soldiers are killed (1:15). In Lam 2:1-9a, in contrast, the focus shifts to Yahweh and his destructive might: he casts down the "splendor of Israel" (2:1b), he destroys dwellings (2:2a), he cuts down the might of Israel (2:3a), he bends his bow like an enemy (2:4a), he destroys palaces and strongholds (2:5b), he breaks down his temple (2:6a), he delivers the city into the hand of the enemy (2:7b), and he breaks the bar to the city gate (2:9a).

d. **External and Metrical Structure**

Unlike the devices and techniques so far discussed, external and metrical structure are not shared by the Mesopotamian laments and

---

[44] Black, 12.

[45] Note that the division of *balag*s in the NA catalogue is not determined solely by the sex of the deity, see Black, 10-11.

Lamentations. The features that define their external structure are fundamentally different in nature. The *kirugu* forms the major structural rubric in the city laments and *balags*.[46] It seems to mark the end of individual songs in a single composition. Lamentations does not have any comparable rubric. However, the poet does shape the individual poems according to the Hebrew alphabet.[47] Lam 1, 2, and 4 are alphabetic acrostics, wherein the first line of each stanza begins with the appropriate letter of the Hebrew alphabet.[48] Although Lam 5 is not an acrostic, it consists of twenty-two lines, the number of letters in the Hebrew alphabet.

Lamentations also has metrical structure.[49] A fully convincing analysis of Hebrew metrics has not yet been forthcoming.[50] Most commentators nevertheless agree that much, though not all, of Lamentations is composed in the so-called *qînāh* meter.[51] According to Karl Budde's classic statement, *qînāh* meter consists of an unbalanced line of poetry wherein the first colon is full, while the second is shorter than normal.[52] In terms of the word count, the bi-colon usually results in a 3+2 pattern (but other unbalanced patterns often occur as well, e.g. 4+3, 4+2, etc.). One need not be bothered by deviations from these normal patterns of the *qînāh* meter, since a poem does not have to be composed

---

[46] See Green, "Eridu," 283-86; *CLAM*, 34; Gwaltney, 204.

[47] See Hillers, *Lamentations*, xxiv-xxvii; Bo Johnson, "Form and Message in Lamentations," *ZAW* 97 (1985) 58-73; Westermann, *Klagelieder*, 90-92.

[48] Lam 3 is also an alphabetic acrostic. It differs from the other three poems in that all three lines of each stanza begin with the appropriate letter of the alphabet.

[49] Fowler (61-62) discusses the relevance of meter in the make up of genres.

[50] Cf. Douglas K. Stuart, *Studies in Early Hebrew Meter* (HSM 13; Cambridge: Havard Semitic Museum, 1976); Michael O'Connor, *Hebrew Verse Structure* (Winona Lake: Eisenbrauns, 1980); James L. Kugel, *The Idea of Biblical Poetry* (New Haven: Yale University, 1981); W. G. E. Watson, *Classical Hebrew Poetry* (JSOT Supplement Series 26; Sheffield: JSOT, 1984).

[51] See Kraus, *Klagelieder*, 7-8; Rudolph, *Klagelieder*, 194-95; Hillers, *Lamentations*, xxx-xxxvii.

[52] "Das hebräische Klagelied," *ZAW* 2 (1882) 1-52.

exclusively in one meter in order for that meter to convey meaning,[53] or be genre-linked.

e. Lists

Among the remaining structural devices and poetic techniques found in the Mesopotamian laments, one deserves mention because of its general prevalence. The Mesopotamian poets often composed with lists.[54] The most prominent examples of this device are the lists of deities who abandon their shrines and cities in LU *kirugu* one and LSUr *kirugu* two. LN makes use of lists (e.g. *kirugu*s one, two, and eight); a short list appears in the curse section of CA (lns. 264-71); and *kirugu* six of LE consists of a brief list of destroyed places. This predilection for lists becomes greatly generalized in the *balag*s and *eršemma*s, accounting for the monotonous and repetitive nature of these compositions. Lamentations does not use this device, however such lists do occur in the Hebrew Bible[55] and will be relevant in the discussion below (see 3.1a.i, ii; 3.2a.i below).

In conclusion, of the structural devices and poetic techniques utilized in the Mesopotamian laments, three (multiple authorial points of view, contrast and reversal motifs, and focus) have significant parallels in Lamentations. Clearly none of these devices or techniques can be said to be more representative of one literary tradition than the other. For two, the multiple authorial points of view and focus, the significance lies in the correspondence of their employment, i.e. the poet's address to the goddess figure, the goddess' address to the deity responsible for the destruction. The use of the contrast motif (and perhaps the reversal motif as well), on the other hand, seems to be emblematic of the wider lament genre (at least in Israel).

---

[53] See Hillers, *Lamentations* (2d), 21-24.

[54] See Krecher, *Kultlyrik*, 42; Green, "Eridu," 287-88; Cooper, *Agade*, 37; Vanstiphout, "Stadtsklacht," 338.

[55] See Gottwald, *Hebrew Bible*, 100; Peter W. Coxon, "The 'List' Genre and Narrative Style in the Court Tales of Daniel," *JSOT* 35 (1986) 95-121.

3. Divine Abandonment

Bertil Albrektson shows that the people of the ancient Near East attributed the course of historical events to the actions or will of the gods.[56] Or as Albrektson puts it, they considered historical events as the proper loci for divine revelation. Human beings learned the gods' disposition by observing what happened:

> Just as unfriendly action in a man indicates that he is angry or injured, so defeats and disasters are interpreted as evidence of the anger or displeasure of the gods, and similarly success and prosperity are held to reveal their favor and mercy.[57]

The ancients exploited this way of thinking in order to interpret defeat or victory in battle. This is nowhere more apparent than in the theme of divine abandonment which pervades the literature of the ancient Near East.[58]

In mythological terms, a city can be destroyed only after its god has left. The vanquished used this theme (which includes within it the notion of divine anger) to rationalize "misfortunes suffered at the hands of an enemy."[59] A defeated people preferred to attribute their loss to the anger and subsequent abandonment of their own gods rather than to the

---

[56] *History and the Gods* (Lund: CWK Gleerup, 1967) 24-41; cf. H. W. F. Saggs, *The Encounter with the Divine in Mesopotamia and Israel* (London: Athlone, 1978) 64-92.

[57] Albrektson, *History*, 100.

[58] See Albrektson, *History*, 24-41, 98-114; Morton Cogan, *Imperialism and Religion: Assyria, Judah and Israel in the Eighth and Seventh Centuries B.C.E.* (Missoula: Scholars, 1974) 9-41; Peter Machinist, "Literature as Politics: The Tukulti-Ninurta Epic and the Bible," *CBQ* 38 (1976) 462-64; J. J. M. Roberts, "Nebuchadnezzar I's Elamite Crisis in Theological Perspective," in *Essays on the Ancient Near East in Memory of Jacob Joel Finkelstein* (ed. M. de J. Ellis; Hamden: Archon Books, 1977) 183-87; Patrick D. Miller, Jr. and J. J. M. Roberts, *The Hand of the Lord: A Reassessment of the 'Ark Narrative' of 1 Samuel* (Baltimore: Johns Hopkins University, 1977) 9-17, 41-43; Daniel I. Block, *The Gods of the Nations* (ETS Monograph Series 2; Jackson: Evangelical Theological Society, 1988) 129-61.

[59] Cogan, 11ff.; cf. Albrektson, *History*, 98-114; Miller and Roberts, 9-17.

power of the victor's gods.[60] From the conqueror's perspective, however, these themes would be recast to tell how his "gods were instrumental in predetermining the outcome of the battle."[61]

Morton Cogan shows how spoliation of divine images gave practical expression to the theme of divine abandonment.[62] Or, put another way, divine abandonment is the mythological expression of the stealing of divine images mentioned throughout Mesopotamian historical texts. From the victor's point of view, the carrying off of the enemy's divine images portrayed the superiority of the victor's own gods. The conquered deity was represented as willfully submitting to the superior power of the victor's god.[63] On the other hand, the defeated normally interpreted this same event as reflecting their own deities' willing departure, thus retaining the deities' autonomy.[64] Occasionally, however, they also shared the victor's viewpoint in that they interpreted the capture and spoliation of the divine image as constituting an involuntary act on the part of their deity. In this case, the defeated people explicitly recognized the superior might of the conqueror's deity.[65] Both the literary theme of divine abandonment and its practical expression in the spoliation of the divine image play prominent roles in the Mesopotamian laments and in Lamentations, constituting another generic link between these texts.

In LU the first *kirugu* consists of a list of city gods and goddesses who abandon their cities and shrines in response to the decision of the great gods (LU 1-39). The second *kirugu* of LSUr comprises a similar register (LSUr 115-284). In LU Ningal is described as a flying bird departing from her city (LU 237-38). The poet in his address to Ningal implores her to return to her city and scolds her for

---

[60] See Miller and Roberts, 11.

[61] Cogan, 11. Cogan points out that this recasting of the divine abandonment theme by the victors was primarily a product of the NA period (21). However, Miller and Roberts (92-93, n. 78) rightly note that such a recasting is already present in the Tukulti-Ninurta Epic, for which see Machinist (455-82, esp. 462-64).

[62] Cogan, 22-41.

[63] See Cogan, 40.

[64] Cf. Roberts, "Nebuchadnezzar," 183-87.

[65] Cf. Miller and Roberts, 41-43.

having abandoned it (LU 373-84). In LSUr Enlil exhorts Nanna to leave his city (370), and Nanna and his consort Ningal ultimately do just that (LSUr 373-76). Later, at the end of the fourth *kirugu*, when the devastation of the city has been completed, Nanna and Ningal return to Ur (LSUr 475-77a). Also, LSUr reports how some of the major deities withdraw their support from the city (LSUr 58-64).

LE reports the departure of Enki and Damgalnunna (LE 1:11-15; 5:1-2). In *kirugu* six a list similar to that found in LU and LSUr appears, only the destroyed cities and temples are said not to have been abandoned by their gods (LE 6:2'-27'). Like Ningal in LU so Enki in LE is implored to return to his city and scolded for having left it (LE 7:1-8:3a). LN briefly describes the departure of the god (LN 80-81, 89) and the return of Enlil and Ninlil (LN 208-9, 214).[66] In LW all the gods and guardian spirits abandon Uruk (LW 2:21'-26'). A version of the abandonment theme also occurs in CA in a difficult set of lines telling of Inanna's abandonment of Agade (CA 60-65). Then several of the major deities withdraw their support from Agade (CA 67-76), and Enlil retreats into his bedchamber (CA 209).[67] This same theme is quite prominent in the *balags*, especially in litanies imploring the deity not to abandon his or her city (e.g. 4:100-27; 5:f+266-77; 6:84-95, b+179-92; 16:c+158-69 [FM]). More often, however, the narrative simply assumes that the deity has abandoned the city and shrine (e.g. *balags* 1:42-45; 3:a+40, 43-44, 55-57; 4:158; 16:a+24-25 [OB]; 42:16 [OB]; 50:b+179-80). The motif also appears in *eršemma* 166.1:16-17.

The spoliation and carrying off of the divine image also appears in many of the Mesopotamian laments. LSUr tells that:

> The statues that filled the treasure house were cut down,
> Niniagara, the great stewardess, ran away from the storehouse,
> Its throne was cast down before it, she sat down in the dust.   (408-10)

CA reports how Naramsin cast down the *lahama*-figures (131-33) and plundered the shrine's treasures (134-45). In LU (275-81) Ningal mourns

---

[66] See Green, "Eridu," 304.

[67] See the discussion by Cooper (*Agade*, 21-23).

the loss of *her* possessions, i.e. Ur's treasures, as does the goddess in *balag* 10 (a+196-203). In both of these passages, the deity and the image are one. An even better example of this identification occurs in *balag* 50 where the poet describes the spoliation of the divine image almost as if it were a rape of Inanna:

> That enemy entered my dwelling-place wearing (his) shoes
> That enemy laid his unwashed hands on me
> He laid his hands on me, he frightened me[68]
> That enemy laid his hands on me, he prostrated[69] me with fright
> I was afraid, he was not afraid (of me)
> He tore my garments off me[70], he dressed his wife (in them)[71]
> That enemy cut off my lapis-lazuli, he placed it on his daughter
>
> (50:b+155-61)

The classic example of the abandonment theme in the Hebrew Bible occurs in Ezek 8:1-11:23, where Yahweh's anger with and abandonment of Jerusalem results in the city's destruction and exile of its population.[72] Miller and Roberts also call attention to how closely the capture of the ark in 1 Sam 4:11 resembles the spoliation and carrying off of divine images practiced throughout the ancient Near East.[73]

An explicit reference to the divine abandonment occurs in Lam 5:20:[74]

> Why have you forgotten us (*tiškāhēnû*) forever?
> Why abandon us (*taʿazbēnû*) for so long?

---

[68] The Sum. actually reads "you frightened me" (mu-e-de₆), but this is probably a graphic mistake for mu-un-de₆, see Black, 52.

[69] Akk. "he killed me."

[70] There is also a Sum. variant kar "to take off."

[71] Cf. *balag* 42:115 (OB).

[72] Cf. Roberts, "Nebuchadnezzar," 184-85, n. 25; Moshe Greenberg, *Ezekiel 1-20* (AB 22; Garden City: Doubleday, 1983) 196-97; Block, 150-59.

[73] Miller and Roberts, 41-43.

[74] Gwaltney, 208.

Notice that the verb √ʿāzab is also used to express Yahweh's abandonment in Ezekiel:

> Yahweh does not see us;
> Yahweh has abandoned (ʿāzab) the land.   (Ezek 8:12; cf. 9:9)[75]

McDaniel and Gwaltney call attention to the abandonment theme in Lam 2:7a:[76]

> The Lord rejected (zānah) his own altar;
>   he spurned (niʾēr) his sanctuary.

McDaniel's contention that this does not contain an exact parallel to the abandonment theme in the Mesopotamian laments seems mistaken.[77] The difference between the guilt of Jerusalem as stated in Lamentations and the innocence of the cities as proclaimed in the Mesopotamian laments has to do with a difference in the assignment of responsibility, not in the concept of abandonment (see 2.4 below).

Lam 2:3b reports that Yahweh withholds his right arm from before the enemy (cf. Ps 74:11). That is, he does not defend Jerusalem from the enemy onslaught as was his duty as divine warrior (see 2.5 below). The "right hand" commonly symbolizes the power of Yahweh as divine warrior in the Hebrew Bible (e.g. Ps 44:4). This withdrawing of military support from Jerusalem is analogous to the withdrawal of divine support found in CA and LSUr:

> Ninurta brought into his Ešumeša
> the regal insignia, the royal crown,
> the ...,[78] and the royal throne which had been given (to Agade),
> Utu took away the city's counsel,[79]

---

[75] See Block (129-61) for full discussion and relevant bibliography; cf. Roberts, "Nebuchadnezzar," 185, n. 25.

[76] McDaniel, "Sumerian Influence," 204; Gwaltney, 208.

[77] McDaniel, "Sumerian Influence," 204.

[78] Sum. ma-an-si-um designates some other unidentified symbol of royalty, see Cooper, *Agade*, 242.

[79] Lit. "words."

> Enki took away its intelligence,
> An brought up into heaven's midst
> its radiant aura that reached heaven,
> Enki tore down into Abzu
> its well-anchored holy mooring pole,[80]
> Inanna took away its weapons.   (CA 67-76)

> An frightened the dwelling of Sumer, the people were afraid,
> Enlil brought about an evil storm,[81] silence was upon the city,
> Nintu put door-locks on the storehouses of the land,[82]
> Enki stopped up the waters of the Tigris and Euphrates,
> Utu took away the pronouncements of equity and justice,
> Inanna handed over (victory in) combat and battle to a rebellious land,
> Ningirsu spilled out Sumer like milk to the dogs.   (LSUr 58-64)

Yahweh's withdrawal of military protection closely parallels that of Inanna in these two passages.[83]

The image of a depopulated Jerusalem (Lam 1:1a) perhaps contains a veiled references to Yahweh's abandonment of the city. Lam 1:1a literally contrasts Jerusalem's deserted present with a past when she "was full of people." In Isa 27:10 *bādād* carries this same connotation of desolation:

> For the fortified city lies desolate (*bādād*; *NJV*),
>   a dwelling deserted (*mĕšullāḥ*)
>   and abandoned (*neᶜĕzāb*) like the wilderness.

However, the loneliness of the city may refer more specifically to the abandonment by Yahweh, an implication of which would be the subsequent destruction of the city and abandonment and desertion by its population. A similar sentiment is related in LSUr 352-56:

---

[80] See Cooper's discussion (*Agade*, 242-43).

[81] Or "a miserable day."

[82] For the various interpretations of Sum. ama$_5$, see Michalowski, *Lamentation*, 76-78; Cooper, *Agade*, 236.

[83] Inanna herself is conceived as a divine warrior; for more about this aspect of Inanna, see Sa-Moon Kang, *Divine War in the Old Testament and in the Ancient Near East* (BZAW 177; Berlin: Walter de Gruyter, 1989) 31-36.

> Oh my father who begot me, return my city, which is all alone, to your
> charge,
> Oh Enlil, return my city, which is all alone, to your charge,
> Return my Ekišnugul, which is all alone, to your charge!
> May you bring forth offspring in Ur, may you multiply the people,
> May you bring back the *me*'s of Sumer which had been destroyed!
>
> (cf. LSUr 512)

This interpretation is supported by the image of the Daughter of Zion as a widow in Lam 1:1a. This widow imagery apparently refers to Yahweh's abandonment of Jerusalem. In Jer 51:5 Jeremiah underscores Yahweh's presence by saying that "Israel has not been widowed (ʾalmān) from his God"[84] (note the paraphrases by the *NRSV* ["Israel and Judah have not been forsaken by their God"] and the *NJV* ["For Israel and Judah were not bereft of their God"]).

Gwaltney cites Lam 2:1c, 6c, 8a, and 5:22a as additional passages that might reflect the theme of divine abandonment.[85]

The anger of Yahweh is a prominent motif in Lamentations (Lam 1:12; 2:1-3, 6; 4:11; 5:22). As noted above this motif is part and parcel of the divine abandonment theme. Lam 2:6c and 5:22 offer the best candidates where anger and abandonment may be wedded together in Lamentations:

> In his fierce anger he spurned
> king and priest.   (Lam 2:6c)

> But instead you have completely rejected us,
> you have been very angry with us.   (Lam 5:22)

One might compare Ps 74:1 and Hos 8:5 for similar language.

---

[84] MT's "and Judah" and "from Yahweh Sabaoth" are probably glosses, so William L. Holladay, *Jeremiah 2* (Hermeneia; Philadelphia: Fortress, 1989) 396.

[85] Gwaltney, 208.

4. Assignment of Responsibility

The Mesopotamian laments characteristically assign responsibility for the destruction of the cities to the decision of the divine assembly.[86] This is most explicit in the fourth *kirugu* of LU where Ningal unsuccessfully pleads with the divine assembly to change its decision. The gods take part in the decision in LSUr 22-26 and 55-57. LW pictures various pairs of gods (e.g. Enki and Ninki, Enul and Ninul, An and Enlil) consenting to the assembly's decision (1:1-13).

But An and Enlil bear most of the responsibility for the destruction. Although An is the highest ranking god in the divine assembly and the ultimate source of authority, he appears most often as a mere figure-head (*balag* 50: b+181-184 and *eršemma* 168:8-12 are notable exceptions), whereas Enlil is the active force in the assembly, the chief administrator of the divine assembly.[87] In literary terms An is a flat character, used primarily to symbolize authority. Enlil, on the other hand, is a very dynamic god who plays an active role in most of the laments (esp. in LU, LSUr, LE, LN, CA, the *balag*s and *eršemma*s addressed to him, as well as most of those addressed to goddesses). Thus, of the two, Enlil is the one ultimately responsible for proclaiming and executing the assembly's decisions; ultimate power and authority, as well as responsibility, reside with him.

After proclaiming the assembly's decision, Enlil's (and An's) word is unchangeable (LU 150-51, 160-61, 168-69; LSUr 57, 365; CA 99; LW 12:38; *balag*s 4:b+235-36; 5:58-59, 72-73, 94; 6:5-6; 10:b+237-38; 11:a+79-80; 13:a+13-14; *eršemma* 160:4-5). The word of Enlil even becomes hypostatized.[88] The destruction usually attributed to the evil storm or foreign invaders becomes associated with the simple proclamation of Enlil's word: "On that day the word was an attacking storm ... / The word of Enlil is destruction ..." (LSUr 163-64). In LW 3:27 the

---

[86] Green, "Eridu," 300-1; Vanstiphout, "Stadtsklacht," 331; Gwaltney, 202, 207; Black, 11.

[87] Cf. Thorkild Jacobsen, *Treasures of Darkness* (New Haven: Yale University, 1976) 95-98, 99-101.

[88] Cf. F. Nötscher, "Enlil," *RlA* 2 (1938) 384.

"word of Enlil" is commanded to return (Sum. gur) just like the storm in LU 111 and LSUr 483 (Sum. ggi₄). This motif becomes greatly expanded in the *balag*s, as, for example, in 9:1-17:

> The honored one of heaven, woe is his word!
> Great An, woe is his word!
> Enlil, woe is his word!
> Let me bring his word to the diviner, and that diviner will lie.
> Let me bring his word to the interpreter, and that interpreter will lie.
> His word afflicts a man with woe, that man moans.
> His word afflicts a woman with woe, that woman moans.
> As his word goes lightly, it destroys the land.
> As his word goes greatly, it destroys the house.
> His word is a covered vat, who knows what is inside it?
> His word, whose inside is unknown, whose outside ...
> His word, whose outside is unknown, whose inside ...
> His word causes men to be sick, it causes men to be weak.
> When his word floats to heaven, indeed the land becomes sick.
> When his word walks on the earth, indeed the land is broken up.
> His word is a storm which drives out five from a household of five.
> His word drives out ten from a household of ten.
>> (cf. *balag*s 5:1-52, b+142-53; 8:1-12 [FM], a+39-57 [OB]; 9:c+137-53; 12:1-13, 19-28 [OB]; 13:a+28-45; 29:c+43-64; 31:a+50-67)

Typically, no fault is found with the city, its ruler, its inhabitants, or its gods. The divine act is arbitrary. In LSUr 366-69 Enlil explains Ur's destruction to Nanna by noting that Ur was not given kingship eternally. This emphasis on the city's guiltlessness remains characteristic of the *balag*s as well.[89] In CA although the initial abandonment of the city is arbitrary, the curse and destruction of Agade is caused by Naramsin's sacrilege (CA 151, 212-14).

In Lamentations the divine act is not arbitrary. Rather, it is motivated by human transgression. Gwaltney correctly recognizes that Yahweh's wrath, resulting in the destruction of Jerusalem, is justified by Israel's sin.[90] Throughout the first chapter the poet recognizes that the

---

[89] See Black, 11.
[90] Gwaltney, 208-9.

devastation and human tragedy, exemplified in the figure of personified Jerusalem, resulted partially from human transgressions (1:5b, 14a[91], 22b [$pš^c$]; 8a [$ht^?$]; 18a, 20b[92] [mrh]). Foremost among the Daughter of Zion's crimes was breach of covenant. Heb. $pš^c$ often signifies political revolt or rebellion against an overlord.[93] In addition Hillers and Albrektson point to a number of passages in Lamentations whose imagery recalls curses commonly associated with treaty-violations, e.g. 1:3, 5, 8, 9, 2:20, 3:45, 4:3-4, 10, 16, 5:12, 18.[94]

Elsewhere, the people in general confess their crimes (3:42; 5:16). The community's leadership must bear its share of the guilt as well: prophets (2:14a; 4:13), priests (4:13), and ancestors (5:7). As seen above the assignment of human guilt has a partial precedent in CA. But clearly the nature of guilt in Lamentations is characteristically Israelite. As Gottwald correctly stresses, the poet of Lamentations has taken over the prophetic concept of sin.[95]

While Lamentations unquestionably acknowledges human sin, Iain Provan is correct in stressing that this is not done in a wholehearted way.[96] In fact from a reading of Lamentations, one could even gain the impression that the sin motif is almost perfunctory in nature. There is never any great specificity as to the nature of the sin involved.[97] This is in marked contrast to the great detail in which the destruction of the city and the suffering of the people is depicted. Moreover, the poem

---

[91] The text here is difficult. Some commentators emend in one fashion or another, e.g. Hillers, *Lamentations*, 11-12; Westermann, *Klagelieder*, 102. Consequently, the reference to transgressions here is debatable.

[92] C. L. Seow questions MT's *kî mārô mārîtî* "for I have been very rebellious" ("A Textual Note on Lamentations 1:20," *CBQ* 47 [1985] 416-19). On the basis of the Vulg., Seow suggests reading *kî mārô mārôtî* "how bitter I am!" This reading does seem to correspond better to the verse's imagery.

[93] Hillers, *Lamentations*, 22.

[94] Hillers, *Lamentations*, 21-22, 24, 87-88, 89, 105; Albrektson, *Studies*, 231-37. See Hillers, *Treaty-Curses*, for a more general treatment of parallels to treaty-curses in the Hebrew Bible.

[95] *Studies in the Book of Lamentations* (London: SCM, 1954) 51, 70.

[96] *Lamentations* (NCBC; Grand Rapids: William B. Eerdmans, 1991) 23.

[97] Cf. Gottwald, *Studies*, 68.

implicitly and explicitly questions the appropriateness and degree of Yahweh's punishment (Lam 1:9c, 11c, 12; 2:20-22; 4:6; 5:1, 20, 22), suggesting a not very repentant point of view. In actuality, however, the poet uses the "orthodox" view of Jerusalem's destruction and the people's suffering as resulting from the punishment of Yahweh for sin as a sort of foil to point up the injustice of the situation no matter what the cause. The poem derives much of its pathos from this protest. With this view in mind, Gottwald correctly compares Lamentations treatment of the problem of suffering to that of Job.[98] Here, then, perhaps one can see something of the poet's creative manipulation of the genre as he molds it to his own purpose.

5. The Divine Agent of Destruction

Throughout the Mesopotamian laments the destructive agent *par excellence* is the storm which ravages the city and the surrounding country-side. McDaniel argues that if some type of relationship existed between Lamentations and the Mesopotamian laments one would expect to see some literal reflex of the storm imagery in the biblical book.[99] That is, McDaniel expects to find a literal reflection of the violent storm in Lamentations. He counts the absence of such a reflection in Lamentations as evidence that no connection exists between Lamentations and the historical city laments. While McDaniel's main point seems true enough -- one should expect to find some counterpart of the storm in Lamentations -- his failure to note the connection between the storm and the god Enlil has kept him from recognizing the reflex in Lamentations, where however, it is functional in nature. In so far as the storm in the Mesopotamian laments is connected prototypically with Enlil, it would be very odd indeed to find a literal reflection of the storm in Lamentations; one would not expect Enlil imagery to show up verbatim in the Hebrew Bible. The functional equivalent of Enlil and the storm in Lamentations is Yahweh, the divine warrior who goes into battle on the Day of Yahweh.

---

[98] *Studies*, 48.
[99] "Sumerian Influence," 207.

Thus, one may agree with McDaniel when he writes that the divine use of fire in Lam 1:13a and LU 259-60 "are only superficially related."[100] Indeed, "there is no need to go all the way to Sumer to find a literary parallel or prototype" for Yahweh's use of fire as a divine instrument.[101] What is significant, however, is that, in the context of city laments, the two fire motifs are functional equivalents. The motif is characteristic of both Yahweh and Enlil; both deities are storm gods of sorts. Other such motifs might also bear superficial resemblances. The Israelite poet placed Yahweh in the role filled prototypically by Enlil in the Mesopotamian city laments.[102] He did not have to import Enlil imagery into his work, because he could make use of his own traditional stock of imagery about Yahweh. Thus, the divine agent of destruction constitutes a fifth generic feature linking Lamentations to the Mesopotamian laments.

More than any other god, Enlil may be considered as the chief antagonist in the Mesopotamian laments. As noted above, he shoulders much of the responsibility for the divine assembly's decision to destroy the cities of Sumer. He also has the task of carrying out the council's decisions by invoking the evil storm (e.g. LU 173; LW 3:2-3) and sending an enemy invasion. As F. Nötscher and Jacobsen note, the storm was both beneficial and harmful to humanity.[103] Some myths emphasize its beneficial effects,[104] while the laments highlight its destructive element. LU 175-76 tells how Enlil takes away the good storm and brings the evil storm in its place (cf. LN 96). The storm ravages the city and the surrounding country-side, indiscriminately killing everything in its path (cf. LU 171-204, 391-415; LE 1:5-10, 19-24; LN 96-107; *balag*s 5:1-12; 9:c+156, 162; 11:a+93-97, 109-19, 12:b+93-101 [OB], a+99-108 [FM]; 13:a+28-45; 43:1-a+57).

---

[100] "Sumerian Influence," 202; cf. Kraus, *Klagelieder*, 11.

[101] McDaniel, "Sumerian Influence," 202.

[102] Gwaltney implies the same thing by comparing Enlil as warrior and Yahweh as warrior (206, 208).

[103] F. Nötscher, *Enlil in Sumer und Akkad* (Hannover: H. Lafaire, 1927); "Enlil," 382-87; Jacobsen, *Treasures*, 98-104.

[104] See Jacobsen, *Treasures*, 99.

The storm may have taken on a life of its own in the laments (esp. in the *balags*), but it nevertheless has its origins in its association with Enlil. This is confirmed by the presence of another instrument associated primarily with Enlil, the pickaxe (Sum. ^{giš}al = Akk. *allu*). The pickaxe, as a counterpart to the spring wind and rains, works the soft earth to prepare for the planting and harvest. This beneficial use of the pickaxe is captured nicely in the "Creation of the Pickaxe."[105] But consider how this use of the pickaxe gets turned around in the laments; just as the storm can symbolize destructive forces, so too can the pickaxe. Instead of working the fertile fields (e.g. LSUr 42), throughout the laments the pickaxe rakes cities into ruins (LU 272; LSUr 80b, 264, 346) and picks apart temples (LU 245, 258, 340; LN 98; CA 125). Thus, the pickaxe and the storm are ultimately associated with Enlil, and are appropriate metaphors for the forces destroying the city.

An enemy invasion constitutes the other principal means of destruction in the city laments. Enlil sends various enemies against Sumer: the Subarians[106] and Elamites (LU 244; LSUr 33; LE 4:10), Elamites (LSUr 166, 254, 257, 261), and Gutians (LSUr 75, 146, 230; LW 4:11; CA 155, 164). Whatever one may deduce about the historicity of these enemies in the laments,[107] their invasion is indisputably a literary motif, analogous to that of the evil storm, symbolizing the destruction of Sumer.[108] As such, storm and invasion imagery become mixed, and the storm sometimes seems to serve as the chief metaphor for the foreign invasion initiated by Enlil.[109] This is most apparent in LSUr 72-84:

This is what Enlil, the shepherd of the black-headed people did:

---

[105] Samuel N. Kramer, *Sumerian Mythology* (Rev. ed. Reprint 1961; Philadelphia: University of Pennsylvania, 1972) 53.

[106] For the equation LÚ.SU = *šimaški*, see Michalowski (*Lamentation*, 73-74), with relevant literature.

[107] E.g. H. L. J. Vanstiphout, "The Death of an Era: The Great Mortality in the Sumerian City Laments," in *Death in Mesopotamia* (XXVI Recontre assyriologique internationale; ed. Bendt Alster; Copenhagen: Akademisk Forlag, 1980) 83-89.

[108] Green, "Eridu," 301; Michalowski, *Lamentation*, 9, n. 49.

[109] Cf. Cooper, *Agade*, 23.

Enlil, to destroy the faithful house, to decimate the faithful man,
To set the evil eye on the son of the faithful man, the first-born,
On that day, Enlil brought the Guti out from the mountains.
Their coming was the flood of Enlil that cannot be withstood,
The great storm of the plain filled the plain, it went before them,
The wide plain was destroyed, no one passed by there.
...

On that bloody day, mouths were crushed, heads were crashed,
The storm was a harrow coming from above, the city was struck by a pickaxe.
On that day, heaven rumbled, earth trembled, the storm never slept,[110]
The heavens were darkened, they were covered by a shadow,...
The sun lay down at the horizon, the dust passed over the mountains,
The moon lay at the zenith, the people were afraid.

(cf. CA 149-61; LW 4:4-12)

The combination of motifs for destruction goes one step further in LW. In LW the gods fashion a monster to destroy Sumer (LW, *kirugu* 1). But the monster must be invoked by Enlil (LW 3:2-3) and imbued with storm imagery (LW 3:4-12). This then gives way to a blend of enemy and storm imagery in *kirugus* four and five.

Although the enemy invasion does not play as prominent a role in the *balags* and *eršemmas*, it nevertheless is present throughout these works.[111]

Enlil, above all others, bears responsibility for the destruction, and is blamed explicitly in the texts (e.g. LU 203, 257-60; LSUr 72, 175-77, 261, 296-99; LN 89-96; *balags* 4:b+253-56; 5:59-60; 6:19-23, 30; 50:b+177-80), especially by the city goddess (e.g. *balags* 5:b+155-62; 10:a+30-36; 43:c+224, d+269-77; 50:b+181-84, 224-28.[112] The various city gods petition Enlil to stop the destruction and devastation.

---

[110] For understanding Sum. igi ... lim as a variant to igi ... lib, see Michalowski, *Lamentation*, 79-80.

[111] Cf. "Index of Sumerian Terms" in *CLAM*, s.v. kur$_2$. Also note the many passages from the *balags* and *eršemmas* cited throughout this study which refer to the invading enemy. The trend away from naming specific enemies begins already in LN, where the enemies are only referred to by (lú) kur$_2$ (LN 64, 95, 155, 159, 169) or (lú) erim$_2$ (LN 136, 266, 302).

[112] Cf. Cohen, *Sumerian Hymnology*, 20; *CLAM*, 15; Gwaltney, 202, 206; Krecher, *Kultlyrik*, 47.

Ningal approaches the entire assembly in the fourth *kirugu* of LU, but she intends her appeal especially for An and Enlil. In LSUr Nanna twice asks Enlil to halt the destruction (LSUr 340-56, 449-58). In the *balag*s and *eršemma*s Inanna (*balag* 8, *eršemma* 32), Nergal (*balag* 31), Ninisina (*balag* 43, *eršemma* 171), and Ninurta (*balag* 9) all approach Enlil.[113]

Throughout the *balag*s and *eršemma*s the plea for Enlil to look upon the destruction he has wrought resounds frequently (e.g. *balag* 16:a+67-71 [OB]; cf. 5:108-19, 120; 6:25, b+121-32, 193-209; 10:a+52-67; 13:c+119-22, CT 42 26: 1-2;[114] 16:c+196-99 [FM]; *eršemma* 1.1:1ff.).[115] Of course the expectation is that Enlil, being so moved by the sight of the destruction, will halt the onslaught. This motif seems related more generally to the notion that Enlil's look alone can determine the fate of Sumer. His frown (CA 1; cf. LSUr 22; *balag* 42:24 [OB; An]) or evil gaze (LE 1:26, 6:4; cf. LN 71, 84) heralds the downfall of Sumer, whereas to look benevolently implies good things for those whom he beholds (LSUr 23; LW 1:19; LN 233; CA 152; cf. LU 431-32 [Nanna]; LW 12:31 [An]; LN 269 [the great gods?]).[116]

While this antagonistic role is filled prototypically by Enlil throughout the genre, other gods on occasion share or appropriate it. In the *balag*s and *eršemma*s, the specific god addressed by the poet will often take over motifs associated originally with Enlil. For example, the set piece characterizing Enlil's word quoted above is altered by simply inserting the name of other gods in the appropriate place. In *balag* 31:a+50-67, addressed to Nergal, the first thirteen lines correspond exactly to *balag* 9:4-16. The fourteenth line is changed from a neutral "*His [Enlil's] word* drives out ten from a household of ten" (9:17) to "*The hero, Nergal,* drives out ten from the household of ten" (31:a+63; cf. *balag*s 3:c+89-109; 25:1-a+26; 26:61-97; 29:c+43-64, 65-81; SBH 7:37-57[117]). Of course, when these other gods take on Enlil's role, the

---

[113] Cf. Cohen, *balag*, 16-30.

[114] *CLAM*, 339-41.

[115] Cf. Wilshire, 243.

[116] Cf. Cooper, *Agade*, 235.

[117] *CLAM*, 526ff.

poets will make use of epithets, motifs, etc. that are specifically associated with them as well.

Many passages in the *balag*s involve the assimilation of a larger group of gods to a single god (usually Enlil), a practice found elsewhere in Mesopotamian literature.[118] For example, as expected the preface to the set piece in *balag* 9:4-17 bewails the word of An and Enlil (9:1-3). In *balag* 5, however, a list of other gods (5:29-34) is appended to An and Enlil (5:25-28; cf. *balag*s 5:1-10; 10:a+52-67, 84-90; 13:b+47-59, f+166-92, 217-46; 16:a+99-111 [FM]).

In *eršemma*s 23.1, 168, and 184, Enlil charges his son Iškur to harness the storm and punish the rebellious lands. But the ultimate responsibility still resides with Enlil.

Turning to Lamentations, one finds that Yahweh fulfills many of the same roles associated with Enlil in the Mesopotamian laments. Analogous to the active role played by Enlil in the Mesopotamian divine assembly, Yahweh presides over the divine assembly in Israel (e.g. 1 Kgs 22:19-23; Ps 82; Isa 6:1-12). This aspect of Yahweh has been most often compared to that of El in the Ugaritic texts.[119] In the Ugaritic texts El, in his capacity as head of the assembly of the gods, makes his will known through his word, which, "in effect," is "the judgment or decision of the divine council":[120] "Your word (*thmk*), O El, is wise, / your wisdom is eternal, / a favorable life is your word (*thmk*)" (*KTU* 1.4.IV.41-44). Likewise, Yahweh's word is sure (e.g. Ps 33:4) and unchangeable (e.g. Num 23:19; Jer 4:28; Ezek 12:25; Isa 40:8; Lam 3:37, 38).[121] By it the world is created (Ps 33:6-9). Yahweh's word is

---

[118] See W. G. Lambert, "The Historical Development of the Mesopotamian Pantheon: A Study in Sophisticated Polytheism," in *Unity and Diversity* (eds. H. Goedicke and J. J. M. Roberts; Baltimore: Johns Hopkins University, 1975) 197-99.

[119] See Frank Moore Cross, *Canaanite Myth and Hebrew Epic* (Cambridge: Harvard University, 1973) 186-90; Patrick D. Miller, Jr., *The Divine Warrior in Early Israel* (Cambridge: Harvard University, 1973) 12-23, 66-74.

[120] Cross, 177.

[121] Especially compare the conception in Num 23:19 ("Does he [God] say and not do, speak and not accomplish it?") with a statement said of Enlil in *balag* 16:a+32 (FM) ("That which you promised [Sum. du$_{11}$/dug$_4$ = Akk. *qabû*], you have accomplished it [Sum. sá ... du$_{11}$/dug$_4$]").

powerful (Ps 147:15-19). Albrektson demonstrates that this motif of the divine word, so characteristic of Enlil, El, and Yahweh, is common throughout the ancient Near East.[122]

Reflexes of the divine-word motif occur in Lamentations, in particular Lam 1:21c ("Oh bring on[123] the day which you proclaimed (qārāʾtā)"), 2:17a ("Yahweh has done what he planned (zāmām), he has accomplished his word (ʾemrātô)"), and perhaps 2:8a ("Yahweh thought (ḥāšab) to destroy the wall of the Daughter of Zion").[124] The latter two verses contain words for planning (zāmām, ḥāšab). This appears to be an uniquely Israelite twist given to the divine word motif as found in the Mesopotamian laments. After surveying the Hebrew terms for divine planning, Albrektson makes a connection between the divine word and the divine plan.[125] This connection is especially clear in Jer 4:28, where dibbartî and zammōtî are in parallel: "for I [Yahweh] have spoken, I have purposed; / I have not relented, and I will not turn back from it."[126] The plan (ʿāṣat) and thoughts (maḥšĕbôt) of Yahweh also figure significantly in Ps 33, a poem which celebrates the creative power of Yahweh's word. Yahweh's plan plays a similar role in passages in Isaiah and Jeremiah which contain other imagery common to city laments (e.g. Isa 23:8, 9; Jer 49:20; 50:45; 51:12, 29; cf. Isa 14:24, 26, 27; 19:12, 17). Thus, as the word of Enlil determines the fate of cities in the Mesopotamian city laments, so does the plan of Yahweh in the Hebrew Bible. McDaniel's arguments to the contrary do not persuade.[127]

The Hebrew Bible characteristically symbolizes Yahweh as a divine warrior (e.g. Exod 15; Judg 5; 2 Sam 22=Ps 18, Ps 29; 68; Hab 3). Yahweh appears as a typical warrior god, most analogous to Baal, but also similar to Anat and El, as well as to other warrior deities from

---

[122] *History*, 53-67.

[123] For the understanding of *hēbētā* as a precative perfect, see Hillers, *Lamentations*, 15.

[124] Cf. Walton, 160.

[125] *History*, 68-97, esp. 86; cf. Kraus, *Klagelieder*, 47-48.

[126] LXX has a different order: "I have spoken and I will not relent; / I have purposed and I will not turn back from it."

[127] "Sumerian Influence," 204-5.

the ancient Near East.[128] Yahweh is armed with bow and arrow (2 Sam 22: 15; Hab 3:9; Ps 7:13; Lam 3:12). His right arm symbolizes the power and strength by which he conquers his enemies (Exod 15:6, 12; Isa 41:10; Ps 44:4; 48:11; 60:7; 77:11; 89: 14; Job 40:14). And the heavenly host often accompany Yahweh into battle (Deut 33:2-3; Hab 3:5).[129]

Like many of the warrior deities, Yahweh is a storm god.[130] Thus, the Hebrew Bible usually portrays his epiphany with storm imagery. In his anger (2 Sam 22:8; Hab 3:2, 12) Yahweh comes forth amidst storm clouds (Judg 5:4; 2 Sam 22:12, 13; Ps 68:5), darkness (2 Sam 22:10, 12), strong winds (Exod 15:8, 10; 2 Sam 22:11, 16; Hab 3:14), and rain (Judg 5:4; Ps 68:9, 10); he thunders (2 Sam 22:14; Ps 68:34) and shoots bolts of lightening (2 Sam 22:15), shakes the earth (Judg 5:4, 5; 2 Sam 22:8; Hab 3:6; Ps 68:9) and spews forth fire (2 Sam 22:9, 13). His look, like Enlil's, portends an inauspicious future for the nations (Hab 3:6), whereas his refusal to look kindly forecasts the same for Israel, implying Yahweh's abandonment (Ezek 9:12).

Attention has already been called to Lam 2:1-9a as a structural unit which focuses on Yahweh's infliction of destruction (see 2.2c above). Much of the imagery in this section portrays the divine warrior in the midst of battle against Jerusalem.[131] He goes into battle angry (Lam 2:1a, 2b, 3a, 6c);[132] fire (Lam 2:3c, 4c; cf. 4:11) and the bow (Lam 2:4a) are his weapons; he destroys houses, palaces and strongholds, the city walls, and the temple (Lam 2:1c, 2ab, 5b, 6a, 7a, 8a, 9a).

Twice Yahweh is explicitly referred to as being like an enemy (2:4b, 5a).[133] This recalls an analogous motif in two of the city la-

---

[128] See Cross, 147-76; Patrick D. Miller, Jr., "El the Warrior," *HTR* 60 (1967) 411-31; *Divine Warrior*, 24-58; Albrektson, *History*, esp. 16-41; Manfred Weippert, "'Heiliger Krieg' in Israel und Assyria," *ZAW* (1972) 460-93; Thomas W. Mann, *Divine Presence and Guidance in Israelite Traditions: The Typology of Exaltation* (Baltimore: Johns Hopkins University, 1977); Kang.

[129] Cf. Miller, *Divine Warrior*, 66-67, 74-128.

[130] Cf. Cross, 156-63.

[131] Cf. Hillers, *Lamentations*, 43.

[132] See McDaniel ("Sumerian Influence," 203) on anger.

[133] Cf. McDaniel, "Sumerian Influence," 203.

ments.[134] In LU 254, 374-75 Ningal stands outside (Sum. bar-ta ... gub) Ur as if she were an enemy (Sum. nu-erím-gin$_7$). Likewise, Enki in LE 1:11-12 stays outside (Sum. bar-ta ... gub) his city as if it were a foreign city (Sum. uru-kúr-gin$_7$). While the martial imagery is not explicit in either of these laments, it is certainly implied.[135]

Alongside the divine warrior imagery in this chapter, one finds the motif of the Day of Yahweh (Lam 2:1c; cf. 1:12c; 2:21c, 22b). Much has been written about the Day of Yahweh,[136] but whatever more one might wish to say about this motif, at the very least it seems to denote the day that Yahweh, the warrior-god, goes into battle, whether against Israel or her enemies.[137] As such, this motif is appropriate in an Israelite city lament.[138]

Two other reflections of divine warrior imagery might occur in this chapter. The "right hand" of Yahweh appears in Lam 2:3b, and perhaps also in 2:4a. The text of the latter verse is suspect, but the MT can be maintained.[139] However, even if one emends the text to read

---

[134] Westermann, *Klagelieder*, 130.

[135] A variant to CA 64 has Inanna attacking Agade, perhaps attesting that such a motif was at least known, see Cooper, *Agade*, 64, 241.

[136] For good reviews of the literature and relevant bibliography, see Hans M. Barstad (*The Religious Polemics of Amos* [Leiden: E. J. Brill, 1984] 89-93) and Oswald Loretz (*Regenritual und Jahwetag im Joelbuch* [UBL 4; Ugaritisch-Biblische Literatur, 1986] 77-79, n. 5).

[137] So Gerhard von Rad, "The Origin of the Concept of the Day of Yahweh," *JSS* 4(1959) 97-108; Cross, 111; A. J. Everson, "The Days of Yahweh," *JBL* 93 (1974) 336; Hans Walter Wolff, *Joel and Amos* (Hermeneia; trans. Waldemar Janzen, S. Dean McBride, Jr., and Charles A. Muenchow; Philadelphia: Fortress, 1977) 33; Barstad, 96.

[138] Interestingly, Barstad locates the original life situation of the Day of Yahweh passages and the prophetic oracles against the nations in the public lament (106-8). The investigation of the prophetic literature conducted below indicates that Day of Yahweh passages, oracles against the nations, and city lament imagery are often found together, thus providing some additional evidence for consideration in conjunction with Barstad's thesis. For the purposes of this study, however, the original life situation of the Day of Yahweh passages has no relevance. The connection between Yahweh as warrior and the Day of Yahweh is sufficient to make the inclusion of the Day of Yahweh motif in Israelite city laments understandable.

[139] So Kraus, *Klagelieder*, 37; Albrektson, *Studies*, 91-92.

something like "the sword-hilt was in his right hand"[140] or "the arrow was in his right hand,"[141] continuity with divine warrior imagery remains. In 2:3b the pronominal suffix is ambiguous. It could theoretically refer to either Israel[142] or Yahweh.[143] To understand Yahweh as the antecedent is the simplest solution since Yahweh is present in the immediate context. The idea, then, is that Yahweh has withdrawn his support from Israel; there is nothing left to defend Jerusalem from the enemy onslaught.

Some translate the *hapax legomenon* $ya\bar{}\hat{i}b$ in Lam 2:1a as "to becloud, overcloud," a denominative verb from the noun $^c\bar{a}b$ "cloud."[144] Others compare Ar. $^c\bar{a}ba$ "to dishonor, disgrace"[145] or Heb. $*w^cb$ (related to Heb. $t\hat{o}^c\bar{e}b\bar{a}h$ "abomination") "to show contempt."[146] All solutions involve some speculation. Because much of the first part of Lam 2 has to do with divine warrior imagery, the translation "to becloud" makes good sense. As has been noted, Yahweh as the divine warrior commonly enwraps himself in clouds (2 Sam 22:12, 13; Ps 97:2; Lam 3:44) or rides upon them through the skies (Ps 104:3; Isa 19:1; cf. 2 Sam 22:11; Ps 68:5, 33). Thus, it seems very fitting that the second chapter begins in the midst of dark storm clouds:

> How the Lord in his anger
> > engulfed the Daughter of Zion in storm clouds!
> He threw down from heaven to earth
> > the Splendor of Israel.
> He did not remember his footstool
> > on the day of his anger.

---

[140] Hillers, *Lamentations*, 37.

[141] Weiser, *Klagelieder*, 59; Rudolph, *Klagelieder*, 216, 218-19; Westermann, *Klagelieder*, 125.

[142] Hillers, *Lamentations*, 36.

[143] Weiser, *Klagelieder*, 63: Kraus, *Klagelieder*, 42; Rudolph, *Klagelieder*, 218; Westermann, *Klagelieder*, 123.

[144] So Weiser, *Klagelieder*, 58, 62; Kraus, *Klagelieder*, 36; Albrektson, *Studies*, 85-86; Westermann, *Klagelieder*, 125.

[145] Rudolph, *Klagelieder*, 218.

[146] Thomas F. McDaniel, "Philological Studies in Lamentations, I," *Biblica* 49 (1968) 34-35; Hillers, *Lamentations*, 35.

Israelite literature used the divine warrior motif as a mythopoetic way to describe Israel's early wars. So too the divine warrior's attack on his own city, Jerusalem, functions mythopoetically to describe the enemy attack. The enemies appear throughout Lamentations (Lam 1:5, 7, 10, 14, 16, 17, 21; 2:7, 17, 22; 4:12). Like Enlil, Yahweh sends the enemies against Israel (Lam 1:17b; 2:22a) or hands Israel over to them (Lam 1:14c, 2:7b). The interpretation of Lam 2:7a as a reference to divine abandonment is further underscored by Lam 2:7b:

> He surrendered (hisgîr) into the hand of the enemy
> the walls of her citadels.

The phrase "to surrender or give (nātan) into the hand" is another way the vanquished can interpret a defeat so that their god's autonomy remains intact.[147] The Sumerian equivalent of this phrase (sum, zé-èm [ES] = Akk. nadānu) occurs in LSUr 63, 181 and 239, balags 2:37, 8:34-35 (FM), 10:a+71-72, 16:a+16-17 (FM), and 50:b+179-80. Sum. šu(-a) ... gi$_4$, "to hand over," occurs in LSUr 172, 175-77,[148] and LN 96.

Finally, Lamentations identifies Yahweh, like Enlil in the Mesopotamian laments, as the one who has caused the destruction (Lam 1:5b, 12c, 13, 14c, 15, 21b; 2:1-9a, 17, 21c). Therefore, Yahweh is implored to look down upon the destruction and have pity upon Israel (Lam 1:9c, 11c; 2:20a; 3:50; 5:1).[149] Such cries are not restricted to Lamentations, but occur often enough in the Hebrew Bible (e.g. Ps 9:14; 25:18, 19; 35:22; 80:15; 102:20; Isa 63:15).[150]

In essence, then, Yahweh conceived as the divine warrior who goes into battle on the "day of his anger" forms a fitting analog to Enlil conceived as the destructive storm who comes "on that day" (Sum. u$_4$-ba).

---

[147] Cf. Albrektson, History, 38-39.

[148] See Michalowski, Lamentation, 88.

[149] Cf. Gwaltney, 208; Walton, 162.

[150] Westermann's observation that such pleas to Yahweh are not found in funeral dirges is absolutely correct (Klagelieder, 115), a further indication that one has to do with more than just funeral dirges in Lamentations.

6. Destruction

The sixth generic feature to be discussed is the description of the destruction. A significant part of the Mesopotamian laments and Lamentations consists of a detailed description of the destruction of the city and surrounding area, the city's buildings and roads, inhabitants, economy, and political, social, and religious customs. It is in this imagery that commentators in the past have identified many parallels between the two groups of texts.

a. City and Environs

The Mesopotamian laments often portray the enemy attack as beginning somewhere in greater Sumer, proceeding to the surrounding countryside and outlying areas of a specific city, and finally reaching the particular city.[151] This attack results in the ruination of the city and the surrounding towns (LU 209, 246, 261-64, 345; LSUr 40; 346-47; LW 4:25; LN 97; *balag* 4:a+210; Cohen, *Analysis*: 15:'2). The cities are turned into tells, becoming haunts for ghosts and wild animals (LSUr 143-46, 222, 346-49; CA 257; LE 4:4-8; LN 100, 103; *balags* 4:a+210, 223; 5:d+179, 194; 10:a+22-27, 31, 122-25; 13:f+212-15). And canals and roadways lie unused (LU 269-70, 367-68; LSUr 38-39, 327-28; CA 264-66; cf. LN 292; *balag* 42:46-48 [OB]). In essence, the city and its environs are completely destroyed.

Lamentations communicates the notion of Jerusalem's total destruction through the use of traditional imagery: it compares Jerusalem with Sodom (4:6), makes Jerusalem the butt of taunts from passers-by (1:7c; 2:15, 16), and depicts Zion as the haunt of foxes (5:18). By far the closest parallel to the Mesopotamian laments consists of the depiction of Zion as a tell, inhabited only by wild animals. Hillers[152] notes that Lam 5:18 ("Over the ruined Mount Zion, foxes prowl") closely parallels the plaint in CA 257 ("May foxes that frequent ruined mounds sweep with their tail") and *balags* 4:a+223, 5:d+192, 6:b+241,

---

[151] See Green, "Eridu," 296; Michalowski, *Lamentation*, 13-14.
[152] *Lamentations*, xxx, 100; *Lamentations* (2d), 33.

and PBS 10/2 no. 12 + VAS 2 12, obv. i:23[153] ("The fox drags his tail there"). He also calls attention to the more widespread use of this motif in the prophets, especially in connection with treaty-curses.[154]

Sodom and Gomorrah are proverbial for emphasizing the utter destruction of a city in Israelite tradition,[155] and no doubt the mention of Sodom in Lam 4:6 was meant to allude to this. This motif is used elsewhere in the Hebrew Bible in passages that contain other city-lament features (e.g. Isa 1:9; 13:19; Jer 49:18; 50:40). Hillers identifies the motif's possible connections with treaty-curses.[156] In Lamentations, however, the image functions chiefly to emphasize Jerusalem's guilt.[157]

Hillers collects evidence showing that the taunt of the passers-by is usually associated with descriptions of ruined cities or land in the prophetic literature.[158] Again his observation is made with reference to treaty-curses. Thus, all three motifs serve to depict ruined cities and are associated with treaty-curses. One can explain the coincidence of these motifs in city laments and treaty-curses in at least two ways. One might suggest that this coincidence has resulted because the two literary genres draw on a common stock of imagery depicting destroyed or ruined cities. This assumes that Israelite writers had a basic stock of literary motifs with which to work, and that they would draw on this body of traditional imagery when penning treaty-curses or the transforms of city laments. Such an explanation may claim some plausibility in light of CA. Much of the imagery in the curse section of CA has parallels in other city laments (and other Mesopotamian literature in general) in non-curse contexts. The fox motif is a case in point. It occurs in the curse section of CA, but in non-curse contexts in the *balags*.

As an alternative explanation one could suggest that the inclusion of these curse motifs in passages with city-lament features resulted from attraction, since the motifs are overtly concerned with ruined cities.

---

[153] *CLAM*, 265.

[154] Hillers, *Treaty-Curses*, 44-54.

[155] Hillers, *Lamentations*, 88.

[156] *Treaty-Curses*, 74-76.

[157] Kraus, *Klagelieder*, 76; Rudolph, *Klagelieder*, 251.

[158] *Treaty-Curses*, 76-77.

Part of the standard imagery in the laments includes the destruction of the city gates, walls, and buildings (e.g. LU 212, 261-64; LSUr 404; LW 5:11-16). In Lamentations compare 1:4b, 2:2a-b, 5b, and 8a.[159] In addition to the parallel to Lam 2:9a ("Her gates are sunk in the ground, he broke[160] her bars") recorded by Hillers ("The doors of all the city-gates of the land lay dislodged in the dirt ..." [CA 168]),[161] one should also note these other parallels: LSUr 292, 404 (only in text II[162]), LE 2:4, eršemmas 163.1:13 and 163.2:a+14.[163]

b. Sanctuary

The enemy attack culminates in the destruction of the temples of the chief gods and goddesses. LE 2:12-3:7 narrates the destruction as it proceeds from the temple walls, through the gates, breaking down the door and bolt and destroying the guardian figures, into the temple itself, where the treasures are stolen. LSUr 407b-48 contains a similar description of the destruction of the Ekišnugal of Nanna, and the destruction of the Ekur of Enlil is described in LN 53-78 and CA 100-

---

[159] Kraus, *Klagelieder*, 11.

[160] MT contains two verbs, ⁾ibbad wěšibbar "he destroyed and broke." As some commentators point out this makes the second colon too long (Hillers, *Lamentations*, 38; Westermann, *Klagelieder*, 125). Therefore, the text has probably incorporated variants, and presents a double or conflate reading.

[161] *Lamentations*, 44.

[162] See Michalowski, *Lamentation*, 173.

[163] The appropriateness of these parallels, however, depends on the meaning of Sum. ᵍⁱˢig ... gub. Bendt Alster (Review of *The Curse of Agade* by Jerrold S. Cooper, *WO* 16 [1985] 162), Wolfgang Heimpel ("The Sun at Night and the Doors of Heaven," *JCS* 38 [1986] 136, n. 29), and Michalowski (*Lamentation*, 94) understand the phrase as referring to doors standing wide open. On the other hand, Green ("Eridu Lament," 146), Cohen (*Sumerian Hymnology*, 189), and Cooper (*Agade*, 250) interpret it to mean "to dislodge a door." The latter interpretation is based to some extent on the Akk. translation of ᵍⁱˢig ... gub in *eršemma* 163.2:a+14: *[d]alātīšu ... tušbalk[it]* "you dislodged ... its doors." While Heb. *tābaᶜ* (lit. "to sink") could conceivably depict a dislodged door, as Hillers contends, a reference to a wide-open door is a bit more problematic.

48 (cf. LU 116-33, 276-81; *balag*s 3:1-28; 4:137-70; 5:e+202-12; 10:a+1-21).

In Lamentations, too, the temple's destruction is a prominent feature.[164] Hillers notes the parallel between Lam 1:10b ("She saw the heathen enter her sanctuary") and *balag* 50:b+155-61, quoted above (see 2.3).[165] The idea that the enemy should not enter the sanctuary, let alone gaze upon the sacred treasures, is common in the Mesopotamian laments (e.g. LSUr 151-52, 197-98, 442; LE 4:9-10, 6:12'; CA 129-30).

Similarly, the plundering of the temple treasures, another common motif in the Mesopotamian laments (LU 133, 239, 275-81; LSUr 169-70; LW 3:29; LN 63, 276-77; CA 136-45; *balag*s 10:a+196-203; 26:57; 27:57; 50:b+226-27), has a counterpart in Lam 1:10a ("The enemy laid his hand upon all her precious things").

The first colon of Lam 2:6a (*wayyaḥmōs kaggan sukkô*) is difficult. Most commentators presume that MT is corrupt.[166] However, Albrektson's suggestion that the preposition *kĕ-* has absorbed the preposition *bĕ-* (**kĕbaggan*) is more plausible in light of two parallels from LU and two from the *balag*s:[167]

My house established by a faithful man
Like a garden hut indeed was thrust on its side.   (LU 122-23)

My faithful house ...
... like a tent, like a pulled-up harvest shed,
like a pulled-up harvest shed indeed was exposed to wind and rain.
                                                                    (LU 125-29)

Enlil, you have turned the faithful house into a reed hut.

[164] See Kraus, *Klagelieder*, 11.

[165] *Lamentations* (2d), 32.

[166] See Albrektson, *Studies*, 95, n. 5 (with earlier literature); McDaniel, "Studies I," 36-38; Hillers, *Lamentations*, 37-38; Westermann, *Klagelieder*, 125.

[167] For Albrektson's argument see his *Studies*, 95; see also his discussion at p. 82, and WOC 11.2.9c. Kraus (*Klagelieder*, 11), Gadd (66), and Westermann (*Klagelieder*, 125) also call attention to the LU parallels.

(*balag* CT 42 26:13;[168] cf. 6:20)[169]

Both the "garden hut" (Sum. gi-sig-kiri$_6$, gi-sig = Akk. *kikkišu* "reed
hut") and "pulled-up harvest shed" (Sum. é-ki-buru$_{14}$-bu) refer to
temporary structures erected during harvesting.[170] Thus, LU compares the
destruction of Ningal's temple to these dilapidated structures after they
have been abandoned following the harvest. This same image occurs in
the two *balags*. Note that the *balags* explicitly mention Enlil as the
perpetrator. Likewise, Lam 2:6a imagines Yahweh as violently destroying the temple as if it were a temporary garden hut. The elliptical nature
of this verse,[171] as compared to the Mesopotamian examples or Isa 1:8
("The Daughter of Zion was left like a booth in a vineyard"), is perhaps
deliberate. The poet might be playing on both the normal meaning of
Heb. *suk/sukkāh* as "a temporary shelter" (Job 27:18; Jon 4:5) and on its
more specialized sense as a designation for the temple (Ps 27:5). Though
precise details of the Hebrew remain problematic, the general sense may
well be that reflected in Albrektson's translation: "He has broken down
his booth as in a garden."[172]

c. Persons

Both Kraus and Westermann recognize how much LU -- and one
should add, the Mesopotamian laments in general -- and Lamentations
are alike in their depiction of the plight of the city's inhabitants.[173] The
people are completely and indiscriminately massacred. As described in
LE 1:20, the storm has "neither kindness nor malice" and knows "neither
good nor evil" (LE 1:20). In LW 4:27 the poet uses a merism to capture

---

[168] The particular text in which this line occurs (CT 42 26) is considered by Cohen
as a part of *balag* 13 (*CLAM*, 339ff.), but by Kutscher as a part of *balag* 16.

[169] CA 193-94 expresses a somewhat analogous sentiment: "On that day Enlil made
small sanctuaries out of the great sanctuaries."

[170] Cf. Thorkild Jacobsen, *The Harps That Once...* (New Haven: Yale University,
1987) 456, n. 22.

[171] See Westermann, *Klagelieder*, 125.

[172] *Studies*, 95.

[173] Kraus, *Klagelieder*, 10; Westermann, *Klagelieder*, 26-27, 30.

this sentiment ("They bludgeoned its population, they finished off young and old"). A similar merism occurs in Lam 2:21:

> Boys and old men
>> lie on the ground in the streets.
> My maidens and young men
>> fall by the sword.

This same attitude is expressed in LU 400-3, LSUr 110-11, LN 67, CA 190-92, and *balag* 43:a+14-19.

The dead were so numerous that piles of corpses filled the streets. Hillers compares Lam 1:15a ("The Lord heaped up[174] in my midst all my strong men") to LU 213-16:

> In the great gate, where there was parading, the corpses were placed;
> In the squares, where feasts were held, they were placed head to head;[175]
> In all the streets, where there was parading, the corpses were placed;
> In the places, where the festivities of the land took place, the people were piled up.[176]

Also compare LE 2:5, LW 2a:6, LN 66[177], *balag*s 2:27-31 and 43:a+36, and *eršemma* 35.2:27-31.

In Lam 4:2 Zion's citizens are said to have been treated like clay pottery (*niblê hereś*). Compare LU 211, where the people are described as littering the tell instead of potsherds, and LSUr 406, "In Ur the weapons attack [the people] like clay pots."[178]

Kraus also observes the general way in which both Lamentations and the Mesopotamian laments treat hunger.[179] More specifically, Hillers

---

[174] See Hillers (*Lamentations*, 12-13) for the understanding of √*slh* "to heap up."

[175] "they were placed head to head" = Sum. sag-bal-e-eš ba-ab-gar

[176] See Hillers, *Lamentations*, 40-41.

[177] Cf. Green, "Eridu," 298.

[178] Cf. Michalowski, *Lamentation*, 100-1.

[179] *Klagelieder*, 11; cf. Lam 4:4 and Cooper, *Agade*, 25-26.

calls attention to two famine parallels.[180] He compares Lam 1:20c
("Outside the sword kills my children, inside it is famine[181]") with LSUr
399-401:

> Inside Ur there is death, outside, there is death,
> Inside, we are being finished off by famine,
> Outside, we are being finished off by Elamite weapons.

He also relates Lam 4:5 ("Those who once ate fine foods are now
desolate in the streets; / those who were brought up in scarlet now
embrace garbage heaps") to CA 249 ("May the aristocrats, who eat fine
food, lie down in hunger"). Additional parallels to the latter pair include:
LSUr 303-8, CA 249-53, *balags* 8:36-37 (FM); 13:b+64-65; 43:a+42-43,
c+214-15.

Another famine related parallel involves Lam 4:9a ("Better are
those slain by the sword than those slain with famine") and LSUr 389
("Those of the city who were not given over to weapons, died of
hunger"). While these do not represent exact parallels, they are very
close in that they both use loss of life from combat and starvation as
their points of reference.

In addition to the images of human slaughter and famine,
Lamentations and the Mesopotamian laments share similar portrayals of
exile. Lam 1:5c, LU 283, and LN 44, 212-23, 219 (cf. LN 2) envision
the city's citizens as going into exile. The motif of young men and
women going into captivity is also common to both Lamentations
(1:18c) and LU (285).

A notice that the king has gone into exile like that in Lamentations (Lam 2:9b; 4:20) appears also in two of the city laments (LSUr 34-
37; LW 2a:3).

---

[180] *Lamentations*, xxx, 14, 88.

[181] Hillers emends MT *kammāwet* "like death" to *kāpān* "famine" (*Lamentations*,
14).

d. **Social, Religious, and Political Customs**

The whole social fabric of the community is destroyed. The family breaks down, family members mourn the death of other family members, and those who survive act unnaturally towards one another. Here the reversal motif predominates, i.e. father abandons his son, etc. (see 2.2b above).

People cannot pursue their jobs, indicating the disruption of normative social functions. Shepherds, field workers, butchers, prostitutes, and merchants do not perform their normal tasks, and those unfamiliar with butter and milk have to make the butter and cream (e.g. LU 265-71; LSUr 42-46, 95-96, 335-36; LW 2:14'-18'; LN 42-43, 212; CA 237-41; *balag*s 4:a+196-97, 198-200, 231-32; 5:d+165-69, 183; PBS 10/2 no. 12 + VAS 2 12, obv. ii:1-2[182]; 42:85-89 [OB]). Priests and other temple personnel neglect their offices (LSUr 447-48; LE 3:15; *balag*s 1:84-89; 3:a+51-54; 4:a+215-19; 5:d+184-88; PBS 10/2 no. 12 + VAS 2 12, obv. ii:16-19[183]; 43:d+276). Canal diggers are cast into the canals (*balag* 1:92-93).

Following this same theme LSUr 251-53 reports that those who normally fetch the water and wood no longer do so:

> In Ur no one went for firewood, no one went for water,
> The one who went for firewood went away from the firewood, and will not
> return,
> The one who went for water went away from the water, and will not return
> (cf. LSUr 293).

The Sumerian word for "firewood," ú, is ambiguous.[184] It can in fact refer to "firewood" (Akk. *iṣu*[185]), or it can mean "food" (Akk. *akalu*[186]). In the *balag*s these same basic lines occur (e.g. *balag* 1:94-97; 42:88-89 [OB]). In *balag* 1:94 the Sum. ú-šè gin-na-mu is translated by Akk. *ša*

---

[182] *CLAM*, 264ff.

[183] Ibid., 264ff.

[184] Cf. Michalowski, *Lamentation*, 93.

[185] Cf. *CAD* I/J, s.v.

[186] Cf. *CAD* A/1, s.v.

ina iṣia illiku. The Akkadian translator clearly understands Sum. ú in this instance as "firewood," and hence the translation above. This seems to be the image which lies behind Lam 5:4:

> Our water we drink in exchange for money[187],
> our wood is brought[188] for a price[189].

This implies that basic commodities like wood and water have to be purchased, presumably from foreigners. The image of gathering firewood and water is a common literary topos. In addition to the biblical references cited by Hillers,[190] the topos occurs in an Amarna letter (*EA* 154:17) and the Keret epic (*KTU* 1.17.III.7-10; cf. 1.17.IV.51-V.2).

The Mesopotamian laments also depict the disruption of the political systems.[191] This is a major theme in LSUr, which Michalowski understands as a propagandistic work of Išbi-Erra and his followers.[192] Ur must be destroyed in order to change the location of kingship (4, 17-19, 28). The king, Ibbi-Sin, is ineffective. He cries bitterly (104-6)[193] and is exiled (34-37). With kingship defiled the land breaks into factions and chaos (99-101). In Lamentations a similar breakdown of law and order results from the exile and flight of the political authorities, i.e. king, princes (Lam 1:6; 2:9b).

Finally, both the Mesopotamian laments and Lamentations characteristically note the interruption of cultic ceremonies (e.g. festivals) and ineffectiveness of cultic personnel as a result of the city's destruction (LU 70, 117, 192, 213-16, 322; LSUr 31, 102, 184, 192, 205, 250, 343-45; LE 1:16; 3:9-14; LN 112, 169-71, 282-85, 302-5;

---

[187] Here the preposition *bě-* in *běkesep* and *bimhîr* governs the price paid (*beth pretii*, see WOC 11.2.5d; GKC 119p).

[188] Here the 3mp verb form is used as an impersonal passive.

[189] Here the preposition *bě-* in *běkesep* and *bimhîr* governs the price paid (*beth pretii*, see WOC 11.2.5d; GKC 119p).

[190] *Lamentations*, 97.

[191] Green, "Eridu," 299.

[192] *Lamentation*, 6-7; Piotr Michalowski, "History as Charter: Some Observations on the Sumerian King List," *JAOS* 103 (1983) 237-48.

[193] See Green, "Eridu," 299.

*balag*s 1:81-89; 3:a+51-54; 4:a+198-232; 5:d+165-201; 6:b+214-246; PBS 10/2 no. 12 + VAS 2 12:obv. col. ii 1-31; 50:a+81-86; *eršemma*s 106; 159; Lam 1:4a-b, 10; 2:6-7, 9c, 14).[194]

7. The Weeping Goddess

One of the more striking motifs in the Mesopotamian laments is what Kramer calls the "weeping goddess."[195] The weeping goddess motif portrays the city goddess grieving over the destruction of her city and temple and the killing, suffering, and dispersement of her people. The prototypical weeping goddess is Ningal in LU. Ningal first appears beginning in the third *kirugu* of the poem. She cries bitterly over the destruction which the storm has caused her city and her house (LU 80-85). She is terrified and cannot get any rest because of the storm. Although she rushes to her city's defence like a bird flapping its wings, she cannot help. The city is destroyed (LU 108-9). In the fourth *kirugu*, set before the onslaught of the menacing storm, Ningal goes before An and Enlil, and then again before the whole assembly of the gods, in order to prevent the destruction. But the divine assembly will not change its decision. Her city and temple must be destroyed (LU 137-72).

Ningal utters another long complaint beginning at the end of *kirugu* six and continuing throughout the whole of *kirugu* seven (LU 252a-327). As she details the destruction of Ur and her temple, the Enunkug, she utters her classic wail, "Alas, my city," "Alas, my house" (LU 247), tears out her hair, beats her chest, and weeps bitterly (LU 299-301).

---

[194] Cf. Green, "Eridu," 299-300. In the *balag*s diviners and dream interpreters are said to lie (5:35-36; 9:4-5), or are otherwise unable to divine or interpret (5:14; 13:f+160). Passages like these illustrate how these prophet-like figures cannot fulfill their normal tasks. However, because they always occur in lists praising Enlil's word, stressing the inability to comprehend Enlil's word, one probably should refrain from making a direct comparison to the passages in Lamentations. The image seems to function quite differently in the two contexts.

[195] "BM 98396: A Sumerian Prototype of the Mater-Dolorosa," *EI* 16 (1982) 141*-46*; "Lisin," 133-44; "Weeping Goddess," 69-88.

In the second *kirugu* of LSUr (115-284), the poet lists the cities of Sumer, noting their destruction, the abandonment by their chief gods, and the goddesses who weep over each city. Two examples will suffice to establish the basic pattern:

> The temple of Kiš, Hursagkalama, was destroyed,
> Zababa seized upon a strange path away from his beloved dwelling,
> Mother Ba'u was weeping bitterly in her Urukug,
> "Alas, the destroyed city, my destroyed temple!" bitterly she wails.
>
> (LSUr 115-18)[196]

> She rode away from her possessions, she went to the mountains,
> She loudly keened a lament over those bright[197] mountains:
> "I am a Lady, (but) I had to ride away from my possessions, and now I am
>   a slave in this land,
> I had to ride away from my precious lapis lazuli, and now I am a slave in this
>   land,"
> ....
> ....
> "Alas, the destroyed city, my destroyed temple!" bitterly she wails.
>
> (LSUr 271-77)

In LE Damgalnunna, the goddess in Eridu, laments the destruction of her city. *kirugu* five portrays Damgalnunna like Ningal, tearing out her hair, gashing herself with sword and dagger, and crying uncontrollably (LE 5:3-6). The rest of the *kirugu* contains her brief lament (LE 5:6-11).

Regarding LW Green notes that somewhere in the broken *kirugus* (7-11) one can expect Inanna's private lament.[198] The weeping goddess becomes a permanent fixture in the *balags* and *eršemma*s (e.g. *balag*s 1:46-63; 2:b+61-75; 3:18, c+65-74; 4:177-95, b+257-60; 7:b+160-68; 20:g+111-20; 43:a+62-94, 58-119, c+239-51, g+338ff; 48:1-21 [FM];

---

[196] The broken parts of this passage can be restored confidently because of the repetitive nature of this *kirugu*.

[197] Michalowski understands Sum. kiš-nu-gál as a variant of giš-nu$_{(11)}$-gal "great light" (1989: 94).

[198] "Uruk Lament," 254.

50:a+42-86, b+186-232, 233-43; *eršemma*s 32; 79; 106; 159; 166.1 and 2; 10).

Only LN lacks the motif of the weeping goddess. In its place Nippur itself complains in first-person Emesal about the distress that surrounds the city (*kirugu* 4 of the LN).[199] This represents the extension of a minor stream of tradition found in the city-lament genre.[200] The poets sometimes personify pieces of the city's architecture, like gates, roads, walls, temples, etc. For example, in the second *kirugu* of LU the cities themselves are addressed in second-person Emesal (LU 40-41, 48-62). In the eighth *kirugu* of LU, the poet speaks to Ningal, trying to convince her to return to her city. At one point he likens Ur, Ningal's shrine, and the wall of the shrine to people in mourning (LU 269-72). Several examples of this type of personification may also occur in LW (1:18-19; 4:29) and LN (53-78). This tendency gets picked up in the *balag*s and *eršemma*s and further elaborated in several recurring lists (e.g. *balag*s 2:1-32; 3:21-28; *eršemma* 35.2:1-14).[201]

Since biblical Yahwism did not tolerate the worship of deities other than Yahweh,[202] one would not expect to find a literal importation of the weeping goddess motif into Lamentations. Rather, the Israelite poet would have had to find a viable substitute for this dominant image. Gwaltney, Westermann, Tikva Frymer-Kensky, and Hillers see in the personified Jerusalem of Lamentations a counterpart to the weeping goddess so familiar from the Mesopotamian laments.[203] The similarities in the poetic elaboration of the two motifs are indeed striking. Specifi-

---

[199] Cf. Kramer, "Nippur," 91-92; Green, "Eridu," 292; Vanstiphout, "Stadtsklacht," 333-34, 339.

[200] This tradition is also found in funeral dirges, cf. Jahnow, 102-3.

[201] Cf. Kramer, "Weeping Goddess," 74; Wilshire, 243.

[202] Cf. Patrick D. Miller, Jr., "The Absence of the Goddess in Israelite Religion," *HAR* 10 (1986) 239-48, esp. 240.

[203] Gwaltney, 208, 209; Westermann, *Klagelieder*, 30; Tikva Frymer-Kensky, *In the Wake of the Goddesses* (New York: Free, 1992) 170; Hillers, *Lamentations* (2d), 34. McDaniel sees no connection ("Sumerian Influence," 201).

For the sake of simplicity, personified Jerusalem is referred to throughout this section (and the whole chapter as well) chiefly as the Daughter of Zion, the most common of her titles.

cally, note the correspondences between the two motifs in the following five areas.

First, Lamentations pictures personified Jerusalem, like the city goddesses in Mesopotamia, as weeping over the destruction of the city and its inhabitants: "She weeps aloud by night, with tears on her cheeks" (Lam 1:2a); "She groans aloud,[204] and turns away" (Lam 1:8c); "Over these things I am weeping, my eyes[205] run with water" (Lam 1:16a); "... and she is bitter" (Lam 1:4c);[206] "Listen[207] to how I groan! There is no one to comfort me" (Lam 1:21a); "Zion stretches out her hands..." (Lam 1:17a); "Lift up your hands to him..." (Lam 2:19c; cf. 2:18-19).

The Daughter of Zion's stretching out and lifting up of her hands to Yahweh in Lam 1:17a and 2:19c also has parallels in the Mesopotamian laments (LU 154[208]; *balag* 42:c+362 [FM]; *eršemma* 79:33[209]).

---

[204] Here compare Heb. *gām* with Ug. *gm* "aloud"; cf. McDaniel, "Studies, I," 31-32; Hillers, *Lamentations*, 10; *contra* Provan, 45.

[205] MT has $^c\bar{e}n\hat{\imath}$ $^c\bar{e}n\hat{\imath}$ "my eye, my eye" as a result of simple dittography. Read $^c\bar{e}n\hat{\imath}$ (cf. LXX, Syr., Vulg., and 4QLam^a).

[206] Following Seow (416-19; cf. Provan, 54-55), one might also cite Lam 1:20b *kî mārô mārôtî* "how bitter I am!" The Daughter of Zion's bitterness here and in Lam 1:4c (*wěhî$^{\circ}$ mar-lāh*) is perhaps not mere happenstance (*contra* McDaniel, "Sumerian Influence," 201). Throughout the Mesopotamian laments the weeping goddess "cries bitterly" (Sum. ér-gig ... še$_8$ = Akk. *bakû* "to cry" and *marṣiš* "bitterly, sickly").

[207] For the understanding that Yahweh is being addressed in this verse, see Kraus, *Klagelieder*, 23; Rudolph, *Klagelieder*, 208; Hillers, *Lamentations*, 14-15; Westermann, *Klagelieder*, 102. Read with Syr. *šěma^c* "Listen!" (Peal Impv. 2ms) for MT *šāmě^{c}û* "they heard," *contra* Provan, 55.

[208] In LU 154 one reads the following:
  úr hé-im-ma-BU-BU   á! hé-im-ma-lá-lá
The second part of this line refers to the stretching out or grasping of the hand. Sum. lá is either equivalent to Akk. *kamû* "to bind" (e.g., "laid hold of arms", see Jacobsen, *Harps*, 457) or Akk. *tarāṣu* "to stretch out" (e.g., "the arms verily I stretched", Samuel N. Kramer, "Lamentation over the Destruction over Sumer and Ur" in *ANET*[3], 1969) 458. The translation of the first part, however, is more difficult. Nevertheless, it most likely refers to a parallel action being done with/to the thigh or leg (Sum. úr = Akk. *sūnu*, *pēm/nu* "thigh, upper thigh"; e.g., "I verily clasped (?) legs", Jacobsen, *Harps*, 457, n. 24). Whatever the correct translation, this appears to refer to some type of mourning gesture with the hands and legs analogous to what is referred to in Lamentations.

Another series of mourning gestures which makes a regular appearance in the Mesopotamian laments consist of the goddess's self-mutilation, i.e. beating or clawing the breast with or without daggers, the tearing out of hair, etc. (e.g. LU 299-301; LE 5:3-6; *balag* 20:g+111-20; *eršemma* 79:25-35). While this motif does not appear in Lamentations, some of the passages from other biblical books examined in the next chapter portray the personified city as either girding on sackcloth and rolling in the dust (e.g. Jer 6:26) or cutting off her hair in mourning over the exile of her children (e.g. Mic 1:16). These gestures, which are not unlike those used to depict the weeping goddess, are typical for mourning someone's death in Syria-Palestine. Note the portrayal of El as he mourns Baal's death:

> He poured dust of mourning on his head,
> > dust of *grieving* on his pate,
> > he covered himself with a garment and loin-cloth.
>
> ....
>
> He lacerated cheek and chin,
> > he did his arm a third time.
> He plowed the chest like a garden,
> > he did the rib cage a third time.
> He lifted up his voice and cried:
> "Baal is dead! What of his people?
> > The son of Dagan! What of his folks?"   (*KTU* 1.5.VI.14-24)

---

[209] In *eršemma* 79:33, just before Ningirgilu begins beating her breast and pulling out her hair, the following line occurs: *šu-ni EL-ta im-ta-zur-zur* $_{zu-ur-zu-ur}$ *èr-gig ì-[še$_8$-še$_8$]*. The meaning of *zur-zur* is problematic. It usually is equated with Akk. *kunnû*, *kutennû* "to treat with care" (Cohen, *Sumerian Hymnology*, 157). Cohen relates *šu LA* to Akk. *esēlu* "to immobilize, to become heavy with movement," and *EL* to *e-la-lu* "cries of mourning" (ibid., 157). He then states: "Perhaps Ningirgilu is described as raising her hands to the sky in wailing, thus causing her hands to become heavy" (ibid., 157). If Cohen's interpretation, which accords well with the immediate context, is correct, then this nicely parallels the Daughter of Zion's actions in Lamentations.

Much of the same imagery is repeated in Anat's lament over Baal (*KTU* 1.6.I.2-6, 9-10).[210]

Second, there are a number of correspondences between the authorial points of view relating to the weeping goddess in the Mesopotamian laments and the Daughter of Zion in Lamentations: (1) like Ningal in LU (*kirugu*s 3-4, and 7), Damgalnunna in LE (*kirugu*s 5 and 6), and other goddesses in the *balag*s and *eršemma*s, the Daughter of Zion utters a complaint (Lam 1:11c-22; 2:20-22); (2) her address to Yahweh (Lam 1:20-22) parallels the addresses made by various goddesses to Enlil (and others) in the Mesopotamian laments; and (3) the poet's address to personified Zion (Lam 2:13-19) parallels similar addresses in the Mesopotamian laments. Also the *focus* of Lam 1, concentrating on the destruction wrought, especially to the temple and the Daughter of Zion, agrees with the *focus* of the weeping goddess passages in the Mesopotamian laments (see 2.2 above).

In the Mesopotamian laments the temple, its treasures, and assorted furnishings are understood as belonging personally to the city goddess. For example, note the following:

> They took my house and my city from me.
> They took the lady (of) my house from me.
> They took my living quarters, my treasure house from me.
> They took my possessions, my furnishings from me.
> They took my property of the Eshumesha from me.
> They took my property of the Erabriri from me.
> They took my throne, my seat from me.
> They took my bed from me.
>> (*balag* 10:a+196-203; cf. LU 133, 275-81; LSUr 169-70, 273-74; *balag*s 1:60, 75-89; 42:122 [OB]; 50:a+54-71; *eršemma*s 166.1 and 2; 171:7-8)

In Lamentations the temple (Lam 1:10b) and the treasures ("The enemy laid his hand upon all her precious things," Lam 1:10a) are similarly

---

[210] Cf. Alster "Mythology," 5; Mark S. Smith, "Baal in the Land of Death," *UF* 17 (1985) 313-14; "Jeremiah," 97-99; "Death," 291; Samuel E. Lowenstamm, "Did the Goddess Anat Wear Side-Whiskers and a Beard?" *UF* 14 (1982) 119-23.

understood as belonging personally to Zion.[211] In fact the reference to the temple as belonging to personified Zion is quite remarkable. In twenty-eight out of the thirty-one occurrences where *miqdāš* refers to the temple and has a pronominal suffix in the Hebrew Bible, the suffix takes Yahweh as the antecedent. Only three times dose the suffix refer to someone else, and only in Lam 1:10b is the suffix feminine, referring to the personified city.

In the Mesopotamian laments the goddesses often bear the title ama "mother" (e.g. LU 28 [um-ma], 378; LSUr 117, 137, 141; LE 1:15; see the numerous references to ama s.v., in Cohen's [*CLAM*] index). At times this metaphor gets extended, and the citizens are characterized as the goddess' children (e.g. LU 369-70; *balag*s 1:76-77; 42:9-11 [OB]; 43:c+239, d+270). In fact throughout the Mesopotamian laments the people are often mentioned as belonging to the weeping goddess (e.g. LU 283, 341, 357, 365-66; *balag* 43:c+234-38, d+270-76; 57.8:46).[212] Moreover, the cow and calf, ewe and lamb imagery commonly applied to the Mesopotamian goddesses also implies the notion of motherhood (e.g. LU 103; *balag*s 5 [N, O, P]:168[213]; 48:b+39-40, 44 [FM]; 49:b+48-49 [OB]; 50:b+129-31).[214]

---

[211] An even closer parallel to Lam 1:10a in phraseology occurs in LU, but without the personal reference to the goddess ("On its possessions which had been placed in the country, defiling hands were placed" [LU 239]).

[212] Cf. Wilshire, 243. One might also call attention to the similar ways in which the Israelites are referred to as Yahweh's people, further attesting that this is a characteristically divine point of view.

[213] *CLAM*, 148.

[214] Interestingly, this animal imagery is also applied to the city (e.g. LU 67-68) as is the conception of the city's inhabitants as the city's children (Sum. tur/di$_4$-di$_4$, *balag* 42:1-3, 9-10 [OB]). Moreover, the cow and calf imagery is applied to the temple in LN 68. This is perhaps significant since LN lacks the weeping goddess motif. In its place the city and perhaps the temple are personified and depicted as mourning the city's destruction.

One should note that the image of goddess as mother was also known in the west, see Aloysius Fitzgerald, "The Mythological Background for the Presentation of Jerusalem as a Queen and False Worship as Adultery in the OT," *CBQ* 34 (1972) 409-10.

Kramer calls attention to the presence of this "weeping mother" motif throughout Sumerian literature.[215] In the *balags* and *eršemmas* the weeping goddess also bemoans the loss of her spouse and son (*balags* 42:68, 100 [OB]; 48:b+37 [FM]; 50:b+224-25, 262; 57.8:43; *eršemmas* 106:15-16; 159:25-26). The identity of the spouse and the son, however, is obscure.[216] Kramer suggests that this motif provides a prototype for Rachel's weeping for her children in Jer 31:15.[217]

Personified Jerusalem is portrayed throughout Lamentations as a mother. In each instance (Lam 1:5c, 16c; 2:19c, 22c) the citizens of Jerusalem are understood as her children.[218] The people in general are construed as belonging to personified Zion (Lam 1:4b-c, 11a, 15; 2:9b-c, 10a, 14, 21b; 4:13).

Finally, the Mesopotamian laments employ exile and enslavement language, especially when the goddess talks about her condition after the city's destruction, presupposing her abandonment of the city (LU 294, 306-8; LSUr 150, 273-74; *balags* 27:58; 50:b+252-57[219]; 57.8:37-54; *eršemma* 32:49-54; 159:26-28; 171:51-55).[220] The point of this imagery is to point up the goddess' reduction in status.[221] The motifs of "exile" and "no rest" in LU 306-7 ("I am one who has gone out of my city" and "I am one who can find no rest/dwelling place") also occur in Lam 1:3a-b:

> Judah has gone into exile after suffering
> and much toil.[222]

---

[215] "Lisin," esp. 136-37.

[216] See Kramer, "Weeping Goddess," 75.

[217] "Prototype," 141*; Hillers, *Lamentations* (2d), 38.

[218] Cf. Hillers, *Lamentations*, 22.

[219] For this passage, see Black, 39, 60-62.

[220] See also Kramer, "Weeping Goddess," 75.

[221] See Black, 60.

[222] Following Hillers (*Lamentations*, 6-7). His understanding of the grammar is superior to any other suggestion; still the exact significance of this phrase eludes this writer. See Robert B. Salters' exhaustive review of the history of exegesis of this verse ("Lamentations 1.3: Light from the History of Exegesis," in *A Word in Season* [*JSOT* Supplement 42; eds. J. D. Martin and P. R. Davies; Sheffield: *JSOT*, 1986] 74-89). See

> She lives now among the nations,
>   and finds no resting place.[223]

Lam 1:1c employs similar imagery.

Thus, the conception of the Daughter of Zion as possessor of the temple and its treasures, her image as mother, mourner, and exiled slave, and the several authorial points of view pertaining to her all have significant correlations with the weeping goddess motif in the Mesopotamian laments.

Another argument in favor of understanding personified Zion as the equivalent of the Mesopotamian weeping goddesses is that her epithets are divine in nature.[224] One of personified Zion's most obvious divine titles is composed of *bĕtûlat* in union with *bat* GN (Lam 1:15c; 2:13b). In the Ugaritic texts Anat's most common epithet is *btlt* ꜥ*nt*.[225]

yōšebet GN/*b*-GN "Enthroned One of GN" or "the One Enthroned in GN" is another divine epithet used to designate the personified cities in the Hebrew Bible. For example, one should compare *hdd ysb skn* "Hadad, the Enthroned One of Sikan" (*Tell Fakhariyeh*, 15-16). In Lamentations this title is used only once in reference to personified Edom (Lam 4:21; for further discussion, see 3.1a.ii below).

McDaniel argues that one should understand *rabbātî* and *śārātî* in Lam 1:1 as the divine epithets "Mistress, Lady" and "Princess."[226] He

---

also Provan's overview (37-39).

[223] This follows Kraus (*Klagelieder*, 270) and Westermann (*Klagelieder*, 111); *contra* Hillers, *Lamentations*, 6-7; Rudolph, *Klagelieder*, 211-12. Whatever the correct translation of 1:3a-b may be, the verse must refer to the exile after the fall of Jerusalem (cf. Salters, 87).

[224] Preliminarily, see F. W. Dobbs-Allsopp, "*bat* GN in the Hebrew Bible." A paper presented to the Hebrew Scriptures and Cognate Literature section at the Annual Meeting of the SBL (Nov 21, 1992; San Francisco).

[225] Cf. Richard E. Whitaker, *A Concordance of the Ugaritic Literature* (Cambridge: Harvard University, 1972) s.v. *btlt*; McDaniel, "Studies, I," 29-31; Fitzgerald, "Background," 409.

[226] "Studies, I," 29-31.

compares these terms to the common use of *rbt* in epithets of Syro-Palestinian goddesses.[227]

Personified Zion's most common epithet in Lamentations, *bat GN*, is used of goddesses elsewhere as well.[228] In a Neo-Babylonian Tammuz lament re-edited by Lambert, the following titles occur: *mārat uruk*[ki] "daughter of Uruk" (ln. 3), *mārat akkade*[ki] "daughter of Akkad" (ln. 3), *mārat larak*[ki] "daughter of Larak" (ln. 4), and *mārat nippuri*[ki] "daughter of Nippur" (ln. 12).[229] The goddess referred to by these epithets is portrayed as a weeping goddess and much of the lament's imagery is characteristic of the city laments.[230] A hymn of Nanâ contains additional examples of the title "*mārat GN.*"[231]

All of these titles fit the metrical pattern of divine epithets known from the Ugaritic texts, confirming their divine nature. *bĕtûlat GN, yōšebet GN/b-GN, rabbātî ʿām, rabbātî baggôyim, śārātî bammĕdînôt,* and *bat GN* correspond to what Richard Whitaker calls "long epithets."[232] Long epithets usually comprise the latter two-thirds of a colon.[233] The titles like *bĕtûlat bat GN* and *yōšebet bat GN* are examples of a "full colon epithet" or "extended epithet."[234] For metrical

---

[227] The Mesopotamian laments furnish numerous examples of Sumerian titles with roughly the same semantic range as *rabbātî* and *śārātî*. For a sample of these Mesopotamian titles and other evidence in support of McDaniel's interpretation, see Dobbs-Allsopp.

[228] For full details, see preliminarily Dobbs-Allsopp.

[229] "Tammuz ," 211-15.

[230] See Lambert, "Tammuz," 214. See also Kramer ("Weeping Goddess") for examples of the weeping goddess motif both in city laments and in Dumuzi laments. Note also that remnants of the Dumuzi myth occur in both *balag*s and *eršemma*s.

[231] See Erica Reiner, "A Sumero-Akkadian Hymn of Nanâ," *JNES* 33 (1974) 221-36). See also K. L. Tallqvist, *Akkadische Götterepitheta* (*StOr* 7; 1938) 125. The "daughter of GN" epithet seems to be Semitic in origin. The writer has not uncovered any Sumerian equivalent to this title.

[232] "A Formulaic Analysis of Ugaritic Poetry" (an unpublished Ph. D. dissertation from Harvard University, 1969) 11-12.

[233] Ibid., 11-12; cf. Hillers, *Lamentations*, xxxvii-xxxix.

[234] Whitaker, "Formulaic," 19.

purposes, "Zion," "Jerusalem," "Edom," etc. are equivalent to Whitaker's "simple name" -- which normally fills one-third of a colon.[235]

In summation, both the correspondences between the personified city motif in Lamentations and the weeping city goddess motif in the Mesopotamian laments and personified Zion's appropriation of divine epithets suggest that the Hebrew poets exploited the Mesopotamian weeping goddess motif (however latent or implicit it may have been in the Israelite literary tradition) when crafting the image of the Daughter of Zion. What results is a vastly complex literary figure, a city and its population embodied in a feminine persona.[236]

The suggestion that the personified city motif depends, at least to some extent, on the Mesopotamian weeping goddess motif indeed seems plausible. As noted such a use of personification has a good parallel within the Mesopotamian city-lament genre in the form of personified Nippur in LN. Moreover, Aloysius Fitzgerald writes the following about the personification of cities in the Hebrew Bible: "For all practical purposes, at least when the imagery is in any way developed, it is limited to a situation in which the city is presented as having suffered or about to suffer a disaster."[237] Barbara Bakke Kaiser makes similar observations about personified Jerusalem in Jer 4 and Lam 1 and 2.[238] Thus, the propensity of the personified city motifs to appear in

---

[235] Ibid., 36.

[236] It is important to stress that the divine attributes identified above *are not* characteristic of the goddesses in the Mesopotamian laments *only*. For example, Kramer documents the use of the weeping goddess motif in a variety of genres ("Lisin"). Moreover, one would expect the Israelite poets to assimilate divine characteristics known from WS goddesses in the literary figure of the personified city. The point of the argument is first to identify the city's divine characteristics, and then to provide a plausible explanation of them. That is, given the existence of other features typical of city laments, the presence of a personified city with divine features may be plausibly explained as resulting from the generic influence of the weeping goddess motif.

[237] "Background," 410.

[238] "Poet as 'Female Impersonator': The Image of Daughter Zion as Speaker in Biblical Poems of Suffering," *Journal of Religion* 67 (1987) 166, 182. She notes that "the poet chooses the female persona to express the intensity of his grief" (166) and "that distinctively female experience was regarded highly enough to function as the

contexts of suffering and disaster correlates well with the idea that they owe something of their existence to the weeping goddess motif in the city laments. Such a connection would also answer Kaiser's query as to why the Israelite poets chose a female persona as the chief metaphor for expressing agony and grief over a city's destruction.[239]

Scholars have only recently become interested in the personification of cities and countries in the Hebrew Bible.[240] Previously, those who noted this phenomenon understood it as a simple case of personification that warranted little comment. However, some of the more interesting recent studies call attention to likenesses in the portrayal of the personified cities/countries in the Hebrew Bible and goddesses from the ancient Near East and classical Greece, thus partially corroborating the analysis of the personified city motif given above.[241] In fact, O. H. Steck refers specifically to the weeping goddess motif in some of the notes to his discussion, as does Frymer-Kensky and Mark E. Biddle.[242] On the

---

chief metaphor through which the poet expressed his own agony over Jerusalem's fate" (182).

[239] Ibid., 166.

[240] E.g. W. F. Stinespring, "No Daughter of Zion, A Study of the Appositional Genitive in Hebrew Grammar," *Encounter* 26 (1965) 133-41; "Zion, Daughter of." in *The Interpreter's Dictionary of the Bible: Supplementary Volume* (ed. K. Crim; Nashville: Abingdon, 1976) 985; Fitzgerald, "Background;" "*BTWLT* and *BT* as Titles for Capital Cities," *CBQ* 37 (1975) 167-83; Chayim Cohen, "The 'Widowed' City," *JANES* 5 (1973) 75-81; Wilshire; John J. Schmitt, "The Gender of Ancient Israel," *JSOT* 26 (1983) 115-25; "The Motherhood of God and Zion as Mother," *RB* 92/4 (1985) 557-69; "The Virgin of Israel: Referent and Use of the Phrase in Amos and Jeremiah," *CBQ* 53 (1991) 365-87; Mary Callaway, *Sing, O Barren One: A Study in Comparative Midrash* (SBLDS 91; Atlanta: Scholars, 1986) esp. 73-90; Elaine R. Follis, "The Holy City as Daughter," in *Directions in Biblical Hebrew Poetry* (*JSOT* Supplement 40; ed. Elaine R. Follis; Sheffield: *JSOT*, 1987) 173-84; Kaiser; John F. A. Sawyer, "Daughter of Zion and the Servant of the Lord in Isaiah: A Comparison," *JSOT* 44 (1989) 89-107; O. H. Steck, "Zion als Gelände und Gestalt," *ZTK* 86/3 (1989) 261-81; Frymer-Kensky, 168-78.

[241] Fitgerald, "Background;" "Titles;" Callaway, 77ff.; Follis, 173-83; Steck, 270, nn. 46 and 51, 273-75; Fyrmer-Kensky, 168-78.

[242] Steck, 270, nn. 46 and 51; Frymer-Kensky, 170; Mark E. Biddle, "The Figure of Lady Jerusalem: Identification, Deification and Personification of Cities in the Ancient Near East," in *The Biblical Canon in Comparative Perspective* (eds. K. L.

whole, Fitzgerald's work in this area is most helpful, although his main thesis that in Syria-Palestine "cities were regarded as goddesses who were married to the patron god of the city" seems improbable.[243] Nevertheless, he and others are on the right track in relating the personified city motif to goddesses.

Evidently, the Hebrew poets used personification to create a literary figure whose presence in the Hebrew Bible would otherwise be abhorrent to orthodox Yahwists. Put simply, personification confers personality on inanimate objects. Claudia V. Camp likens personification to a sentence which has a literal subject and a metaphorical predicate.[244] The subject consists of the object to be personified. The poet intends the subject to be taken literally, thus its meaning is usually unambiguous and is always present at some level. The metaphorical predicate provides the persona and any "second-order referents." It is the predicate which engages the reader or hearer.

In the case of the personified city or country in Lamentations, the city (Jerusalem) or country (Judah, Israel) constitutes the literal subject. In BH the word for city ($^c\hat{\imath}r$) can refer to the actual physical entity of mortar and brick, roads and houses, or by metonymic extension to the inhabitants of the city.[245] Similarly, the words for country (^cam, $g\hat{o}y$)

Younger, Jr., W. W. Hallo, and B. E. Batto; Lewiston: Edwin Mellen, 1991) 182.

[243] Fitzgerald, "Titles," 405; see the similar assessment of Fitzgerald's thesis by Frymer-Kensky (269, n. 13).

[244] *Wisdom and the Feminine in the Book of Proverbs* (Bible and Literature Series 11; Sheffield: Almond, 1985) 217-22. The present discussion of personification depends on Camp's treatment of the subject. References to the relevant literature can be found in her work.

[245] See BDB, s.v. For the concept of metonymic extension, see conveniently Taylor, 122-30. The names of cities (i.e Jerusalem) and countries (i.e. Judah) function similarly. In the case of city names, however, this may not be as apparent. City names are grammatically feminine in BH. This is reflected frequently in translation by the use of feminine pronouns to refer to cities, often giving a mistaken impression that personification is implied. Such an impression is no doubt further influenced by the poetic image of the city or country as a woman (e.g. Hosea). However, it does not necessarily follow that every time a feminine pronoun or verbal form is used in conjunction with a city name that some type of personification is involved. Strictly speaking, gender is a grammatical category which need not have anything to do with

can refer to either the political entity or the populace.[246] A variety of feminine imagery forms the metaphorical predicate, the persona which enlivens the figure of the Daughter of Zion. Thus, personified Zion is both Jerusalem-as-city (physical entity, inhabitants) and Jerusalem-as-female.[247] Sometimes the city imagery dominates the feminine, other times it is the reverse, and still other times both images are complexly interwoven.

As an example, take Lam 1:1c and 3a-b. At the literal level these verses refer to the exile of the community. However, at the level of personification, the concepts of exile, enslavement, and restlessness have their background in the plight of the weeping city goddess in the Mesopotamian laments.[248]

Although the Hebrew poets rationale for using personification is clear enough, the decision to personify cities (and countries), as opposed to other entities, and place them in the role of the weeping goddess needs explaining. It is likely that this results from the particularly close identification of goddesses with their cities. One of the main functions of goddesses in the ancient Near East was to protect a people, city, or individual.[249] The goddess as protectress of the city and its well being is represented graphically by her turreted crown (*Mauerkrone*) in ancient iconography.[250] According to Monika Hörig, the "turreted crown" motif dates back to OB terra cotta reliefs from Mari.[251] However, the best examples of this motif come from the depictions of the Hellenistic *tychē poleōs*.[252] The *tychē poleōs* is the deified personification of "chance,

---

sex-based gender (cf. WOC 6.3.1.). Rather, it is often the case that the inhabitants of a particular city are referred to by the city name and whatever feminine grammatical elements are relevant. This is a form of metonymic extension, not personification.

[246] See BDB, s.v.

[247] Lanahan, 42.

[248] *Contra* McDaniel, "Sumerian Influence," 201-2.

[249] Cf. Urs Winter, *Frau und Göttin* (OBO 53; Göttingen, 1983) 239-51.

[250] Monika Hörig, *Dea Syria* (AOAT 208; Neukirchen-Vluyn: Neukirchener, 1979) 129-97.

[251] Ibid., 197-91. Biddle calls attention to the turreted crown motif in Mesopotamian and Israelite literature (175-79, 182-86).

[252] See Fitzgerald, "Background," 406-7; Hörig, 138-54.

fortune, or fate." She becomes assimilated with other goddesses and eventually gains her own cult.[253] The weeping goddesses in the Mesopotamian laments are clearly portrayed as being responsible for protecting the well being of the city and its inhabitants. Thus, this traditional association of the protective city goddess with her city would seem to provide the likely background of the personified city motif in the Hebrew Bible. This movement from city goddess to personified city is prefigured by personified Nippur in LN and culminates to some extent in the figure of the Hellenistic *tychē poleōs*.

In addition to the image of the personified city, a related use of personification arises at several points in Lamentations. In Lam 1:4a-b "the roads of Zion" are said to mourn ($\sqrt{bl}$) while the gates lie desolate, and in Lam 2:8c Yahweh causes the walls and ramparts to mourn ($\sqrt{bl}$).[254] Particularly close parallels to Jerusalem's groaning walls occur in the laments from Mesopotamia (LSUr 380; LN 141; CA 227). The city gate and its surrounding walls were evidently prime loci for lamentations.[255]

One last example of personification in Lamentations deserves comment. In Lam 2:18a the poet addresses the "wall of the Daughter of Zion." Many commentators emend MT's *hōmat*.[256] The motivation for the emendation, namely to have the poet addressing the Daughter of Zion, is well reasoned. The wider context compels one to understand

---

[253] Cf. Martin P. Nilsson, *A History of Greek Religion* (2d ed.; Oxford: Clarendon, 1945) 284-85; Fitzgerald, "Background," 413; Michael Avi Yonah and Israel Shatzman, *Illustrated Encyclopaedia of the Classical World* (New York: Harper & Row, 1975) s.v. *tyche*; Hörig, 138-54; Michael L. Barré, *The God-List in the Treaty between Hannibal and Philip V of Macedonia: A Study in Light of the Ancient Near Eastern Treaty Tradition* (Baltimore: Johns Hopkins University, 1983) 64-65; Pierre Grimal, *The Dictionary of Classical Mythology* (trans. A. R. Maxwell-Hyslop; New York: Blackwell, 1986) s.v. *tyche*.

[254] Cf. McDaniel, "Sumerian Influence," 205.

[255] Green, "Eridu," 313.

[256] E.g. <*ni*>*hhemet* "repentant, remorseful" (Hillers, *Lamentations*, 40), *hěmî* "wail" (Weiser, *Klagelieder*, 60; Kraus, *Klagelieder*, 38; Rudolph, *Klagelieder*, 220; Westermann, *Klagelieder*, 126), *hômat* "tumultuous" (McDaniel, "Sumerian Influence," 204).

personified Zion as the addressee. The verse falls within the poet's broader address to the Daughter of Zion (2:13-19). The reference to "your children" in 2:19c demands Zion as the pronoun's antecedent -- note the motherhood imagery discussed above. And lastly, the personified city begins her address to Yahweh in Lam 2:20.

However, emendation is unnecessary. As Provan rightly stresses, the address to the "wall of the Daughter of Zion" involves synecdoche, i.e. the wall stands for the whole city/temple, and thus is not so odd.[257] More significantly, however, the peculiar nature of the imagery in 2:18a seems to have come about as a result of the fusion of two distinct motifs, the weeping goddess and the personification of the city's architecture. For the most part, these motifs are kept apart in the Mesopotamian laments. But in Lamentations, because personified Zion embodies both goddess and city imagery, the two motifs merge quite naturally, both at the literal (walls form part of the natural structure of cities and temples) and the metaphorical (walls and the city/temple are both personified) level. Therefore, the poet's address to the "wall of the Daughter of Zion" involves no incongruity. In fact, the image reminds one very much of an often repeated line in the *balags*: "Its lofty brickwork sits in tears like a mother crying" (57.3:44; cf. 3:22; 4:146).[258]

8. Lamentation

Bewailing the death of friends and relations, and the destruction of city and temple is a commonplace in the Mesopotamian laments and Lamentations, and gave the Mesopotamian genre and biblical book their name. In fact, mourning is the proper reaction of the people to the city's destruction (LW 3:22). These laments consist of short refrains typical of expressions found in funeral dirges.[259] For example, a mother mourns her child, "Oh, my child!" (*balag* 10:a+113, 115), a girl her brother, "Oh,

---

[257] Provan, 76.

[258] This line in the *balags* specifically describes the destroyed shrine. Whether the "wall of the Daughter of Zion" refers to the city wall, or more specifically to some wall associated with the temple precinct, is not made clear.

[259] See Jahnow, 92-93.

my brother!" (*balag* 10:a+114), and a child her father, "Oh, my father!" (*balag* 10:a+116; cf. *eršemma*s 1.1:25-29; 1.2:38-42). In *balag* 48:9 the goddess mourns "Alas, my mother! Alas, my child!" (cf. *balag* 50:b+262). Dumuzi is mourned, "Alas, the young man!" (*eršemma* 88:4-9). Phrases like these surely lie behind the weeping goddess' most common plaint, "Alas, my city! Alas, my house!" (LU 247-248; cf. LU 261-264, 329; LSUr 118, 122, 126, 135, 138, 142, 148, 154, 162, 182, 190, 203, 209, 213, 217, 220, 248, 277; LE 1:27; 2:19; *balag*s 3:a+44, 45; 42:62 [OB]; 45:1 [OB}; 48:1-2, 8 (FM); 57.2:6-7; *eršemma*s 10:15; 32:1-9; 166.1:1-7; 166.2:1-10). This becomes especially clear in passages like *eršemma* 79:31 where the plaint "Alas, my destroyed city!" parallels the phrase "Alas, [my] men!", or *balag* 16:a+25-26 (FM)[260], where the plaint "Alas, my house!... my city!" coincides with "Alas, my baby!... my big one!" Similarly, in *eršemma* 10 the goddess' lament "Alas, my city! Alas, my house!" (10:15) is followed directly by the lament "Alas, my spouse! Alas, my child!" (10:16). The poets place similar plaints in the mouths of others as well (CA 202-4; LN 65).

Another typical plaint asks *how long?* (Sum. èn-šè, me-na-šè = Akk. *adi mati*; LU 374; LSUr 398, 451; LE 6:27'; LN 31, 36, 37, 80; *balag*s 4:195; 6:24-29, a+107-19; 8:b+77-82 [OB]; 16:a+33-36 [OB], a+28-30, 99-111 [FM]; Kutscher, 56, ln. 27; Black, 25, ln. 223; *eršemma*s 29:20; 160:36; 163.1:19). Lamentations also appear more generally throughout the city laments (e.g. LU 231-34; LSUr 361-62, 479-81; LN 30, 41, 43, 46, 53-78; CA 196-209; *balag*s; 3:13-28; 4:137-70, a+207-32; 5:e+202-12; 10:a+10-21; 16:a+2-8 [OB]; 23:a+36-41)

The biblical book of Lamentations is filled with references to weeping, crying and mourning (Lam 1:4, 11a; 2:5c, 10, 11; 3:48-51; 5:15, 17). The exclamatory interjection ᵓ*êkāh* "how!" (Lam 1:1; 2:1; 4:1) is a typical mourning cry,[261] corresponding to Sum. ù-a, ù, or a "woe!, alas!" and me-le-e-a "woe!, alas!" (and functions like other

---

[260] Kutscher, 56, lns. 25-26.
[261] Jahnow, 136.

Hebrew interjections, e.g. *hôy*, *hô*, and *ᵓôy*).[262] McDaniel correctly
contends that such general lamentation imagery alone does not prove
literary dependence on the Mesopotamian city laments.[263] But it is genre
marked, and thus, like the generic features subject and mood, merits
citation as evidence that Lamentations participates in the city lament
genre.

9. Restoration of the City and Return of the Gods

The final generic feature common to both the Mesopotamian
laments and Lamentations concerns the restoration of the city and return
of the gods. These two themes make an appearance in most of the city
laments[264] and many of the *balag*s and *eršemma*s. Restoration themes
occur in LU 423, 435, LSUr 352-56, 460-74, 493-518, LE 8:1, *balag*s
3:e+141-49, 7:b+84-85, 8:c+89-e+137 (OB), VAS 2 16 rev. col. vi:6-
18[265], etc. In LN the restoration theme has undergone a change in scale
Fowler calls *macrologia*, the magnification of one of the generic
features. It enlarges to form over half of the lament (LN *kirugu*s 6, 8-
11).

It has been frequently posited that the city laments functioned in
restoration ceremonies of the specific temples and/or cities.[266] This
contention is supported by the many *balag*s in which the concluding line
explicitly states that the *balag* was meant to function as an appeal for
restoration (e.g. *balag*s 5:f+279; 10:c+384; 12:e+292 [OB]; 29:f+248;
48:e+172 [FM]).[267] The return of divine support was an essential element
for a city's restoration and the hoped for reversal of the gods' abandon-

---

[262] Cf. Krecher, *Kultlyrik*, 114-15; Jahnow, 83-87. This does not imply that the
Hebrew somehow depends on the Sumerian (so McDaniel ["Sumerian Influence," 202]
in response to Kraus [*Klagelieder*, 10]). McDaniel is undoubtedly correct that Heb.
ᵓêkāh is a good Northwest Semitic particle. The point of comparison lies in the fact
that both Sumerian and Hebrew use short, ejaculatory phrases to express woe.

[263] "Sumerian Influence," 200-1.

[264] Green, "Eridu," 305-6.

[265] *CLAM*, 267-68.

[266] See *CLAM*, 38-39.

[267] Ibid., 38-39.

ment. LU and LE plead for Ningal (LU 331-84) and Enki (LE 7:1-24) to return. LSUr (475-77a) and LN (207-14 and *kirugu* 8) narrate the return of the deities. In the *balag*s and *eršemma*s, desire for the deities return is usually implicit in questions such as, Why will he not rise? (e.g. *balag* 13:c+111-18), or, How long will he sleep? (e.g. *balag* 8:b+77-82 [OB]), though explicit references to the god's return also occasionally appear (e.g. *balag*s 6:c+247-57; 8:e+137 [OB]). The final *kirugu*s of all of the Sumerian city laments consist of a prayer to a god.[268] Similar prayers are scattered throughout the *balag*s and *eršemma*s (e.g. *balag*s 3:e+141-49; 5:f+225-65; 6:43-83; 8:c+89-e+137 [OB]; 12:e+161-280 [OB]; 15:a+177ff.; 16:b+112-25 [FM]; SBH 7:58-98[269]).

CA shows that these themes become even more powerful in their absence. CA functions rather differently than the other Mesopotamian laments. Instead of looking toward Agade's future restoration, as would be natural at cultic ceremonies where the razing of old foundations took place, the poem emphasizes the exact opposite, that Agade will not be restored. The poem's last line makes this interpretation very explicit, in case one missed the point of the curse section: "Agade is destroyed! Praise Inanna!" (281). The force of the curse section (CA 210-80) and the haunting doxology (CA 281) is all the more powerful when read/heard with the expectations of the city-lament genre. Here, then, one has a nice example of how a poet plays upon the generic expectations of his audience while not actually fulfilling them. In doing so he is able to give a whole different feel to his text.

The theme of restoration is perhaps present in Lamentations, but only implicitly, and only referred to in passing. Lam 4:22 ("Your punishment is complete, O Zion") perhaps signals the end of the destruction, carrying a similar sentiment as the interjection múš-àm (Akk. *ahulap*) "enough! have mercy!" found in LU 381 ("May An, the king of the gods, say about you, "Enough!"; cf. LN 161, 199).[270]

---

[268] Green, "Eridu," 307-10.
[269] *CLAM*, 526-30.
[270] Kraus, *Klagelieder*, 11; Gwaltney, 209.

Like the Mesopotamian laments, Lam 5:21 contains a short prayer for restoration (see esp. LSUr 352-56).[271] However, Lamentations does not tell of Yahweh's return to Jerusalem. Rather, it seems to do just the opposite, reaffirming his absence via the divine abandonment theme (Lam 5:22).[272] This affirmation of Yahweh's absence serves to undercut much of the force of the prayer, as does the prayer's extreme brevity (cf. the prayers in the Mesopotamian laments).[273] Here Lamentations bears some affinity to CA. The poet of Lamentations, like the poet of CA, uses the generic expectations associated with the city-lament genre to set up his audience. Rather than fulfilling these expectations, he explodes them. By including the one-line prayer, the poet heightens the conventional expectations only so he can dash them in the very next line. Thus, it seems unlikely that Lamentations was composed explicitly for the razing and rebuilding of the temple.[274] If this were the case, one would expect a more hopeful treatment of the restoration and return themes along the lines of the Mesopotamian laments. But Jerusalem's restoration is nowhere in sight. Rather, it seems more likely that the poems of Lamentations were composed to give voice to the community's profound grief and to protest the injustice of the city's destruction and the people's suffering. Indeed if there is any hope in Lamentations, it lies in the book's eloquent protest.

---

[271] Cf. Gwaltney, 209.

[272] The fullest literary expression of the return of Yahweh to Zion in the Hebrew Bible occurs in Ezek 40-48, cf. Block.

[273] The precise nature of the connection between vv. 21 and 22 is disputed (see Rudolph, *Klagelieder*, 257-58, 262-63; Albrektson, *Studies*, 205-7; Hillers, *Lamentations*, 100-1; R. Gordis, *The Song of Songs and Lamentations* (3d ed.; New York, 1974) 289-93; Westermann, *Klagelieder*, 178-79; Provan, 133-34). Nonetheless, one can agree with Provan that whatever the exact connection, "it is clear ... that the poem does not have a confident ending" (134).

[274] As suggested by Gwaltney (210).

10. Summary

Lamentations shares a number of generic features common to the Mesopotamian laments, thus one can legitimately categorized the book generically as a city lament. Even the general similarity in subject matter (e.g. lamentations, depiction of destruction), which often leads to a certain affinity in imagery but does not necessarily imply the constitution of exact parallels, can become genre-linked, and thus has relevance for this study.[275]

However, Lamentations does not simply mechanically reproduce features from the Mesopotamian genre. Rather at almost every step along the way one is confronted by Israelite literary traditions and imagery. Moreover, the Israelite city-lament features do not conform to their Mesopotamian counterparts in a simple straightforward manner. Rather, they exhibit a variety of relationships with their corresponding Mesopotamian feature. For example, the theme of divine abandonment surfaces throughout ancient Near Eastern literature, and thus has roughly the same meaning in both Lamentations and the Mesopotamian laments. Other features, however, while treating similar subject matter (e.g. the divine agent of destruction), differ markedly in actual content (e.g. the evil storm as opposed to the divine warrior). This difference usually results from the use of traditions and imagery peculiar to each of the specific cultures in question. Sometimes the difference entails the process of adaptation (e.g. the personification of Jerusalem as an adaptation of the weeping goddess motif).

The existence of such a variety of correlations is comprehensible in light of the understanding of genre presented above[276] and results

---

[275] *Contra* McDaniel ("Sumerian Influence," 200-1) and Jacobsen (Review of *Sumerians*, 147, n. 32).

[276] Longman's treatment of the genre of *Fictional Akkadian Autobiography* may serve as another example of the elasticity required in generic studies. The fifteen texts he treats are generically related principally on formal grounds: they are (1) fictional, (2) written in Akkadian prose, and (3) autobiographies (199). Regarding content, however, these fifteen texts diverge greatly. Comparatively, the city laments form a more cohesive genre in that they share formal as well as substantive features. Yet, differences among individual city laments remain.

more particularly from the cultural differences involved.[277] This suggests the existence of a native Israelite genre, as does the presence of distinctly Israelite imagery in Lamentations. The plausibility of this hypothesis will be tested, as far as possible, in the next chapter. That is, if one can find similar evidence of a city-lament genre elsewhere in the Hebrew Bible, then the hypothesis of an native Israelite city-lament genre is made more likely.

---

[277] One should note that a certain amount of flexibility exists in the Mesopotamian genre itself, see Green, "Eridu," 294-95.

3
The City-Lament Mode
in the Prophets and Psalms

In the past a few scholars have asserted that some of the prophetic laments (especially those in the OAN) resemble the Mesopotamian laments.[1] However, no evidence in support of these claims was ever provided. More recently, and independent of these early assertions, Hillers has made similar observations and provided initial data supporting them.[2] Building on and amplifying the seminal insights of Hillers and others, this chapter charts the use of the city-lament mode through the Prophets and Psalms.

As defined earlier (see 1.4 above), a mode is an abstraction of a genre, usually containing only an incomplete repertoire of the genre's features. It typically lacks external structure and varies widely in how many of a genre's features it incorporates. A mode represents generic mixture below the level of hybridization (where the complete repertoires of two or more genres are joined). This concept is especially useful in the present study, because it allows one to call attention to the presence of city-lament features without committing oneself to a classification of the material in which they are embedded or presuming that an actual city lament existed for every city or country mentioned. That is, it enables a more precise literary analysis to be undertaken without overstepping the bounds of evidence, which at the present, only permit one to extract evidence that the city-lament genre was present in the Israelite literary tradition. Perhaps at some later date it may be possible

---

[1] Kramer, "Sumerian Literature," 201, n. 1; G. Ernest Wright, "The Nations in Hebrew Prophecy," *Encounter* 26 (1965) 233-34.

[2] *Lamentations* (2d), 35-39.

to fine tune the analysis offered here, specifying more precisely the type of generic mixture involved.[3]

Identification of the city-lament mode is determined by the clustering of features characteristic of the genre, inclusive of one or more of the genre's diagnostic features, i.e. subject matter, the use of *qînāh* meter, the personification of the city or country like a weeping goddess figure, etc. The greater the number of city-lament features in a given biblical text the greater the probability is that the text has been modified by the city-lament mode.[4] Such a methodology will enable one to identify the best examples of the city-lament mode in the Hebrew Bible. But since the scope of modal extension varies greatly, the actual use of the city-lament mode may be more widespread than indicated in this study.

Although it seems unnecessary to defend the notion that mixed genres existed in antiquity, perhaps the presentation of some examples involving the city-lament genre may prove helpful. The example of CA as a possible modulation of the city-lament genre with the literary-historical genre has already been cited (see 1.4 above). City laments and Dumuzi laments seem to mix freely in the *balag*s (e.g. 42, 48, 49, etc.) and *eršemma*s (e.g. 60, 88, 97, 165, etc.). Also note the same phenomenon in Lambert's Tammuz lament.[5] Kramer shows that the weeping goddess motif occurs in a variety of genres besides the city lament.[6] Machinist argues convincingly that the Tukulti-Ninurta Epic has incorporated the divine abandonment motif from the Sumerian city laments.[7] And finally, A. L. Oppenheim notes that Marduk's lament over the destruction of Babylon in the Erra Epic (IV:36-45) "takes up an old Sumerian literary tradition, the lamentations over destroyed temples and

---

[3] E.g. see Gale A. Yee's analysis of Isa 14 as a parody of a funeral lament ("The Anatomy of Biblical Parody: The Dirge Form in 2 Samuel 1 and Isaiah 14," *CBQ* 50 [1988] 565-86).

[4] See Hirsch, 173-80, esp. 179.

[5] "Tammuz."

[6] "Lisin," 133-37. This may represent what Fowler calls topical invention (170-71). Topics (topoi) may be transformed from one genre to another. In the case of the weeping goddess, the direction of transformations is not easily discernable.

[7] Machinist, 462-64.

cities."[8] Thus, some evidence involving the Mesopotamian lament genre does exist for the type of generic mixture to be analyzed below.

In what follows, exegesis and discussion of passages are restricted to those matters which bear directly on the present thesis. The search for the city-lament mode is conducted at the level of the basic unit of interpretation, the individual oracle.[9] While disagreement often exists over what constitues the higher compositional levels of prophetic books, most scholars would submit that many of the individual oracles in these books originally circulated separately. Empirical support for this position may be found in the collection of the OAN in Jeremiah. The LXX of Jeremiah differs from the MT both in its placement of the collection (after 25:14 as opposed to after 46:1 in MT) and in the order of the oracles within the collection.[10] This suggests that the oracles were transmitted separately at one time.[11] It is perhaps legitimate, then, to assume that this situation also holds for the other collections of the OAN as well as other prophetic oracles in general (at least when there is no evidence to the contrary).[12]

In the main, the chapter is divided between oracles against foreign nations and oracles about Israel and/or Judah. Within each of these two major sections, passages are discussed according to the relative degree of modal extension they exhibit. The chapter concludes by considering some psalms which display evidence of the city-lament mode.

---

[8] *Ancient Mesopotamia* (rev. ed.; Chicago: University of Chicago, 1977) 268; cf. Müller, 235-36. Note the following in support of Oppenheim's supposition: 1) prior to Marduk's lament, Babylon's destruction is narrated (IV:1-35); 2) the destructions of Sippar, Uruk, Dur-Kurigalzu, and Der are narrated next (IV:50-86); and 3) Erra's instructions for Akkad's restoration (V:20-38) remind one of the similar restoration passages in the city laments, especially Enlil's pronouncement in LSUr 460-74.

[9] Cf. J. J. M. Roberts, *Nahum, Habakkuk, and Zephaniah* (OTL; Louisville: Westminster/John Knox, 1991) 10.

[10] Cf. Holladay, *Jeremiah 2*, 312-14.

[11] Cf. John Bright, *Jeremiah* (AB 21; Garden City: Doubleday, 1965) 307.

[12] Cf. Walther Zimmerli, *Ezekiel 2* (Hermeneia; trans. James D. Martin; Philadelphia: Fortress, 1983) 3; Roberts, *Nahum*, 195.

1. Oracles Against the Nations

a. Comprehensive Modulation

The first group of OAN to be discussed exhibit a relatively high degree of city-lament modulation. That is, they contain a large number of the generic features surveyed in the previous chapter as well as an array of individual motifs found in Lamentations and/or the Mesopotamian laments. Thus, these passages provide some of the best evidence of the city-lament genre outside of Lamentations.

i. *Isa 15:1-16:14*   This *maśśā*[13] against Moab abounds with problems. Fortunately, however, many of these can be sidestepped in the present investigation. Attention will focus especially on Isa 15:1-9 and 16:6-11.[14] Wright compares these poems to LU and Hillers notes the presence of specific city-lament features (Isa 15:2, 5; 16:9-11).[15]

These chapters somberly depict the ruination of Moab and its chief cities, thus subject matter and mood agree with that of the city-lament genre. The next thing that one notices about the oracle is the profusion of place names. The prophet[16] portrays the destruction as

---

[13] As Roberts recognizes (*Nahum*, 40), the term is undoubtedly related to the idiom *nāśā* + a word for voice or message. Especially noteworthy is the fact that both Amos (5:1) and Ezekiel (26:17; 27:1) use the idiom *nāśā* + *qînāh* "to lift up a dirge" in laments over cities/countries. *maśśā* occurs in other oracles in Isaiah containing the city-lament mode (Isa 13:1; 14:28; 22:1; 23:1).

[14] For divisions of the text which recognize the unity of each of these passages, see A. H. Van Zyl, *The Moabites* (Leiden: E. J. Brill, 1960) 20ff.; Otto Kaiser, *Isaiah 13-39* (OTL; trans. R. A. Wilson; Philadelphia: Westminster, 1974) 65ff., 73ff.; Hans Wildberger, *Jesaja 13-27* (BKAT 10; Neukirchen-Vluyn: Neukirchener, 1978) 615ff., 624ff., 626ff.; John Oswalt, *The Book of Isaiah: Chapters 1-39* (Grand Rapids: Wm. B. Eerdmans, 1986) 333ff., 343ff. (note, however, that Wildberger partitions these passages even further).

[15] Wright, 233-34; Hillers, *Lamentations* (2d), 38.

[16] Whether this is Isaiah or a member of his school is immaterial for the purposes of this study.

affecting the whole "territory of Moab" (Isa 15:8)[17] by enumerating a large number of place names: Ar and Kir (15:1),[18] Dibon/Dimon (15:2, 9),[19] Nebo and Medeba (15:2), Heshbon (15:4; 16:8, 9), Elealeh (15:4; 16:9), Jahaz (15:4), Zoar, Luhith, and Horonaim (15:5), "the waters of Nimrim" (15:6), Eglaim and Beer-elim (15:8), Kir-hareseth (16:7), Sibmah and Jazer (16:8, 9), and Kir-heres (16:11). This predominance of geography reminds one of a similar motif in the Mesopotamian laments. The enemy attack (or the onslaught of the storm) is portrayed as moving through greater Sumer and ultimately culminating at a particular city. For example, the whole state of Sumer comes into focus in the second *kirugu* of LSUr (115-284). Here the poet narrates the abandonment and destruction of Sumer's cities and temples. The destruction finally reaches Ur in the third *kirugu*, with the final onslaught occurring in the fourth *kirugu* (377-407a), after Nanna and Ningal abandon the city (371-76). A similar but much shorter list occurs in the midst of Damgalnunna's lament in *kirugu* six of LE (6:2'-24'). In LE the attacking storm progresses from the city gate of Eridu to the temple itself (*kirugu*s 2-4). Similarly, in LW the attackers move through Sumer until they reach Uruk (4:22-5:22). In CA Enlil releases the Gutians (149-57) who ravage all of Babylonia (158-92). This leads eventually to the gods' curse of Agade (210-81). This listing of affected cities becomes widespread in the *balag*s and *eršemma*s.[20]

In the above lists the city goddess usually utters a brief lament as the storm or enemy approaches her city. In Isa 15-16 it is the personified cities (15:4) and country (15:2; 16:7)[21] which cry out. Note

---

[17] See Wildberger, *Jesaja 13-27*, 592.

[18] Assuming these are names of cities. See the commentaries for more general discussions of the geographical names in these chapters.

[19] Even if one does not read *dybwn* with 1QIsa[a] in 15:9, *dibōn* and *dimôn* should still probably be identified with one another, see Wildberger, *Jesaja 13-27*, 592.

[20] In LN 218-50 the motif is used to recount the restoration of Sumer-Akkad city by city.

[21] In the personification of Moab and the emphasis placed on the country as a whole, one can clearly see the prominence of the nation state assert itself. This may perhaps account for the confusion in the gender of the suffixes throughout Isa 15:1-9. Who is the main character, personified Dibon or personified Moab? A similar change

also that the personified city motif emerges if one emends the difficult text of Isa 15:2a to read, "the Daughter of Dibon goes up to the high places to cry."[22] The Daughter of Dibon's weeping would be paralleled in 15:2b by Moab's wailing, thus fitting in nicely with the geographical motif.

This use of the geographical motif effectively signals the city-lament mode's presence in this oracle. However, other city-lament features and motifs further color these chapters. The prophet employs several different authorial points of view. He functions as an impartial narrator in Isa 15:1-4, 6-8, and 16:8. But as in Lamentations and the Mesopotamian laments, he abandons this role for that of an internal observer who is personally moved by the destruction of Moab (Isa 15:5;[23] 16:9-11). This switch in "spatial level," common in the city-lament genre, better explains the prophet's otherwise jarring empathy for one of Israel's enemies. The prophet's distress over the destruction of an enemy heightens even further the severity of the situation.[24]

Note that the prophet's reaction to the destruction in Isa 16:11 ("my stomach groans like a lyre for Moab, my liver for Kir-heres") is

---

in gender occurs once in Lamentations. Zion's female persona is clearly present in Lam 1:17a and c. In v. 17a Zion's mourning gesture parallels similar gestures made by the weeping goddess (see 2.7 above). In v. 17c the image is that of a menstruating woman. But when the poet uses "Jacob," a distinctly masculine noun, in v. 17b, it triggers masculine agreement in the following pronominal suffixes. That is, the grammatical gender conflicts with the gender of the personification, resulting in a certain grammatical inconsistency. When the poet uses a long epithet (e.g *bat ʾĕdôm*, Lam 4:22), the country will also be personified as a female. But when the simple name is used masculine agreement may be triggered.

[22] D. Bernh. Duhm, *Das Buch Jesaia* (AT; Göttingen: Vandenhoeck & Ruprecht, 1892) 103-4; T. K. Cheyne, *The Book of the Prophet Isaiah* (Leipzig: J. C. Hinrichs'sche, 1899) 119; Wildberger, *Jesaja 13-27*, 590; John D. W. Watts, *Isaiah 1-33* (WBC 24; Waco: Word Books, 1985) 226; Hillers, *Lamentations* (2d), 38; cf. Targ. and Syr.

[23] LXX reads *hē kardia* and the Targ., *blybhwn*, for MT *libbî*. But MT is the more difficult text and supported further by similar first person addresses in Isa 16:9 and 11, see Hans Wildberger, *Jesaja 1-12* (BKAT 10; Neukirchen-Vluyn: Neukirchener, 1978) 591.

[24] Cf. Kaiser, *Isaiah 13-39*, 68.

not unlike the poet's in Lam 2:11 ("my stomach churns" and "my liver spills on to the ground").[25] This motif seems related to the conventional reaction to bad news identified by Hillers.[26] In Isa 21:3-4 the prophet reacts to the destruction of Babylon in the conventional language identified by Hillers[27]:

> Therefore my loins
>   are filled with anguish;
> pangs have seized me,
>   like the pangs of a woman giving birth;
> I am contorted from hearing (it),
>   I am troubled from seeing (it).
> My heart reels,
>   shuddering falls upon me.[28]

Similarly, Moab's loins quiver[29] and his soul shudders (Isa 15:4) in reaction to the destruction. Compare Zion's reaction in Lam 1:20 ("my stomach churns" and "my heart turns within me").

The prophet switches to Yahweh's point of view in Isa 15:9. Many commentators understand Isa 15:9b as a late addition to the text[30]

---

[25] Cf. Wildberger, *Jesaja 13-27*, 629.

[26] "A Convention in Hebrew Literature, the Reaction of Bad News," *ZAW* 77 (1965) 86-89. Whether the motif depicts a reaction to the news of the city's impending destruction (as in the cases cited by Hillers) or to the city's actual destruction (as reflected in the Mesopotamian laments) must remain unresolved. Resolution of the problem depends on how one understands the specific oracles in question. Do they reflect prophecies of future events? Or, do they lament actual events which are already in the past? The city-lament mode could be used equally plausibly in both situations.

[27] "Bad News," 89.

[28] Other city-lament features are prominent in Isa 21:1-10: (1) Yahweh is conceived as the agent of destruction who orders the Elamites and Medes to lay siege to Babylon (v. 2); (2) Babylon falls (v. 9b); and (3) the divine images are shattered (v. 9c) -- occasionally instead of carrying off the divine images, the victor would destroy the defeated people's images (see Cogan).

[29] Reading MT as if from √*yrᶜ*.

[30] E.g. Duhm, 105; Cheyne, *Book*, 120; Kaiser, *Isaiah 13-39*, 69; Wildberger, *Jesaja 13-27*, 599; Ronald E. Clements, *Isaiah 1-39* (Grand Rapids: Wm. B. Eerdmans, 1980) 153.

and some emend the text, removing the reference to a lion and understanding the verse as a continuation of the prophet's first person speech begun in Isa 15:5.[31] However, recognition of the city-lament mode in these chapters permits one to understand 15:9 as an address by Yahweh, which is integral to the poem in Isa 15:1-9.

The multiple points of view encountered in city laments allow for easy assimilation of additional points of view. Moreover, the divine agent of destruction is sometimes given voice in the Mesopotamian laments (see 2.2a above). Thus, the use of a judgment speech made by Yahweh (a commonplace in the prophetic literature) in 15:9 is appropriate for a passage modulated by the city-lament genre.

Israel's assignment of Moab's destruction to Yahweh and thus the depiction of Yahweh as the agent of destruction makes good sense in Israelite city laments (even if the Moabites would not have necessarily interpreted their destruction in this manner). The notion that Yahweh will place "even more" (nôsāpôt) devastation on Dibon/Dimon assumes that Yahweh was responsible for the destruction all along. As Wildberger notes, the lion in the Hebrew Bible is used commonly as a metaphor for the attacking enemy.[32] Thus, one has the common city-lament motif of Yahweh's sending of the enemy.[33]

---

[31] Cf. BHS, NJV, and the discussions by Wildberger (Jesaja 13-27, 592) and Watts (Isaiah, 227).

[32] Jesaja 13-27, 619; cf. Hillers, Lamentations, 68; Oswalt, 339.

[33] MT's ᵓǎdāmāh "land" is either understood as a place name, "Adama," or emended, most often to ᵓêmāh "terror," see Wildberger (Jesaja 13-27, 592) and Watts (Isaiah, 227) for discussions of the issue. One might suggest ᵓōrēb "ambush" as a better emendation. The image of a lion lying in wait has good parallels in Lam 3:10 and Ps 10:9. In BH words with the same semantic range as √šyt are used to set an ambush: √śym (Josh 8:2, 12; Judg 20:29), the Hiphil of √qwm (1 Sam 22:8; although the Qal is also used in 22:13), and the Hiphil of √kwn (Jer 51:12). daleth and resh and mem and beth were easily confused in the Hebrew scripts of many periods. A scribe's interpretation of šěᵓērît as a construct (i.e. "the remnant of one who lies in wait") would have facilitated the corruption to the more common phrase "remnant of PN or people" (e.g. Jer 6:9; 24:8; 25:20; 40:15; Ezek 9:8; Amos 1:8; 9:12). Thus, one could translate accordingly: "surely I will set upon Dimon even more / for the refugees of Moab, a lion, and for the remnant, an ambush." Note that Moab is gapped in the second colon of the last bicolon, resulting in qînāh meter.

The reversal motif is clearly present in Isa 16:10.[34] Note especially how joy and gladness are taken away and songs are no longer sung, comparing the similar motif in Lam 5:14-15.[35] The prophet uses the *qînâh* meter throughout both of these sections (Isa 15:2a-b, 3a [MT], 3b, 4b, 5a,[36] 6a, 9b; 16:6a, 7a,[37] 8a,[38] 9a, c, 10b,[39] 11).[40]

Although not found in Lamentations, the disruption of agriculture and alteration of the water supply are motifs used commonly in the Mesopotamian laments to depict the city's destruction.[41] In Isa 15:6 the waters of Nimrim dry up and the green vegetation withers. The disruption of agriculture continues as the primary motif in Isa 16:8-11.

The people respond to Moab's destruction by lamenting or undertaking other mourning gestures (see esp. Isa 15:2-3; 16:7).[42] Here, then, in addition to individual motifs such as the geographical motif and the disruption of agriculture and alteration of the water supply, perhaps as many as five city-lament features appear (2.1, 2a, b, d, e, 5, 7, 8), thus strongly marking the city-lament mode in this oracle.

ii. *Jer 48:1-47*   Like Isa 15-16, this chapter comprises an oracle (or oracles) against Moab and features the geographical motif. Much of

---

[34] Cf. Kaiser, *Isaiah 13-39*, 74.

[35] The contrast motif might occur in Isa 16:8, if one understands the "lords of the nations" as striking down the vines (v. 8b) which used to supply a wide area with wine (v. 8c-d; see Kaiser, *Isaiah 13-39*, 57ff.; Watts, *Isaiah*, 224ff.; Oswalt, 343-46), however, the verse is extremely difficult.

[36] MT's *ʿeglat šĕlîšiyyāh* is most likely a gloss for *ṣōʿar*, Wildberger, *Jesaja 13-27*, 591.

[37] Delete *lĕmôʾāb* following Wildberger (*Jesaja 13-27*, 594); cf. Clements, *Isaiah*, 155.

[38] A verb, *šuddĕdû* "are destroyed," has probably dropped out of the text, the scribe's eye skipping from the sequence of *šd* in *šddw* to the *šd* in *šdmwt*. This yields a 4+3 meter.

[39] LXX lacks *haddōrēk*, yielding 4+2 meter.

[40] Cf. Duhm, 103-8; Cheyne, *Book*, 119; Kaiser, *Isaiah 13-39*, 65; Wildberger, *Jesaja 13-27*, 611, 615, 624, 626-27.

[41] See Cooper, *Agade*, 25-26.

[42] In Isa 15:2 the LXX contains a different mourning gesture, the laceration of the arms.

the chapter's second part (vv. 29-47) contains, in William L. Holladay's words, "duplications and reminiscences" of Isa 15-16.[43] The city-lament mode's appearance in this material was just discussed. Yet, much of the material not duplicated from Isaiah also seems to be modulated by city-lament features. The chapter as a whole concerns itself with the destruction of Moab and its major cities. More than any of the passages to be discussed, Jer 48 maintains its *focus* specifically on the destruction of the country. While the poem clearly identifies Yahweh as the one responsible for the destruction (48:12, 33 [MT], 35, 38, 44), conspicuously it lacks any explicit reference to the divine warrior. The poem does refer several times to the enemy (i.e. "destroyer," 48:8, 18, 32).

The first ten verses resemble the litany of place names found in Isa 15-16 (see 3.1a.i above) and its parallel in Jer 48:29-39. Holladay also compares Mic 1:10-15.[44] Robert Carroll observes that this collection of place names gives "the impression of the deity roaming about the land of Moab slaughtering everything he encounters."[45] Of course, the geographical motif in the Mesopotamian laments gives the same impression, only in them it is the storm or enemy which does the slaughtering.

Jeremiah sounds the divine abandonment theme in 48:7.[46] Cries of lament and related mourning gestures pervade the poem (48:2,[47] 4, 5, 18, 20, 31-32,[48] 37-39). The lament particles *hôy* (48:1) and *ʾôy* (48:46) come at the beginning and the end of the poem. The restoration theme may also occur (48:47). The mention of Moab's restoration and that of Egypt (46:26b [MT]), Ammon (49:6 [MT]), and Elam (49:39), like Isaiah's and Jeremiah's (see 3.2a.ii below) mourning over the destruction

---

[43] *Jeremiah 2*, 346; cf. the commentaries, esp. Wildberger, *Jesaja 13-27*, 605-11.

[44] *Jeremiah 2*, 349; see 3.2a.i below.

[45] *Jeremiah* (OTL; Philadelphia: Westminster, 1986) 781.

[46] Reading *kĕmôš* with Q; cf. Block, 149.

[47] *gam-madmēn tiddōmmî* "Aloud, O Madmen, you will weep (√*dmm* II)!" cf. McDaniel, "Studies, I," 31-32.

[48] The identification of the "I" in these verses is not entirely clear. In light of the obvious parallels with Isa 16:9-11, one should perhaps understand Jeremiah as the one grieving the destruction of Moab. However, Holladay's contention that Yahweh constitutes the proper antecedent cannot be ruled out (*Jeremiah 2*, 352).

of foreign nations, seems somewhat jarring at first glance. However, undoubtedly Carroll is correct in maintaining that this theme is conventional in nature.[49] Yahweh brings about the destruction of a foreign nation, and the nation's subsequent survival represents Yahweh's restoration of its fortunes. This conventionalist interpretation corresponds well with the fact that restoration is a common feature in city laments.

The images of personified Dibon and Aroer dominate 48:17-20:

> Console[50] him,[51] all you who are round about,
> all you who know his name!
> Say: "How the mighty rod is broken,
> the glorious staff!
> Come down from glory and sit[52] in filth,[53]

---

[49] Carroll, 796.

[50] This is Hillers' translation (*Lamentations* (2d), 38. Also see D. Paul Volz's "have compassion on him" (*Der Prophet Jeremia* [KAT 10; 2d ed.; Leipzig: A. Deichertsche, 1928] 406). Most commentators, however, translate "mourn" or the like, e.g. D. C. H. Cornill, *Das Buch Jeremia* (Leipzig: Tauchnitz, 1905) 466; F. Giesebrecht, *Das Buch Jeremia* (HAT 2/1; Göttingen: Vandenhoeck & Ruprecht, 1907) 235; Artur Weiser, *Der Prophet Jeremia 25:14-52:34* (ATD 21; Göttingen: Vandenhoeck & Ruprecht. 1955) 401; Bright, 315; Carroll, 785; Holladay, *Jeremiah 2*, 342. In support of Hillers' translation, one may note that friends and neighbors were expected to comfort the grieving person. Rachel refuses such comfort (Jer 31:15) and in Lamentations, as in laments in general (see Hillers, *Lamentations*, 19), Zion complains that her neighbors do not comfort (√nhm) her (Lam 1:2, 9, 16, 21). The meaning "to comfort, console, take pity" falls within √nwd's semantic range (Jer 15:5; Ps 69:21; Job 2:11; 42:11). Here those who live near Moab and know him are urged to console him.

[51] Note that Moab's gender varies throughout this chapter, see especially v. 20.

[52] Reading ûšĕbî "and sit" with many Heb. Mss, the versions, and Q.

[53] Read baṣṣōʾāh "in filth" for MT's baṣṣāmāʾ "in thirst," so Cornill, 466-67; Volz, 409, n. q; Weiser, *Jeremia 25*, 401; Bright, 315; Wilhelm Rudolph, *Jeremia* (HAT 12; 3d ed.; Tübingen: Mohr, 1968) 276; Carroll, 786; Holladay, *Jeremiah 2*, 342-43. The conventional image is that of a god or goddess coming down from his or her throne and sitting on the ground, in the dust. Thus, revocalizing MT to baṣṣāmēʾ "on parched ground," so *NRSV*, cf. Isa 44:3. has some appeal. However, in the first half of the colon the prophet speaks hyperbolically, substituting the more figurative or abstract glory for the concrete throne. So one might suppose he does the same thing in the second half of the colon, substituting the hyperbolic filth for the more conventional ground or dust.

> O Enthroned One, Daughter of Dibon!
> For the destroyer of Moab has come up against you,
>   he has destroyed your strongholds.
> Stand by the way and look,
>   O Enthroned One of Aroer!
> Ask the man fleeing and the woman escaping,
>   say, 'What has happened?'
> Moab is ashamed,[54] she is terrified,
>   wail and cry out!"[55]
> Tell it at the Arnon
>   that Moab is destroyed.

The passage is enveloped by mp imperatives addressed to Moab's neighbors (*nūdû* and *ʾimrû*, v. 17; *haggîdû*, v. 20). That is, the dirge (vv. 17b-20a) has been put into the mouths of Moab's neighbors.[56] In these verses note the presence of *qînāh* meter, the female mourning figures, and the image of the enemy in 48:18.[57]

In this dirge personified Dibon and Aroer are referred to by the term *yōšebet* (or *yôšebet*). Most interpreters translate *yōšebet* here and elsewhere with a variety of terms meaning "to live, dwell, or inhabit."[58] However, Holladay is surely correct in arguing that the figure designated by the phrases *yōšebet bě-GN/yōšebet (const.) GN* is the enthroned city.[59] These phrases were titles borne by kings and gods in Israel and the ancient Near East.[60] In particular note the following titles: *hdd ysb skn* "Hadad, the Enthroned One of Sikan" (*Tell Fakhariyeh*, 15-16), *l-yhwh yōšēb ṣiyyôn* "to Yahweh, the Enthroned One of Zion" (Ps 9:12),

---

[54] Emend MT's *hōbîš* (ms) to *hōbîšāh* (fs) corresponding to *hattāh* (fs), so Holladay, *Jeremiah 2*, 343; *contra* Rudolph, *Jeremia*; Carroll, 787.

[55] Reading *hêlîlî ûzeʿāqî* (fs imperatives) with LXX and Q, so Cornill, 467; Weiser, *Jeremia 25*, 401; Holladay, *Jeremiah 2*, 343. Either Aroer (cf. Cornill, 467) or Moab is being addressed.

[56] Cf. Hillers, *Lamentations* (2d), 39.

[57] Cf. Giesebrecht, 235; Volz, 413; Rudolph, *Jeremia*, 277; Hillers, *Lamentations* (2d), 39.

[58] Cf. *NRSV* and *NJV* at v. 19.

[59] *Jeremiah 1* (Hermeneia; Philadelphia: Fortress, 1986) 341.

[60] See the convenient discussion by Francis I. Andersen and David Noel Freedman (*Amos* [AB 24a; Garden City: Doubleday, 1989] 253-54).

and *hayyōšĕbî baššāmāyim* "the one enthroned in heaven" (Ps 123:1; cf. 2:4). Interpretation of Isa 47:8 as a reference to the Daughter of Chaldea's secure enthronement seems most logical, since her lack of a throne is explicitly mentioned in 47:1, implying that she was indeed previously enthroned (this is further supported by the Ugaritic parallel cited below; cf. Zeph 2:15). The same image occurs here in v. 18, only *yōšebet* is clearly used as a title. Moreover, the divine title interpretation corresponds well with the personified cities' other divine epithets (see 2.7 above). In fact, such an interpretation is demanded by passages such as Lam 4:21: "Rejoice and be glad, O Daughter of Edom, you who are enthroned in the land of Uz" (cf. Jer 22:23).

Lastly, a number of individual motifs recall motifs from Lamentations and/or other passages colored by the city-lament mode. The description of a Moabite city as "the glory of Moab" (*tĕhillat mô°āb*; Jer 48:2) corresponds nicely to the descriptions of Babylon ("the splendor and pride of the Chaldeans" *tip°eret gĕ°ôn kaśdîm*; Isa 13:19) and Jerusalem ("the splendor of Israel" *tip°eret yiśrā°ēl*; Lam 2:1b). In Jer 48:25 Moab's horn (*qeren*) is hewn down (√*gd°*) as is Israel's in Lam 2:3a. And perhaps a variation of the taunt of the passers-by occurs in Jer 48:39: "And Moab will become a laughingstock and terror to all those round about him" (cf. Lam 1:7d; 2:15, 16; 2.6a above).

Here again the use of the city-lament mode is indicated by a large number of identifiable city-lament features (2.1, 2c, d, e, 3, 5, 6a, 7, 8, 9) and related motifs. The use of the geographical motif and the *focus* on destruction stand out in this oracle.

iii. *Isa 47:1-15*   McDaniel observes that the image of personified Babylon in Isa 47:1-5 closely resembles that of the Daughter of Zion in Lamentations.[61] In fact, this chapter contains one of the most developed depictions of the personified city motif in the Hebrew Bible outside of Lamentations. However, Isa 47 contains other city-lament features as well. The subject of the chapter is Babylon's destruction (Isa 47:11). The poet clearly casts much of the chapter in *qînāh* meter, especially Isa 47:1-9 where most of the city-lament imagery occurs (vv. 1a-c, 2a-b, 5a-

---

[61] "Studies, I," 31.

b, 6a, and 9a-b).[62] The poet contrasts personified Babylon's past status as the "tender and delicate" "Mistress of Kingdoms" with her present station, a slave grinding flour (Isa 47:1-2, 5).[63] Yahweh is the agent of destruction. He becomes angry with his people (Isa 47:6a; √qsp, cf. Lam 5:22), pollutes his heritage (Isa 47:6a; cf. Lam 2:2c; 5:2), and gives them into Babylon's hands (Isa 47:6b; ntn ... byd). The divine abandonment theme appears in Isa 46:1-2 (these verses narrate how the prostrated images of Bel and Nebo are borne away into captivity),[64] anticipating the account of Babylon's destruction in Isa 47. Finally, two individual motifs have parallels in Lamentations: compare lōʾ zākart ʾaḥărîtāh in Isa 47:7b with lōʾ zākĕrāh ʾaḥărîtāh in Lam 1:9a[65] and note how the plight of the elderly emerges in Isa 47:6c and Lam 1:19b-c, 2:21a, and 5:12.[66]

The most striking image remains that of personified Babylon. The poet gives her several divine epithets: "Maiden, Daughter of Babylon" (Isa 47:1a), "Daughter of Chaldea" (Isa 47:1b, 5a), and "Mistress of Kingdoms" (Isa 47:5b). The image of a widowed and childless, personified city occurs in Isa 47:8-9. The Daughter of Babylon's words in Isa 47:8 and 10, ʾănî wĕʾapsî ʿôd ("I am, and there is no other but me"), further elaborate the portrayal of the personified city as a divine figure. They closely resemble Yahweh's own words in Isa 45:5 (ʾănî yhwh wĕʾēn ʿôd zûlātî ʾēn ʾĕlōhîm "I am Yahweh and there is no other, besides me there is no god"), 45:6 (kî-ʾepes bilʿādāy / ʾănî yhwh wĕʾēn ʿôd "for there is no other besides me / I am Yahweh and there is no other"), and 46:9 (kî ʾānōkî ʾēl wĕʾên ʿôd ʾĕlōhîm wĕʾepes kāmônî "for I am god and there is no other god, and there is no one like me").[67]

---

[62] See Sidney Smith, *Isaiah Chapters XL--LV: Literary Criticism and History* (London: Oxford, 1944) 88.

[63] Christopher R. North, *The Second Isaiah* (Oxford: Clarendon, 1964) 169; Claus Westermann, *Isaiah 40-66* (OTL; trans. D. M. G. Stalker; Philadelphia: Westminster, 1969) 190.

[64] Cf. Block, 149.

[65] North, 171; Hillers, *Lamentations*, 24; Westermann, *Klagelieder*, 114.

[66] Westermann, *Isaiah*, 191.

[67] Cf. North, 171.

Isa 47:1-3a, 5 are extremely well crafted verses. Most commentators recognize the contrast between queenly and enslaved Babylon at play here. However, this is only the tip of the iceberg. This portrait of personified Babylon seems to combine the motif of the weeping goddess with that of the plundering of the divine image. Westermann correctly notices the close Ugaritic parallel[68]:

apnk. ltpn. il dpid.	Thereupon Ltpn, Kindly El
yrd. lksi. yṯb lhdm	came down from the throne (and) sat on the footstool,
[w]l. hdm. yṯb lars	and from the footstool, he sat on the ground.
	(*KTU* 1.5.VI.11-14)

Similarly, the Daughter of Babylon is commanded to come down (✓*yrd*) and sit (✓*yšb*) on the ground (ᶜ*āpār*, ᵓ*āreṣ*) where there is no throne (*kissēᵓ*). However, Westermann fails to mention that El's actions form part of the gestures which accompany his lament over the death of Baal, just as personified Babylon's actions are in response to the predicted destruction of Babylon. Hillers connects the Ugaritic text to the tradition behind the imagery in Lam 1:4, especially that of the grieving virgins and bitter, personified Zion.[69] Another parallel occurs in LSUr 408-10, where Niniagara sits down in the dust to mourn the destruction of her temple (see 2.3 above). The goddess in Lambert's NB Tammuz lament also complains that her throne has been overturned (ln. 22: ᵍⁱˢ*kussî nēmettīya ultabalkitannu*). Thus, as McDaniel argues, the imagery in Isa 47:1 undoubtedly relates to personified Babylon's bewailing the destruction of her city (see Ezek 26:16-17 and Lam 2:10 for biblical examples of these gestures).[70]

Mixed in with the city goddess image is the motif of the looting and carrying off of the divine image. It has already been observed that occasionally in the Mesopotamian laments the divine image and the

---

[68] *Isaiah*, 190.

[69] "'The Roads to Zion Mourn' (Lam 1:4)," *Perspective* 12 (1971) 123-30.

[70] Note further that in Isa 47:5 personified Babylon is told to sit and wail (✓*dmm* II). For the concepts of "mourning" and "darkness" together, see Jer 4:28 (ᵓ*bl/qdr*) and 14:2 (ᵓ*bl*, ᵓ*ml*, *swh/qdr*).

goddess become one. The best example of this happens in *balag* 50:b+155-61 quoted above (see 2.3 above). In this *balag* the enemy enters the temple and approaches the cultic barge. The barge's bow houses the goddess' treasure and the stern, her divine image. The enemy physically abuses Inanna/the divine image. They tear off her garments and steal her lapis-lazuli. The goddesses' garments are removed in the NB Tammuz lament as well (lns. 2, 18; cf. *balag* 42:115 [OB]). Similarly in Isa 47:2-3 the Daughter of Babylon's veil[71] and robe[72] are stripped off, and she is perhaps even sexually abused.[73] John L. McKenzie strongly rejects the suggestion that Isa 47:2-3 alludes to the punishment of the adulterous wife described in Ezek 16:37 and Hos 2:10.[74] He is surely correct, since there is no mention of adultery in Isa 47.[75]

The Daughter of Babylon "crosses the river" into exile and enslavement (Isa 47:2).[76] This, of course, calls to mind both the exile of the weeping goddess and the victor's carting off of the conquered people's divine images.

Another concept related to the divine abandonment theme may be relevant for the interpretation of Isa 47. In Mesopotamian theology when a god leaves his or her throne, chaos and destruction ensue. This

---

[71] The word translated "veil" (*sammāh) occurs elsewhere only in the Song of Songs (Cant 4:1, 3; 6:7), where much of the imagery is taken from the description of statues, see Jerrold S. Cooper, "New Cuneiform Parallels to the Song of Songs," *JBL* 90 (1971) 160; Marvin H. Pope, *Song of Songs* (AB 7c; Garden City: Doubleday, 1977) 72.

[72] 1QIsa[a] reads the more common *šwlyk* (cf. Jer 13:22, 26; Nah 3:5; Lam 1:9) for MT's *hapax legomenon šōbel*.

[73] North, 170; John L. McKenzie, *Second Isaiah* (AB 20; Garden City: Doubleday, 1968) 92.

[74] McKenzie, 91.

[75] This shaming sanction (see Lyn M. Bechtel, "Shame as a Sanction of Social Control in Biblical Israel: Judicial, Political, and Social Shaming," *JSOT* 49 [1991] 47-76) was of course mirrored on the human level, whereby prisoners of war in the ancient Near East were commonly stripped and lead naked into captivity (Bechtel, 63-67).

[76] See McKenzie, 91.

is best illustrated in the Erra Epic.[77] When Erra urges Marduk to leave
his throne in order to get his statue refurbished, Marduk tells of the
destruction which resulted the last time he became angry and left his
throne (I:132-48) and of the destruction which will surely follow if he
does so again (I:170-77). The dethronement of the Daughter of Babylon
thus poignantly symbolizes Babylon's destruction.

Thus, Second Isaiah seems to have crafted his oracle around the
figure of personified Babylon, while incorporating other prominent city-
lament features (2.1, 2b, d, 3, 5) and characteristic motifs. The city-
lament mode is very pervasive here. If the oracle was truly penned by
Second Isaiah, then it also represents one of the latest samples of the
city-lament genre in the Hebrew Bible (i.e. mid-sixth century B.C.E.).

iv. *Jer 50:1-51:58*   This oracle(s) against Babylon is by far the most
extensive OAN in Jeremiah. Like Lam 2:1-9a, but unlike many of the
other prophetic passages under discussion, Jer 50-51 *focuses* chiefly on
Yahweh's destructive power. Yahweh is the main actor throughout these
chapters. As the divine warrior (50:25; 51:25) and the one who rouses
the enemy to attack (50:3, 9 [√⁻wr], 41 [√⁻wr]; 51:1-2 [√⁻wr], 11-12
[√⁻wr], 14), he causes Babylon's destruction (50:32; 51:6, 25, 55).
Yahweh's anger is kindled against Babylon (50:13; 51:45) and he carries
out his plan (50:45; 51:11-12, 29). The enemy attack is depicted quite
literally (50:14, 21-22, 26-29, 41-42; 51:27-28), which has good parallels
in the Mesopotamian city laments (e.g. LU 219-25; LSUr 381-88; LW
5:11-19).

Jer 51:9 ("For her judgement has reached to the heavens and is
lifted up unto the clouds") may be a veiled reference to the divine
assembly's confirmation of Babylon's fate.[78]

The divine abandonment theme emerges twice, albeit in very
polemical garb. Bel/Marduk does not actually abandon Babylon. Rather,
Babylon is captured presumably while he is still present (50:2), implying

---

[77] See Luigi Cagni, *L'Epopea di Erra* (Studi Semitici 34; Rome: Universita di
Roma, 1969) 70-77, 184-86; *The Poem of Erra* (SANE 1/3; Malibu: Undena, 1974)
32-34, esp. 33, n. 36.

[78] Cf. Holladay, *Jeremiah 2*, 422.

a humiliating defeat at the hands of Yahweh. Bel's punishment by Yahweh is made explicit in 51:44.[79]

Descriptions of Babylon's destruction appear periodically in the poems, often in motifs familiar from the city-lament genre. The city walls, gates, and buildings are demolished (50:15; 51:30, 44, 58) and the corpses of Babylon's soldiers are stacked in her streets and squares (50:26, 30; 51:4, 47). The city becomes deserted (50:12, 13; 51:42-43), only inhabited by wild animals (50:39-40; 51:37). It is likened to Sodom and Gomorrah (50:40). Seeing the once glorious city in this condition, passers-by hurl taunts at her (50:13; 51:37).

Babylon is held responsible for her own destruction. But unlike other OAN, Jer 50-51 repeatedly refer to Yahweh's punishment of Babylon (√pqd; 50:18, 27, 31: 51:18, 44, 47, 52) and Yahweh's vengeance (nĕqāmāh; 50:15, 28; 51:6, 11) and recompense (√šlm; 51:24, 56). As is usual in the OAN, Babylon is accused of extreme hubris (50:24, 29). But it is doubtful that hubris alone accounts for such strong language. Rather, one notes that chief among Babylon's other crimes is the profanation of the Jerusalem temple (51:11, 51). Such sacrilege by itself would incur talk of punishment and revenge. Note the same sentiment on Enlil's part in CA 151:

> Enlil, concerning his Ekur which was destroyed, what should he destroy (in revenge)[80] for it?

The profanation of the temple mentioned in 51:51 provides the rationale (lākēn, at least at a redactional level) for Yahweh's punishment referred to in the following verse.[81] Jer 51:11, secondary addition[82] or not,

---

[79] Note that bēl bĕbābel represents the divine name type "DN in GN" (for which see P. Kyle McCarter, Jr., "Aspects of the Religion of the Israelite Monarchy: Biblical and Epigraphic Data," in *Ancient Israelite Religion* [eds. P. D. Miller, Jr., P. D. Hanson, and S. D. McBride; Philadelphia: Fortress, 1987] 140), signifying the local manifestation of Bel in Babylon.

[80] Cooper shows that this phraseology is used elsewhere in Sumerian literature to introduce vengeful acts (*Agade*, 248-49).

[81] Cf. Carroll, 850.

[82] So Bright, 347; Rudolph, *Jeremia*, 308; Carroll, 839; Holladay, *Jeremiah 2*, 397.

explicitly connects Yahweh's vengeance with the profanation of his temple.

The Daughter of Babylon is present in the oracle (e.g. 50:42; 51:13, 33), but her character is flat, not fully developed. She is most often only the object of destruction and abuse. Although brief the portrait of Babylon as a grieving and broken mother is poignant:

> Your[83] mother is very ashamed (*bôšāh*),
> she who bore you is humiliated.[84]
> Look! The last of nations[85] is (now)
> a wilderness, dry and wasted! (Jer 50:12)

Personified Israel's widowhood is briefly mentioned (Jer 51:5) and the "Enthroned One of Zion" utters a mock dirge over Babylon (Jer 51:35).

The mention of lamentation is also at a minimum in these chapters. Only once is the call to lamentation issued: "Suddenly Babylon has fallen and is shattered, wail over her!" (Jer 51:8; cf. Ezek 26:15-18; Amos 5:2). Jeremiah employs the *qînāh* meter sparsely but consistently (e.g. Jer 50:11a, 12a, 22, 23, 27b, 28a, 31b, 41, 42c; 51:1b, 2b, 4, 5b, 8, 13a, 35, 37a, 41, 44b),[86] and brief dirges arise at times. For example, note the following:

> How she has been hewn down and shattered,
> the hammer of all the earth!
> How she has become a desolation,
> Babylon among the nations! (Jer 50:23)

---

[83] The 2 mp suffix refers to Babylon's populace, her children, addressed with 2 mp verb forms in v. 11 (reading with Q).

[84] The image is one of shame and humiliation at personified Babylon's reversal of status.

[85] Perhaps "the last of the nations" refers to Babylon, all alone after the surrounding towns have been destroyed and abandoned, but just prior to the final assault. A similar image of Uruk appears in LW 5:9: "The surrounding villages were scattered, Uruk stood all alone." The image, then, is the still proud but solitary Babylon which is instantly (*hinnēh*) turned into a wasteland. A few lines later in LW, this same sentiment is rendered: "Uruk, the good place, is (now) ... with dust" (5:16).

[86] Cf. Rudolph, *Jeremia*, 301, 303, 305, 311, 313.

How she has been captured and seized,[87]
    the glory of all the earth![88]
How she has become a desolation,
    Babylon among the nations!   (Jer 51:41)

Note especially the plaint in Jer 50:23b and 51:41b. It is very close to the plaints in Lam 1:1: a) they lament the desolation of a city; b) *ʾêk* and *ʾêkāh* are semantic equivalents; c) *ʾêk hāyětāh lěšammāh* is very close to *ʾêkāh...hāyětāh kěʾalmānāh/hāyětāh lāmas*; and d) *bābel baggôyim* is reminiscent of *rabbātî baggôyim* and *śārātî bammědînôt*.

The only restoration referred to is that of Israel (50:4-5, 19; 51:5, 45). Indeed, it is effected as a result of Babylon's destruction. Thus, all nine features surveyed in Chapter Two appear in this oracle, though most do not seem to be as developed as they are in some of the other passages treated in this study. Nonetheless, the city-lament mode's presence is unmistakable.

v. *Isa 23:1-14*   Verses 1a and 14 form an inclusio delimiting the original oracle. Commentators disagree whether this oracle originally addressed all of Phoenicia or only one city, Tyre or Sidon. The resolution of this debate does not bear significantly on the present study. However, the prominence of Sidon in the poem leads one to follow Kaiser and others who believe that the oracle originally addressed Sidon.[89]

The presence of Tyre does not necessarily have to result only from the recasting of the oracle which accompanied the addition of vv. 15-18.[90] It has been frequently noted that city laments, while focusing on one city, also have a larger geographical area in their purview. Thus,

---

[87] Following LXX, which lacks the secondarily inserted athbash *šēšak*, see Cornill, 518; Giesebrecht, 254; Volz, 438; Weiser, *Jeremia 25*, 433; Bright, 358; Carroll, 846; Holladay, *Jeremiah 2*, 399.

[88] Again the familiar description of the city with *těhillat* (or its synonyms) occurs.

[89] Kaiser, *Isaiah 13-39*, 162-63. See discussions by Wildberger (*Jesaja, 13-27*, 859-61) and Clements (*Isaiah*, 191-92).

[90] Kaiser, *Isaiah 13-39*, 162-63.

the inclusion of Tyre and other Phoenician localities in this oracle may be original.

The destruction of Sidon and greater Phoenicia forms the primary subject matter of the poem (Isa 23:1, 9, 10, 11, 13, 14). Immediately one recognizes a common city-lament motif in the description of the destruction, Sidon[91] is to be turned into a ruin (*mappēlāh*), a lair for wild animals (*siyyîm*; Isa 23:13). The poet calls on people (Isa 23:2,[92] 6) as well as the "ships of Tarshish" (Isa 23:1, 14) to lament over this destruction. Jahnow correctly notes that the personified ships parallel the personified roads, gates, and city walls which cry out in Lamentations and other city laments.[93] The dominant image of Phoenician shipping here exerts itself over the more typical imagery usually associated with cities.

Structurally, the poet employs *qînāh* meter throughout the poem (Isa 23:1b, 2a, 2γ-3α,[94] 4δ-ε, 10,[95] 11a-b).[96] He also uses the contrast

---

[91] This verse is hopelessly corrupt, however, the 3fs suffixes (*yĕsādāh*, *śāmāh*) certainly refer to the Daughter of Sidon in Isa 23:12.

[92] Derive MT's *dōmmû* from √*dmm* II "to wail," cf. Akk. *damāmu*; Wildberger, *Jesaja 13-27*, 856.

[93] Jahnow, 194. The other nine times that *ᵓŏniyyôt* (*ᵓŏnî* 1 Kgs 10:22, 22) *taršîš* occurs, it is used in a natural sense (1 Kgs 22:49; 2 Chron 9:21; Ps 48:8; Isa 2:16; 60:9; Ezek 27:25).

[94] Here read: *ᶜōbĕrîm yām malᵓākêkem / bĕmayim rabbîm* "whose messengers cross over the sea / on mighty waters" (cf. Ps 107:23, LXX, 1QIsaᵃ, Kaiser [*Isaiah 13-39*, 160]). MT, LXX, and 1QIsaᵃ have all suffered haplographies:

MT   =   ᶜbr   y̱m̱ mlᵓwk wbmym rbym
LXX   =   ᶜbrẙm̱ y̱m   bmẙm̱ rbym
1QIsaᵃ   =   ᶜbṟw̱ y̱m mlᵓkyk wbmym rbym

Wildberger suggests that the suffix on "messengers" should be 3fs, identifying the antecedent as Sidon (*Jesaja 13-27*, 856). However, the antecedents must surely be the vocatives "inhabitants of the coastlands" and "merchants (reading a plural construct with LXX, Syr., and Targ.) of Sidon."

[95] Read: *ᶜibrî ᵓarsēk bat-taršîš / ᵓên māhōz ᶜôd* "Cross over to your land, O Daughter of Tarshish, / this is a harbor no more." LXX lacks MT's *kayᵓōr*, thus it is deleted here as a gloss (Kaiser, *Isaiah 13-39*, 161; Clements, *Isaiah*, 194). MT's *mēzah* "girdle" makes no sense. Many critics read *māhōz* "harbor, wharf" (cf. Ps 107:30), assuming that the final two consonants have been metathesized (*BHS*; Kaiser, *Isaiah 13-39*, 161; Clements, *Isaiah*, 194; see Wildberger [*Jesaja 13-27*, 857] and Watts

motif in Isa 23:7, 8, and 12.[97] Each of these verses presents an image of
the past which, of course, is to be contrasted with the present desolation
of Sidon, Tyre, and Phoenicia.[98] Jahnow also calls attention to the use
of questions in Isa 23:7 and 8, a commonplace in laments in general (cf.
Lam 2:13a-b, 15c).[99]

The poem identifies Yahweh as the agent of destruction. As the
divine warrior, Yahweh stretches his hand over the sea and causes the
kingdoms to quake (Isa 23:11a).[100] Yahweh plans (Isa 23:8-9) and
commands the destruction. And if Isa 23:13 can be trusted (?), he uses
Assyria as his instrument.

The personified city motif is also present in the poem. The
prophet specifically gives Sidon and Tarshish divine epithets (bětûlat
bat ṣîdôn, Isa 23:12; bat taršîš, Isa 23:10). Like the Daughter of Zion
(Lam 1:3b) and her Mesopotamian counterparts, there is no rest for the
Daughter of Sidon (Isa 23:12b). And Isa 23:4 pictures Sidon as a divine
mother in mourning.[101]

The latter verse contains a number of problems. The versions
provide little help, so most commentators result to some kind of

---

[Isaiah, 303] for other suggestions). As an alternative to MT's ʿibrî, one might follow
LXX and 1QIsaᵃ, which read ʿibdî "work, till."

[96] Cf. Wildberger, Jesaja 13-27, 862.

[97] Cf. Jahnow, 194. Note that in both Isa 23:7 and 12 words derived from √ʿlz "to
exult" are used to describe the city's past status. This suggests that Isa 22:2a also
involves the contrast motif. In this verse Jerusalem, "the noisy city, exultant town," is
filled with the sounds of destruction (těšuʾôt; see Job 36:29 [the sound of thunder]
for the semantic ranges of šôʾāh and měšôʾāh). That is, the past sounds of normal
city life are replaced by the din of battle. Isa 22:2b, then, would refer to death by
disease and famine which always accompanied war in the ancient Near East.

[98] The reversal motif would be present if one emended dōmmû in Isa 23:2 to
nidmû ("the inhabitants of the coastlands are ruined/quieted") with Kaiser (Isaiah 13-
39, 160, 164-65) and Clements (Isaiah, 193). This deathly silence would contrast with
the past bustle of Phoenician trading. This writer, however, opts to understand the
verse differently, avoiding the need for emendation (see above).

[99] Jahnow, 196.

[100] Kaiser, Isaiah 13-39, 167.

[101] Jahnow, 194.

emendation. Many delete *mā̄ʿôz hayyām* as an explanatory gloss.[102]
lēʾmōr is prosaizing and is lacking in the Syr., and thus should be
deleted.[103] Still, one cannot determine why the sea should be speaking.
As some scholars argue the speech must be personified Sidon's.[104] The
content suggests this as does the *ʾmrh* of 1QIsaᵃ. The image is that of
a woman who either has not borne and raised children or can do so no
longer.[105] A woman's value in much of antiquity was dependent upon the
number of children she could bear.[106] Thus, personified Sidon's present
status is one of a childless woman, typical of goddesses in the Mesopotamian city laments.

This speech can be related to a similar statement in Isa 47:8.
There the Daughter of Babylon boasts that she will never experience
widowhood or loss of children:

> Now hear this, O lover of pleasures,
>   who sits securely enthroned,
>   who says in your heart,
> "I am, and there is no one besides me,
>   I will not sit as a widow,
>   and I will not know childlessness."

The following verse reports that personified Babylon will become
childless and widowed (Isa 47:9), which of course is the basic sense of
personified Sidon's speech in Isa 23:4.

The two speeches differ in that Sidon's is not a boast but a
lament. This is indicated by Heb. *bwš* "to be ashamed." The word is
often used in lament contexts (e.g. Isa 19:9; 29:22; Jer 14:3-4; 48:1, 20,

---

[102] E.g. Duhm, 143: Cheyne, *Book*, 93; Kaiser, *Isaiah 13-39*, 160; Wildberger, *Jesaja 13-27*, 856.

[103] Cf. Duhm, 143; Cheyne, *Book*, 93; Wildberger, *Jesaja 13-27*, 856.

[104] Jahnow, 194; Paul Auvrey, *Isaïe 1-39* (Paris: Librairie Lecoffre, 1972) 217; Kaiser, *Isaiah 13-39*, 160; Clements, *Isaiah*, 193.

[105] The grammar is ambiguous. If the comparison with Isa 47:8 is accurate, then it is perhaps best to see Sidon as no longer being able to bear or raise children. Put differently, Sidon's loss is so great that it is as if she never had children, cf. Jahnow, 194; Clements, *Isaiah*, 193.

[106] Wildberger, *Jesaja 13-27*, 873.

39; 49:23; 50:2; Joel 1:11). Although such a concept of shame is strange to modern western ears, Holladay may nevertheless be correct in suggesting that the translation "shame" be maintained. He notes that different cultures may have different concepts of shame.[107] Here personified Sidon's shame combines with grief at the reversal of her fortunes and her inability to live up to societal norms.[108] A similar notion of shame characterizes the grieving city/country in Jer 48:20, 49:4, and 50:12.

Note that personified Babylon is addressed with an imperative (*šimᶜî*) and that the vocative (*ᶜădînāh*) is continued by relative clauses consisting of definite feminine singular participles (*hayyôšebet, hāᵓōmĕrāh*).[109] Isa 23:4 may be understood in a similar fashion, translating as follows:

> Be ashamed, O Sidon, you who utter aloud,[110]
> > "I cannot labor nor give birth,
> I cannot raise up young men,
> > nor bring up young maidens."

---

[107] *Jeremiah 1*, 431.

[108] Cf. Bechtel.

[109] For this peculiarity of vocative addresses, see Delbert R. Hillers, "*Hôy* and *Hôy*-Oracles: A Neglected Syntactic Aspect," in *The Word of the Lord Shall Go Forth* (eds. C. L. Meyers and M. O'Connor; Winona Lake: Eisenbrauns, 1983) 185-88.

[110] MT has been emended to read *bwšy sydwn hᵓmrh gm*. Kaiser proposes a similar emendation (*Isaiah 13-39*, 160), only he deletes *yām* and reads a different form of the feminine participle (*hāᵓōmeret*). The emendation suggested here has the advantage of being able to explain how *yām* came into the text. *yām* would have entered the text via a graphic confusion between *gimel* and *yod*. Confusion between these two letters is common. Moreover, *gam* "aloud" has been plausibly identified in at least three similar lament contexts: Jer 48:2, Lam 1:8c, and Ps 137:1 (McDaniel, "Studies, I," 31-32). The preference for *hāᵓōmĕrāh* derives from the reading of 1QIsaᵃ (*ᵓmrh*).

Clements' emendation ("she cries in her shame [*bĕbōšet*]"), which follows *NEB*, has similar implications as the emendation offered here (*Isaiah*, 193), but it involves a more radical departure from MT and the versions and fails to account for *yām*.

Thus, perhaps as many as six city-lament features (2.1, 2, 5-8) have been incorporated into this oracle.

vi. *Zeph 2:13-15*   The last section of Zephaniah's speech against the foreign nations in 2:4-15 is cast in the form of a short dirge over the destruction of Nineveh:

> He will stretch out his hand against the north
>> and destroy Asshur.[111]
> He will make Nineveh into a ruin,
>> dry as a desert.
> Flocks will lie down in her midst,
>> all the wild animals of the meadow.[112]
> The hawk and the hedgehog
>> will lodge on her capitals.
> The owl[113] will sing out in the window,
>> the raven,[114] on the threshold < >[115]:

---

[111] It is ambiguous as to whether the country or city is intended here. Roberts suggests that reference to the city Asshur would make a good parallel to Nineveh (*Nahum*, 203).

[112] Emending MT's *gôy* to *nāway*, which Wilhelm Rudolph understands as a byform of *nāweh* "habitation, abode" (*Micha, Nahum, Habakuk, Zephanja* [KAT 13; Gütersloher: Mohn, 1975] 278, n. 14b). Others emend to *gayᵓ* "valley," so *BHS*; D. Ernst Sellin, *Das Zwölfprophetenbuch* (KAT 12/2; Leipzig: A. Deichertsche, 1930) 431. The LXX's reading *tēs gēs* should be rejected. It is probably substituting the more common phrase *haytô-ᵓāres* for MT (note the Syr. follows MT here). Moreover, the phrases "the wild animals of the land" and *haytô-śādāy* "the wild animals of the field" do not fit the context here. These phrases only occur when the wild animals are sent to consume the land. Here it is a matter of animals dwelling amid the destroyed city's ruins.

[113] Emending MT's *qôl* to *kôs* "owl," so *BHS*; *NRSV*; Sellin, *Zwölf* (2), 431; Friedrich Horst, *Die Zwölf kleinen Propheten: Nahum bis Maleachi* (Tübingen: J. C. B. Mohr, 1938) 191. Rudolph adds *kôs* after *qôl* (*Micha*, 278, n. 14f). Roberts takes *qôl* as a bird name (*Nahum*, 194, n. 24).

[114] Reading *ᶜōrēb* with the LXX for MT's *horeb* "desolation," so *BHS*; *NRSV*; *NJV*; Sellin, *Zwölf* (2), 431; Horst, 191; Rudolph, *Micha*, 278, n. 14h; Roberts, *Nahum*, 194, n. 26. Cf. Isa 34:11.

[115] Delete the last colon in MT *metri causa*. See Rudolph (*Micha*, 278-79, n. 14i) for discussion. No solution has yet emerged for this crux.

"(So) this is the exulted city,
> she who sat securely enthroned,
who said in her heart:
> 'I am and there is no one else!'
How she has become a desolation,
> a lair for wild animals!
Everyone who passes by her,
> hisses and shakes his fist."

(Zeph 2:13-15)

Though brief, the existence of the city-lament mode in this dirge is unquestionable. *qînāh* meter dominates the dirge.[116] Nineveh's past glory (2:15a-b) is contrasted with her present desolation (2:15c-d). Zeph 2:13 attributes Nineveh's destruction to Yahweh. Language very similar to 2:13b is used to describe Babylon in Jer 50:12-13. The motif of the dwelling-place of animals occurs in 2:14, conventionally depicting Nineveh's ruination. Notice the unique twist added by Zephaniah, however. The owl and raven sing a dirge within a dirge. Part of the second dirge (2:15aβ-b) occurs also in Isa 47:8aβ-b (see 3.1a.iii above), verifying the prophet's personification of Nineveh like a weeping goddess. This interchangeability reminds one of how stock phrases are used in the *balags*. The adjective *hā⁻allîzāh* "exulted" (2:15) is used in dirges over Jerusalem (Isa 22:2) and Sidon (Isa 23:7). The familiar taunt of the passers-by appears in 2:15d. Also compare Zeph 2:15c with Jer 50:23b and 51:41b and Lam 1:1b.

b. **Moderate Modulation**

This group of passages on the average contains fewer city-lament features than those discussed above. Yet, the city-lament mode's presence in these passages nevertheless seems certain. That is, the city-lament mode in these texts seems diminished only in scope.

i. *Isa 13:1-22* There remains some debate concerning the integrity and delimitation of Isa 13 and the identity of the nation upon which the

---

[116] Cf. Sellin, *Zwölf* (2), 432; Horst, 189; Rudolph, *Micha*, 283.

chapter focuses.[117] These matters, however, do not bear directly on the question at hand. For the purposes of this study, Isa 13 is interpreted as a single unit addressing Babylon.

Several features of Isa 13 resemble features known from the city lament's generic repertoire, especially in vv. 14-22. These latter verses depict the destruction of Babylon. The people flee (13:14) or are killed (13:15-16, 18). A number of individual motifs closely correspond to motifs found in Lamentations: women are raped (Isa 13:16, √*šgl*; cf. Lam 5:11, √*'nh*); the total destruction of Babylon, like that of Jerusalem (Lam 4:6), is compared to Yahweh's devastation of Sodom and Gomorrah (Isa 13:19); the description of Babylon's past status as "the glory of kingdoms" (Isa 13:19; *şĕbî mamlākôt*) and "the splendor and pride of the Chaldeans" (Isa 13:19; *tip⁾eret gᵉ⁾ôn kaśdîm*) reminds one of Jerusalem, "the joy of all the earth" (Lam 2:15c; *māśôś lᵉkol-hā⁾āreş*) and "the splendor of Israel" (Lam 2:1b; *tip⁾eret yiśrā⁾ēl*); and like Jerusalem (Lam 5:18) Babylon will become a haunt for wild animals (Isa 13:20-22).

Furthermore, the poem portrays Yahweh as the divine agent of destruction. He rouses the Medes against Babylon (Isa 13:17).[118] His wrath is kindled because of evil and iniquity (Isa 13:11). These images are compatible with the picture of Yahweh in the first part of the poem (Isa 13:1-13). These early verses depict Yahweh as the divine warrior who goes into battle on the day of his anger.[119]

The prophet uses *qînāh* meter periodically throughout the poem (cf. vv. 4, 5, 8a, b; 9a; 11a; 19; 21b), especially in vv. 2-5.[120] And he summons the victims of Yahweh's onslaught, presumably the Babylonians, to wail (Isa 13:6).

---

[117] E.g. Wildberger, *Jesaja 13-27*, 505-9; Clements, *Isaiah*, 132-33.

[118] The Heb. word "arouse" (√*'wr*) is commonly used for Yahweh's summoning of the enemy in other passages marked by the city-lament mode (Jer 6:22; 50:9, 41: 51:1, 11).

[119] Cf. Miller, *Divine Warrior*, 102-3; Kaiser, *Isaiah 13-39*, 13-18; Wildberger, *Jesaja 13-27*, 508-9; Watts, *Isaiah*, 195-6.

[120] Cf. Duhm, 89-92; Cheyne, *Book*, 123; Kaiser, *Isaiah 13-39*, 9; Wildberger, *Jesaja 13-27*, 509.

Thus, while the overall number of city-lament features in this poem is not large, the subject matter, *qînāh* meter, and some of the motifs signal a moderate level of modal extension.

ii. *Jer 46:14-24*   The divine abandonment theme and personified city motif clearly call attention to the city-lament mode in this short oracle. The divine abandonment theme is reflected in 46:15 (cf. 46:26). Most commentators follow LXX's reading, *dia ti ephygen ho Apis* "on account of what has Apis fled?" (=*nās hap* instead of MT's *nishap*).[121] Apis' abandonment is of course related as seen from the Israelite perspective. Yahweh being the superior deity has set Apis to flight.

In 46:19 the "Enthroned One, Daughter of Egypt" is commanded to ready her bags for exile because Memphis will be made into a ruin. In 46:20-23 the attacking army is likened to a swarm of "gadflies (*qeres*) from the north" and locusts (*ʾarbeh*). The references to *hayil* "army, force, strength" in v. 22 and *ʿam-ṣāpôn* "army from the north" in v. 24 confirm that the insect imagery is a metaphor for the invading army. In Jer 4:7 and 8:17 Holladay questions whether similar animal imagery should be understood literally (see below). Finally, notice that in v. 24 the Daughter of Egypt is given into the hand (*ntn byd*) of the army from the north, presumably by Yahweh.

iii. *Jer 49:1-6*   This short oracle against Ammon focuses on the destruction of Rabbah and her daughter villages (49:2). In Jer 49:3 the prophet commands the "daughters of Rabbah" to grieve over this destruction. The Hebrew *bĕnôt rabbāh* combines the image of professional mourners, a role traditionally filled by women in the ancient Near East (e.g. 2 Sam 1:24; Jer 9:16-21),[122] with the personification of the city weeping, i.e. the prophet charges the villages surrounding Rabbah to wail (note the parallel in the first colon where Heshbon is ordered to cry). The theme of divine abandonment appears in the last bicolon of

---

[121] Cf. Cornill, 402; Giesebrecht, 229; Bright, 303; Carroll, 768; Holladay, *Jeremiah 2*, 323; *NRSV*.

[122] Cf. Jahnow, 60-73, 81-82, 159.

49:3.[123] Jer 49:4 has a form similar to Isa 47:8 (and Isa 23:4, see 3.1a.v above):

> Why do you boast in your ebbing strength,[124]
>   O shamed Daughter,[125]
> you who trusts in your[126] treasures, who says,[127]
>   "Who can come against me?"

As in the two passages from Isaiah, the city speaks. The treasures referred to probably include the riches found in the temple (cf. Jer 48:7; 50:37). On the inviolability of the city, compare Lam 4:12.

Yahweh causes the destruction (49:5) and effects Ammon's restoration mentioned in 49:6 (though LXX lacks the latter verse). Thus,

---

[123] Cf. Block, 149. Reading *milkōm* with the LXX, Syr., and Vulg. for MT's *malkām* "their king."

[124] This follows Holladay's suggestion, *bĕᶜimqēk hazzāb* (*Jeremiah 2*, 366). MT is conflate, reading *bāᶜămāqîm zāb ᶜimqēk* lit. "in the valleys flowing your valley." LXX has the equivalent of "in the valleys."

√*mq* carries the meaning of "strength" in Ugaritic, see Mitchell Dahood, "The Value of Ugaritic for Textual Criticism," *Biblica* 40 (1959) 166-67.

[125] Read *bat bûšāh* or *habbat habbûšāh* with LXX (*thygatēr atimias* [vocative]; a few of the Lucianic minuscules supply the definite article). Some critics retain MT, e.g. Giesebrecht, 239; Weiser, *Jeremia 25*, 411; Bright, 324; while others emend to *habbat haššaᵓănannāh* "O complacent Daughter," e.g. *BHS*; Cornill, 476; Rudolph, *Jeremia*, 286; Holladay, *Jeremiah 2*, 366. While most scholars correctly hold MT in suspicion (the epithet does not seem to fit the present context and occurs elsewhere in Jer 31:22) one is puzzled by the dismissal of LXX in favor of an emendation. As has been pointed out previously, √*bwš* is at home in lament contexts. Thus, to address the city as the "shamed Daughter" seems perfectly acceptable (cf. "Be ashamed, O Sidon" in Isa 23:4). After the metathesis of the *bet* and *shin*, a scribe read the epithet in light of Jer 31:22.

Regardless of how one resolves the verse's textual problems, the question is clearly addressed to the personified city.

[126] The use of the vocative accounts for the variation in 2nd and 3rd person references, see Hillers, "*Hôy*," 185-88.

[127] Reading *hāᵓōmĕrāh* with the versions. This also corresponds to the form of Isa 23:4 and 47:8.

in the space of six verses, six city-lament features are touched upon (2.1, 3, 5-8).

iv. *Ezekiel*   Ezekiel specifically uses the term *qînāh* for a dirge over a destroyed city or country in at least three places: 26:17, 27:2, and 32:16. In Ezek 26:15-18 Tyre falls (v. 15) and "all the princes of the sea" (v. 16) descend (*yrd*) from their thrones, strip off their royal garments, sit (*yšb*) terrified on the ground, and raise a short dirge over the fallen city:

> How you have disappeared[128] from the seas,[129]
>   O renown city! < >[130]
> You who dispensed your terror[131]
>   to all of the dry land![132]
> Now the coastlands shudder
>   on the day of your fall! < >[133]

Note that *qînāh* meter is used throughout the dirge.[134] Tyre's title, *hāʿîr hahullālāh*, parallels the similar titles of Jerusalem, Babylon, and

---

[128] Following the LXX, read *nišbatt* for MT's *nôšebet* and delete *ʾābadt*, see C. H. Toy, *The Book of the Prophet Ezekiel* (Leipzig: J. C. Hinrichs'sche, 1899) 20; D. Johannes Herrmann, *Ezechiel* (KAT 11; Leipzig: A. Deicherische, 1924) 162, n. 17b; Alfred Bertholet, *Hesekiel* (HAT 13; Tübingen: J. C. B. Mohr, 1936) 94; G. A. Cooke, *The Book of Ezekiel* (ICC; New York: Charles Scribner's Sons, 1937) 293, 295; Georg Fohrer, *Ezechiel* (HAT 13; Tübingen: J. C. B. Mohr, 1955) 151; Walther Eichrodt, *Ezekiel* (OTL; trans. C. Quinn; Philadelphia: Westminster, 1970) 366; Zimmerli, *Ezekiel 2*, 30. Cf. Isa 14:4 and 17:3.

[129] Or "sea" with LXX.

[130] LXX lacks 26:17c; cf. Toy, 20, 81.

[131] Read *nātĕnāh hittîtāh* with LXX for MT's *nātĕnû hittîtām*, which has probably been influenced by the addition of v. 17c, so Toy, 20; Herrmann, 162, n. 17e; Bertholet, 94; Fohrer, 171; Eichrodt, 367; Zimmerli, *Ezekiel 2*, 31. Again note the use of the 3rd person with a vocative.

[132] Emend MT's *yôšĕbeyhā* "her inhabitants" to *hayyabbāšāh*, so NRSV, NJV; cf. Bertholet, 94; Cooke, 293, 295; Eichrodt, 366. Here too MT may have been influenced by the addition in v. 17c.

[133] LXX lacks 26:18b; cf. Toy, 20, 81.

[134] Bertholet, 93; Fohrer, 152.

especially Damascus (ʿîr těhillāh, Jer 49:25). The contrast motif appears internally within the first bicolon. The first two bicola, depicting Tyre's glorious past, also contrast with the third, describing the present (ʿattāh) terror of the city's destruction.

Ezekiel's lament over Tyre (Ezek 27:1-11, 26-36) provides another example of an oracle with only a moderate amount of modal extension. In this oracle Ezekiel is instructed to "raise a lament over Tyre" (śāʾ ʿal-ṣōr qînāh). While present, city-lament features are not very prevalent, because imagery derived from the basic metaphor of a Tyre as a great ship dominates the lament. Nonetheless, qînāh meter predominates throughout the lament.[135] The contrast motif has structural significance: the first part (27:1-11) of the lament presents Tyre's glorious past, while the second (27:26-36) depicts the present destruction. Tyre's title, "she who is enthroned at the entrance of the sea"[136] (Ezek 27:3), is reminiscent of like divine titles in Isa 47:8, Jer 10:17, 22:23, 46:19, 48:18, 19, and Lam 4:21. Tyre's boast in the same verse, "I am the perfection of beauty" (kělîlat yōpî), is exactly what was said about Jerusalem before her fall (Lam 2:15).[137] Formally, the boast is like the boasts of personified Babylon (Isa 47:8) and Rabbah (Jer 49:4). The ship is shattered (√šbr) by the east wind (27:26, 34). The nominal form of √šbr, šeber, is a term used commonly to refer to the city's ruin in other city-lament contexts, e.g. Jer 8:21, Lam 2:11. Mourning and lamentation occur in 27:28-32. Note that the rhetorical question in 27:32 ("Who has ever been destroyed[138] like Tyre in the midst of the sea?") resembles similar questions in Lam 2:13 and the Mesopotamian laments (see 2.2a above). Finally, there is a bit of a taunt in 27:35-36.

At the close of the dirge over Pharaoh (Ezek 32:1-16), it is reported that the "daughters of the nations" should keen (těqônēnnāh) this lament (qînāh) over Egypt. This further demonstrates that Ezekiel

---

[135] Bertholet, 95; Fohrer, 154; Zimmerli, *Ezekiel 2*, 53.

[136] Reading hayyōšabtî ʿal-měbôʾ hayyām, so *BHS*; K; Herrmann, 163, n. 3a; Fohrer, 153; Eichrodt, 380; Zimmerli, *Ezekiel 2*, 42.

[137] Cf. Cooke, 296.

[138] Reading nidmāh with Theodotion and Vulg., see *BHS*; *NRSV*; Herrmann, 169, n. 32d; Cooke, 307, 312; Fohrer, 155; Eichrodt, 382; Zimmerli, *Ezekiel 2*, 52.

was familiar with city (or nation) laments. It also raises the question
whether or not Pharaoh is understood in this instance as merely a
representative of the Egyptian state. That is, in reality the dirge laments
the destruction of Egypt, just not the death of the Egyptian king.[139] One
notes that the last few verses of the lament have a wider purview than
simply the person of the Pharaoh; the whole country comes into view.
However, for obvious reasons this study must refrain from treating
laments over individual kings (e.g. Isa 14:3-23; Ezek 28:1-10, 11-19).
Therefore, although Ezekiel does not use the city-lament mode exten-
sively, there are at least three places in the book which indicate that the
prophet knew of the genre.

v. *Nahum*   Jack M. Sasson remarks on the general resemblance
between Nahum and CA: "Both texts include vivid, often figurative
descriptions of the fortification and fall of cities, divine curses against
them, and laments over their demise."[140] In addition one recognizes more
specific city-lament features in at least three places in Nahum. Most of
Nah 2:4-14 depicts the enemy's assault on Nineveh. The realistic nature
of the assault corresponds to CA's presentation of Naramsin's destruction
of the Ekur. The "river gates" in 2:7 stand wide open to enemy attack.
The same image appears in Nah 3:13 as well (these verses may offer
better parallels to CA 168; see discussion at 2.6a above).

Nah 2:8a contains a longstanding *crux interpretum*.[141] Two lines
of interpretation appear attractive. One understands the fs verbs in 2:8a
to refer to Nineveh, the other thinks they refer to the city goddess,

---

[139] Jahnow proffers a similar suggestion concerning Ezek 19. That is, the
destruction of the political state is represented as the personal destruction of its kings
(Jahnow, 201). The allegorical nature of this chapter, however, obscures any attempt
at interpretation.

[140] Jack M. Sasson, *Jonah* (AB 24b; Garden City: Doubleday, 1990) 22, n. 20.

[141] For reviews of suggested solutions, see J. M. P. Smith *et al, Micah, Zephaniah,
Nahum, Habakkuk, Obadiah and Joel* (ICC 14; New York: Charles Scribner's Sons,
1911) 320-21; Sellin, *Zwölf* (2), 368-69; Rudolph, *Micha*, 168, n. 8a.

Ištar.[142] If it is correct to see the city-lament mode in operation here, then a combination of these two interpretations fits perfectly. That is, Nineveh personified as a goddess figure is the subject of 2:8. Roberts comes to a somewhat similar conclusion.[143] Thus, following Kevin Cathcart and others, one should emend MT's *wĕhussab* to *hassĕbî* "beauty."[144] Though against Cathcart, *hassĕbî* must refer to the personified city, not simply to the statue of Ištar -- the entire oracle focuses on Nineveh (cf. esp. 2:9). Furthermore, the word is used commonly to designate cities or the land of Israel (Jer 3:19; Ezek 20:6, 15; 25:9; Dan 8:9; 11:16, 41, 45), especially in some of the city-lament passages discussed above (Isa 13:19; 23:9; other synonymous terms have also been noted throughout this chapter). One can translate the verse as follows:

> The Beauty has been stripped and carried off,[145]
> > her slave-girls are lead away,[146]
> moaning[147] like the sound of doves,
> > beating their breasts.

---

[142] See Smith *et al*, 320, 321; John D. W. Watts, *The Books of Joel, Obadiah, Jonah, Nahum, Habakkuk and Zephaniah* (Cambridge: Cambridge University, 1975) 113.

[143] *Nahum*, 66.

[144] Kevin J. Cathcart, *Nahum in the Light of Northwest Semitic* (BibOr 26; Rome: Pontifical Biblical Institute, 1973) 96-98; cf. Rudolph, *Micha*, 168, n. 8a.

[145] Rudolph (*Micha*, 168, n. 8a) and Roberts (*Nahum*, 60, n. 17) prefer the alternative emendation *wĕhussĕbāh baggālût hāᶜătallah* "the princess is made to stand among the captives," which permits the same general line of interpretation as suggested above. If the emendation "the beauty" makes sense, as this writer argues, then it may perhaps be preferred over Rudolph's and Roberts' proposal, which requires a more radical alteration of the consonantal text.

[146] Reading *mĕnuhăgôt* as a Dp participle derived from √*nhg* I "to drive, lead away" with LXX, Targ., and Vulg., so Sellin, *Zwölf* (2), 365, 369; Roberts, *Nahum*, 60, n. 18; cf. Karl Elliger, *Das Buch der zwölf Kleinen Propheten 2* (ATD 25; Göttingen: Vandenhoeck & Ruprecht, 1951) 10. See below for further justification.

[147] Reading *hōgôt*, cf. Targ. and Vulg. Apparently the verb fell out of the text due to homoioarkton, so *BHS*; Sellin, *Zwölf* (2), 365, 369; Elliger, 10; Rudolph, *Micha*, 168-69, n. 8b; R. Renaud, *Michée, Sophonie, Nahum* (Paris: Librairie Lecoffre, 1987) 300, n. 8c; Roberts, *Nahum*, 61, n. 19.

The stripping and forceful exile of the personified city is a common city-lament motif in Israel, which has been discussed previously. As Smith *et al* point out, the slave-girls would correspond to the Mesopotamian goddess' devotees.[148] In LU 283 Ningal laments that her slave-girls (ES gi₄-in = geme₂ = Akk. *amtu*) have been exiled. Note that the goddess' *guzilītu*, presumably some type of female servant,[149] departs (*paṭāru*) in Lambert's NB Tammuz lament (ln. 2). This image also occurs in the *balag*s (e.g. 42:127 [OB]). The presence of these attendants further underscores the divine background of the personified city metaphor.

Interestingly, LU 282 (the line immediately preceding the reference to Ningal's slave-girls) portrays Ningall's birds as also being exiled. Thus, the dove imagery in 2:8b is perhaps not accidental. Cathcart correctly cites the mourning bird parallel in CA 219: "May its pigeon moan in its hole!" (cf. LN 82). The pigeon/dove (tu^mušen) and francolin (dar^mušen) are commonly associated with a city's destruction throughout the *balag*s (e.g. 3:19; 4:143, a+224; 5:d+193; 6:b+242; 10:a+12). The image in 2:8b, then, is that of the personified city's attendants in mourning, crying and beating their breasts.

The familiar reaction to the city's destruction occurs in 2:11. In 2:12-13 a brief dirge is raised over Nineveh, metaphorically represented as a lion's den.

Another dirge is uttered over Nineveh in 3:1-7. The city is addressed derogatorily throughout, e.g. "city of blood" (3:1), "harlot" (3:4),[150] "mistress of sorcery" (3:4). Yahweh promises to lift her skirts over her face and reveal her nakedness to the nations (Nah 3:5; cf. Lam 1:8b). Roberts notes that the motif of public exposure both maintains the harlot imagery and describes the enemy's treatment of the conquered city (see 3.1a.iii above).[151] The familiar motif of corpses piled up in the

---

[148] Smith *et al*, 321; cf. Watts, *Books*, 113.

[149] Cf. *CAD* s.v.

[150] Interestingly, Watts (*Books*, 116) observes that this depiction of Nineveh owes something to the way Ištar is normally presented.

[151] *Nahum*, 73.

streets and squares occurs in 3:3 (see 2.6c above).[152] Nah 3:7 concludes
the dirge with a set of questions similar to those rhetorically asked of
Jerusalem (Lam 2:13) and other cities:

> Nineveh is destroyed,
> > who will grieve for her?
> Where will I seek
> > comforters for you?[153]

Nah 3:8-11 compares Nineveh to Thebes, "who is enthroned at
the Nile." Personified Thebes is exiled and her children are dashed in
pieces (cf. Isa 13:16, 18) "at the head of every street" (cf. Lam 2:19d).
The implication is that these same things, and more, will happen to
Nineveh.

Thus, Sasson's comparison of Nahum with CA seems appropriate.
Bits and pieces of city-lament features and motifs are woven in
throughout the book.

c. **Local Modulation**

In the final group of passages discussed in this section, the city-
lament genre has been extended only locally. That is, only slight touches
of the mode, sometimes just a single motif, have been used to color an
oracle. Obviously, the existence of a single motif does not yield as
convincing a case for the city-lament mode as does a larger number of
features and motifs. Nonetheless, the nature of the motifs or features
cited are often compelling by themselves, though some doubt will
invariably persist.

---

[152] Cf. Cathcart, 128-29.

[153] For the need of comforters, see Lam 1:2b, 9b, 17a, 21a. The confusion of
person (Nineveh is addressed in the third [3:7b, c (LXX)] and second [3:7a, c (MT)]
persons) perhaps reflects the grammatical ambiguity usually associated with *hôy*
oracles (cf. Hillers, "*Hôy*").

i. *Jer 49:23-27*   A short dirge over Damascus occurs in 49:25-26:

> How utterly[154] abandoned[155] is the glorious city,
>   the town of joy![156]
> Therefore her young men will fall in her squares,
>   and all her warriors will lie silent!

Note that the description of Damascus as a "glorious city" (*ʿîr tĕhillāh*) and "town of joy" (*qiryat māśôś*) parallels similar descriptions of Jerusalem (Lam 2:1b, 15c), Babylon (Isa 13:19), and the Moabite city in Jer 48:2. For the image of the dead corpses filling the streets and squares, compare the motif in Lam 1:15 and the Mesopotamian laments (see 2.6c above). These two motifs may be positively associated with the Israelite city-lament genre.

A third city-lament feature may also be present. Jer 49:25 is usually taken to refer to a deserted city, i.e. devoid of population. However, such an interpretation is somewhat incongruent with the following verse.[157] That is, if v. 25 states that the city is deserted, then what is the sense of "therefore" (*lākēn*) in v. 26? The translation of *NJV*, "Assuredly," simply glosses over the problem. On the other hand, if one understands v. 25 to refer explicitly to the abandonment of Damascus by its gods, then v. 26 follows naturally from it. The abandonment of Damascus by its gods results in the loss of the city's divine protection, and "therefore" its soldiers will be slaughtered and their corpses piled up in the city's squares. Heb. *ʿzb* is used elsewhere in the Hebrew Bible to refer to divine abandonment (e.g. Jer 12:7; Ezek 8:12; 9:9; Lam 5:20). While such a concise context does not allow for certainty, the interpreta-

---

[154] Understanding MT's *lōʾ* as a mistake for the emphatic *lamed* (cf. Bright, 333; WOC 11.2.10i; John Huehnergard, "Asseverative *la and Hypothetical *lu/law in Semitic," *JAOS* 103 [1983] 569-93). Others would delete *lōʾ* with Vulg., e.g. *BHS*; Giesenbrecht, 241; Weiser, *Jeremia 25*, 419; Rudolph, *Jeremia*, 292; Holladay, *Jeremiah 2*, 379. For other suggestions, see Cornill (485), and Volz (419).

[155] The verb form is probably best identified as a Gp, rather than the Dp pointed by the Masoretes. A D of √*ʿzb* is not otherwise attested in the Hebrew Bible.

[156] Deleting MT's 1cs suffix with most of the versions.

[157] Cf. Bright, 335.

tion suggested here makes the relationship between the two verses easily discernable. However, either interpretation of the city, as deserted of people or abandoned by the gods, is compatible with the city-lament mode.

ii. *Jer 46:3-12*   This oracle against Egypt mostly contains a description of the enemy attack and imagery associated with the divine warrior and the Day of Yahweh. In 46:11-12, however, brief mention is made of the "Maiden, Daughter of Egypt" lamenting over the destruction of her country.

iii. *Isa 14:28-32*   The personification of the city and gates as mourning figures in Isa 14:31a corresponds to similar personifications in city laments:

> Wail, O gate; cry out, O city;
>> Melt in fear, all of Philistia!

Note the use of *qînāh* meter (4+3). Furthermore, the charge to the Philistines not to rejoice is reminiscent of the sarcastic charge to the Daughter of Edom in Lam 4:21. The call to rejoice and the like seems to be characteristic of the restoration theme.

iv. *Jer 47:1-7* This short oracle against Philistia has features compatible with the city-lament mode, (e.g. lamentations, enemy attack, Yahweh as the divine warrior), yet there is one motif that has extremely close parallels in the Mesopotamian laments. In 47:3 fathers are so frightened by the enemy onslaught that they do not turn back for their children. Concerning this unnatural behavior, Holladay remarks, "I am aware of no parallel for this description."[158] This motif is common in the Mesopotamian laments:

> The mother left before her child's eyes...   (LU 233)

---

[158] *Jeremiah 2*, 338.

The father turned away from his child...   (LU 234)

The mother turned away from her child...   (LSUr 96; cf. LN 212)

The birth mother[159] abandoned her child...   (*balag* 6:32; cf. 5:99)

The wife of a warrior abandoned the little child, her child.
                                                   (*balag* 6:33; cf. 5:100)

2. Oracles About Israel and Judah

a. Comprehensive Modulation

As in the OAN, the city-lament mode is found in oracles about Israel and/or Judah. Mic 1 and the cycle of poems in Jer 4-6 and 8-10 constitute the best examples of such oracles. These passages also show the most comprehensive use of city-lament modulation in oracles concerning Israel and/or Judah.

i. *Mic 1:2-16* At places Micah 1:2-16 displays familiarity with the city-lament mode. While not insisting that each of the three sections of Mic 1 (1:2-7, 8-9, 10-16) were written at the same time, many critics agree that Mic 1 can be read intelligibly as a coherent unit.[160] Mic 1:8-9 fuses the oracles in 1:2-7 and 10-16.[161] In these verses the prophet laments the destruction of Samaria (cf. 1:2-7) and Judah and Jerusalem (cf. 1:10-16).[162] The term *makkāh* "wound" is used elsewhere in the city-lament genre to designate the devastation of a conquering enemy (Isa 1:6; Jer

---

[159] Lit. "the actual mother who gave birth" (Sum. ama-gan-zi-da). For ama-gan as "the mother who gave birth," see Alster, "Mythology," 7.

[160] E.g. Rudolph, *Micha*, 37-39; James L. Mays, *Micah* (OTL; Philadelphia: Westminster, 1976) 38; Delbert R. Hillers, *Micah* (Hermeneia; Philadelphia: Fortress, 1984) 22-23.

[161] Rudolph, *Micha*, 42-43; Hillers, *Micah*, 22-23.

[162] See Rudolph, *Micha*, 42; Leslie C. Allen, *The Books of Joel, Obadiah, Jonah and Micah* (NIC; Grand Rapids: Wm. B. Eerdmans, 1976) 274; Mays, 51; Hillers, *Micah*, 23; Hans Walter Wolff, *Micah* (trans. Gary Stansell; Minneapolis: Augsburg, 1990) 48.

14:17).[163] This short lament reminds one of similar laments offered by Isaiah, Jeremiah (see 3.2a.ii below), and the poet of Lamentations upon witnessing the destruction of various cities.

The text of Mic 1:10-16 is extremely difficult, nevertheless, most commentators agree that the oracle addresses cities which have suffered or expect to suffer destruction at the hands of an invading army.[164] One begins to feel the movement of the invading army (identified metaphorically as Yahweh, the divine warrior [1:2-7], a wound [1:9], disaster [1:12], and conqueror [1:15]) already in 1:9 as it reaches Jerusalem. This sense of movement is continued in 1:12, and 15.[165]

Scholars recognize the poem's connection with the funeral dirge and laments over the fall of nations or cities.[166] The *qînāh* meter predominates in those verses which permit judgment (e.g. 1:11b, 12a, b, 13a, 14b, 15a, 16b).[167] The towns affected by the enemy attack are beckoned to cry (1:10) and mourn (1:11), roll in dust (1:10), go about naked (1:11), writhe in anguish (1:12),[168] and shave off hair (1:16) as the invader passes through. Five of the cities are addressed with the divine title "Enthroned One of GN" (Shaphir and Zaanan in v. 11; Maroth in v. 12; Lachish in v. 13; Mareshah in v. 15). The Daughter of Zion is addressed in v. 13, and most commentators agree that personified Zion or Jerusalem is addressed in v. 16, though the text lacks a specific addressee.[169] In the main, then, the passage lists a group of personified

---

[163] Cf. Mays, 55.

[164] E.g. Theodore H. Robinson, *Die Zwölf kleinen Propheten: Hosea bis Micha* (Tübingen: J. C. B. Mohr, 1938) 132; Rudolph, *Micha*, 50-51; Allen, 278: Mays, 50, 54; Hillers, *Micah*, 24; Artur Weiser, *Die Propheten Hosea, Joel, Amos, Obadja, Jona, Micha* (ATD 24; Göttingen: Vandenhoeck & Ruprecht, 1985) 240ff.; Wolff, *Micah*, 53-54.

[165] Cf. Mays, 54.

[166] Robinson, 132; Mays, 54; Weiser, *Propheten*, 240; *contra* Wolff, *Micah*, 49.

[167] Robinson, 132; Mays, 51; Weiser, *Propheten*, 240; Wolff, *Micah*, 49.

[168] Though MT's reading has been questioned, e.g. Robinson, 132; Allen, 276: Hillers, *Micah*, 26; Weiser, *Propheten*, 239.

[169] See D. Ernst Sellin, *Das Zwölfprophetenbuch* (KAT 12/1; Leipzig: A. Deichertsche, 1929) 313; Rudolph, *Micha*, 37; Allen, 283; Mays, 50, 52, 60; Hillers, *Micah*, 28; Weiser, *Propheten*, 240; Wolff, *Micah*, 45, 64. The first colon of v. 16a

cities in Judah lamenting or performing other mourning gestures in
response to the invasion of their country.

This perhaps provides the best example of the geographical motif
in the Hebrew Bible (cf. Isa 15-16; Jer 48:1-9). It is especially close to
the motif as found in the second *kirugu* of LSUr, where in addition to
abandoning their cities and temples, the city goddesses cry over the
destruction that Enlil brings on Sumer; one city goddess after another
cries out as the storm passes through their cities (cf. Lambert's NB
Tammuz lament). The Micah passage obviously does not portray the
abandonment of the personified cities, since this theme could only be
applied to Yahweh in an Israelite context. While the textual difficulties
does not permit one to be confident about any interpretation of this

---

is too short, suggesting that a word has fallen out of the text. The fs imperatives in v.
16 make it likely that the word was a city name or its equivalent. Some commentators
therefore add Zion, Jerusalem, or the like at the beginning of the colon, e.g. Sellin,
Zwölf (1), 313; Weiser, *Propheten*, 240. However, Rudolph commendably searches for
a word whose loss can be better accounted for text critically. He suggests that perhaps
qiryāh "town" was lost through haplography (*Micha*, 37, n. 16a). But this would be
a fairly bland choice of terms given the extensive use of personification elsewhere in
the passage. Moreover, two items strongly suggest that the city is to be personified like
a weeping goddess: LXX's reference to widowhood in v. 16b (*tēn chēreian sou*) and
that the mourning gestures are commanded because the missing city's children have
gone into exile.

Therefore, as an alternative one may suggest reading *bat yiśrāʾēl* "the
Daughter of Jerusalem," which LXX reads at the end of v. 15 in the place of MT's
"Israel," cf. Wolff, *Micah*, 45. The original text of the end of v. 15 and beginning of
v. 16 would have read as follows: *kĕbôd yiśrāʾēl // bat yiśrāʾēl qārĕhi wāgozzî. bat
yiśrāʾēl* was lost from MT via homoioteleuton. LXX's loss of *yiśrāʾēl* is not so easily
explained. Either it was simply an inadvertent oversight, or perhaps a scribe thought
his *Vorlage* contained a conflation of two variants, of which he chose one.

In light of the intensive use of personification in these verses, perhaps one
should also emend the problematic "houses (*bāttê*) of Achzib" in v. 14 to read either
"the Daughter of Achzib" (cf. *NJV*, n. f-f; Sellin, *Zwölf* (1), 316; Rudolph, *Micha*, 37,
n. 14f) or the mixed form <*yś*>*bty* (cf. Jer 10:17, 22:23, and Lam 4:21; Mays, 49, n.
u).

passage, the apparent presence of a list of personified cities mourning an enemy invasion nonetheless remains very suggestive.[170]

The divine warrior imagery in Mic 1:2-7 is compatible with the city-lament imagery in the rest of the poem. As Mays notes, the theophany of the divine warrior "may have been developed by Micah with the lament [vv. 8-16]," the latter providing a portrayal of the former's effect.[171] Furthermore, note that Samaria is to become a ruin (v. 6) and that she is at least partially personified (see ʾetnan zônāh "whore's fees" in v. 7).

Thus, city-lament features may appear in all three sections of Mic 1, giving the poem its sense of coherence. A total of five city-lament features occur in Mic 1 (2.1, 2d, e, 5, 7, 8), plus the predominant geographical motif in 1:10-16.

ii. *Jer 4-6, 8-10, etc.* Chapters 4-6 and 8-10 contain a cycle of poems whose coherence hinges on a variety of common motifs, the most prominent of which is the foe from the north (4:5-8, 13-18, 29-31; 6:1-6, 11-12, 22-26; 8:10, 14-17; 9:9-10; 10:17-22).[172] Carroll observes that these chapters also share common features with the OAN in Jer 46-51.[173] If he is correct, then it is not surprising that identifiable city-lament features arise in chapters 4-6 and 8-10 (plus some individual poetic units

---

[170] Isa 10:27c-34 may constitute another example of the geographical motif, but the evidence there is less compelling. Note, though, the use of *qināh* meter (10:27c-28a, 30a, 32b), the personification of Gallim (10:30) and Jerusalem (10:32; reading *bat* with Q, 1QIsaᵃ, LXX, Syr., and Vulg. for K's *bayit*), the call to lament (10:30), and the portrayal of Yahweh as the enemy.

[171] Mays, 51.

[172] Cf. Bright, 33; William L. Holladay, *The Architecture of Jeremiah 1-20* (Lewisburg: Bucknell University, 1976) 108-9; *Jeremiah 1*, 132-38; Carroll, 757; Thomas W. Overholt, "Jeremiah," in *Harper's Bible Commentary* (ed. James L. Mays; San Francisco: Harper & Row, 1988) 599, 612, 615.

[173] Carroll, 754-57. He further suggests that the material in chapters 4-6 and 8-10 be conceived of as "a transformed mode" of the OAN genre (757). In light of the present thesis, it is better to suppose the opposite. That is, that the OAN represent "a transformed mode" of the city-lament genre.

in chapters 14, 22, and 31)[174] as well, since the city-lament mode is most
pronounced in the OAN. Since commentators disagree widely on the
division of this material into smaller and larger units,[175] it will suffice to
point out the more obvious city-lament features which appear throughout
this material.

The dominant subject matter in these chapters is the destruction
of Jerusalem and Judah (e.g. 4:6-7, 20, 23-26; 6:1, 6, 23; 8:14-23; 9:10;
10:18-20; 14:17-18). Jeremiah repeatedly uses *qînāh* meter throughout
these chapters. Holladay notes the striking interchange of speakers that
pervades these chapters.[176] At times as many as five different speakers
appear: Yahweh, Jeremiah, the enemy, the community (1cp), and the
personified city/country. Holladay, like most commentators, does not
distinguish between the personified city and the community. However,
surely Carroll is correct in stressing the need to distinguish between the
personified city, community, and prophet "in the fictive mode of
representation."[177] Whoever speaks for the personified city, for she is but
a metaphor, "speaks of the city's responses to the disaster," not his or
her own feelings.[178] While an attempt to chart all the viewpoint shifts in
these chapters will not be made, the identification of the speaker is
especially crucial in one area. In both Lamentations and Isaiah, the
poet/prophet and personified city/country react to the destruction of the
city/country in a way similar to the conventional reception of bad news.
In these chapters, there are at least three comparable passages: 4:19-21,
8:18-23, and 10:19-21.

In 4:19 the writhing of the stomach (√*hwl*, *mēʿay*) and pounding
of the heart (√*hmh*, *lēb*) reminds one of similar language in Lam 1:20,

---

[174] Holladay recognizes a kinship between 22:20-23 and Jer 4-6 (*Jeremiah 1*, 602)
and Carroll notices an affinity between 30-31 and the OAN (756; cf. Overholt, 643).
Jer 14:17-18 preserves two good city-lament motifs: lamentation and the making of
Jerusalem into a lair for wild animals.

[175] Cf. Holladay, *Jeremiah 1*, 133.

[176] *Jeremiah 1*, 137-38. However, Holladay is mistaken in his assumption that this
switching of speakers is unique to Jeremiah in the prophetic literature. As has been
observed, the changing of authorial points of view is a characteristic of city laments.

[177] Carroll, 235-36.

[178] Ibid., 236.

2:11, Isa 15:4, 16:11, and 21:3-4. Note further that as in Isa 21:3-4, the reaction is caused by sight and sound (Jer 4:21). Most commentators understand the "I" of 4:19-21 to refer to Jeremiah,[179] Paul Volz, Carroll, and Kaiser, however, argue that personified Jerusalem constitutes the proper antecedent.[180] The latter are undoubtedly correct. In 4:20 MT reads a plural, "my tents are destroyed," while the LXX, Syr., and the parallel in 10:20 have the singular, "my tent is destroyed." Holladay argues convincingly that the latter is the better text and must be a reference to the temple.[181] But he is then forced to see v. 20 as the lament of the community (in 1 cs?), not Jeremiah. Thus, he has two separate "I's" in these three verses. A more prudent solution is to have the personified city speaking throughout these verses. The reference to "my tent" and "my curtains" as spoken by personified Jerusalem parallels the similar conception of possession in Lam 1:10b ("her sanctuary," i.e. Zion's).

In 8:18-23 again many commentators understand Jeremiah as the main speaker,[182] and again Carroll holds the minority view that sees the personified city speaking.[183] This time, however, one must side with the majority of critics. In vv. 19a-b and 22 the personified city, the "Daughter of my people," is presented in the third person. In vv. 21 and 23 the one speaking in the first person refers again to the "Daughter of my people" in third person. Compare v. 21 ("I am shattered *because of the ruin of the Daughter of my people*") with Lam 2:11, where the poet's weeping and anguish are "*because of the ruin of the Daughter of my people.*" Both verses contain the phrase ^ᶜ*al šeber bat-*^ᶜ*ammî.*

---

[179] E.g. Cornill, 52; Artur Weiser, *Der Prophet Jeremia 1-25:13* (ATD 20; Göttingen: Vandenhoeck & Ruprecht, 1952) 45; Bright, 34; Rudolph, *Jeremia*, 33; Holladay, *Jeremiah 1*, 147, 151; William McKane, *Jeremiah* (ICC 11/1; Edinburgh: T. & T. Clark, 1986) 102.

[180] Volz, 56; Carroll, 167; Kaiser, 166-74.

[181] *Jeremiah 1*, 162.

[182] E.g. Cornill, 121; Giesebrecht, 56; Volz 1928, 111; Weiser, *Jeremia 1*, 81; Bright, 65; Holladay, *Jeremiah 1*, 289; McKane, 193.

[183] Carroll, 235.

In 10:19-21 Holladay believes the people are the main speakers (vv.19-20)[184] and William McKane says that Jeremiah "takes to himself the shattered body politic and experiences the reality of it as his own pain and incurable sickness."[185] Both interpretations are illegitimate because they do not abide by the literary distinctions made in the text. Rather, one must agree with Carroll and Kaiser that the city as a bereaved mother is here lamenting the loss of her children.[186] In 10:17 "the one enthroned (yōšebet, so Q) under siege," i.e. the personified city, is addressed. In 10:20 reference is again made to "my tent" and "all my tent-cords," and in addition, to "my children" who "have gone away from me and are no more (wĕ⁾ênām)." The latter clearly implies the mother city. Compare this to the personification of the city\country as Rachel in Jer 31:15.[187] She mourns the loss of her children "because each is no more (kî ⁾ênennû)."[188]

Jeremiah laments over the ruin of the city in a least one other place, Jer 14:17.[189] In addition to Jer 31:15, the personified city/country bewails the destruction in 4:31 ("the Daughter of Zion"), 6:26 ("Daugh-

---

[184] *Jeremiah 1*, 339; cf. Giesebrecht, 67; Volz, 126; Weiser, *Jeremia 1*, 96.

[185] McKane, 230; cf. Cornill, 140; Bright, 73.

[186] Carroll, 261; Kaiser, 168-69.

[187] Cf. Kramer, "Prototype," 141*; Carroll, 596-98; Hillers, *Lamentations* (2d), 38.

[188] Some scholars suspect that this latter part of 31:15 has been corrupted, e.g. Cornill, 337; Giesebrecht, 168; Weiser, *Jeremia 25*, 271; Holladay, *Jeremiah 2*, 186-88. However, the lack of ⁽al-bāneyhā in the LXX (cf. Syr.) could be due to homoioteleuton. ⁽al-bāneyhā kî ⁾ênennû may be considered as a variant to ⁽al-bāneyhā mē⁾ānāh lĕhinnāhēm; the text is conflate. The first two bicola may be read in qînāh meter, see Giesebrecht, 168; Bright, 275; Hillers, *Lamentations* (2d), 38. The second bicolon read either "Rachel weeping *over her children, / refusing comfort*," or "Rachel weeping *over her children, / because each is no more*," see Volz (286, n. 57) for the originality of the latter phrase. Thus, kî ⁾ênennû as the shorter member of a bicolon in qînāh meter is perfectly acceptable, *contra* Holladay, *Jeremiah 2*, 187.

[189] MT appears to be expansionistic here, the LXX lacks both gādôl and bĕtûlat, but the title bĕtûlat bat-⁽ammi is unique in the Hebrew Bible, and thus may be original. bĕtûlat perhaps fell out of the LXX due to homoioarkton. The sense of the verse is not affected either way. The presence of the title bĕtûlat bat-⁽ammi at whatever level of the text further corroborates the titular nature of bat-⁽ammi.

ter of my people"), and 22:23 ("you who are enthroned[190] in Lebanon").
Moreover, the first two passages contain typical mourning gestures.
Compare especially the stretching out of the hands in Jer 4:31 with the
same gesture in Lam 2:19c.

Other city-lament features appear in these chapters. The poem
depicts Yahweh as the agent of destruction. It identifies him as the cause
of the destruction (6:8; 8:14; 9:10; 10:18). He sends the enemy against
Jerusalem (4:6b). Sometimes the enemy is depicted metaphorically as
wild animals, such as a lion (4:7; cf. Isa 15:9) or snake (Jer 8:17). Note
that CA 158-59 likens the attacking Guti brought by Enlil to a horde of
locusts.[191] The attack motif (i.e. when the enemy attack is often
graphically and literally depicted; cf. 3.1a.iv above) is present (4:13, 16-
17, 29; 6:1-8, 22-23; 8:16). And note the reference to Yahweh's word
and plan (4:28).

The questions, "Is Yahweh not in Zion? Is her king not in her?"
in 8:19 may reflect the divine abandonment theme.[192] Several common
destruction motifs are found in theses chapters as well. The temple is
destroyed (4:20; 10:20). In 9:10 Yahweh states that he will make
Jerusalem into a ruin, a lair for jackals. For the motif of unsafe roads
(and canals in Mesopotamia) in 6:25, compare LU 367-68, LSUr 38-39,
94, CA 163-4, 166-67, and *balag* 42:46-48 (OB).[193] And the motif of the
sword outside and famine inside occurs in 14:18 (cf. Lam 1:20c; 2.6c
above).

---

[190] GKC (sec. 90n) considers *yōšabt* a mixed form, combining the G fs part. with
the G perf. 2 fs. It is best to read it as a feminine participle, like in Isa 47:8, Jer 10:17,
and Lam 4:21.

[191] Holladay questions whether the attack of the wild animals should be taken
literally (*Jeremiah 1*, 292). In support of a more literal reading, he cites the similar
treaty-curse imagery presented by Hillers (*Treaty-Curses*, 54-56, esp. 55). The affinity
between some city-lament imagery and the imagery in treaty curses which focus on
the destruction of cities and/or countries has already been noted. This perhaps is
another example of a common store of poetic images for the destruction of cities. The
"evil from the north" in 4:6 and the sound of the enemy's horses in 8:16 may favor the
metaphorical understanding of the lion and snake imagery in these verses.

[192] Block notes similar questions which imply divine abandonment (150, n. 35).

[193] Cf. Cooper, *Agade*, 26.

Judah's guilt is underscored frequently (e.g. 4:14, 17-18, 22; 6:6-7; 8:14; 10:21). Lamentation is prevalent among the people (4:8; 9:9 [LXX]; 9:16-21). And even some references to restoration occur in 31:4-5 and 21-22 (note the presence of the personified city in both of these contexts). Thus, one can clearly see a clustering of city-lament features throughout chapters 4-6 and 8-10 (2.1, 2a, d, 3-5, 6a-c, 7-9). This clustering is especially significant if scholars are correct in their assessment of Jer 4-6 and 8-10 as a semi-coherent cycle of poems.

b. Moderate modulation

The use of the city-lament mode in Isa 22 and Amos 5 is less extensive than in Mic 1 or Jer 4-6, 8-10, still its presence is easily observable.

i. *Isa 22:1-14* There is much in this poem which remains obscure or problematic for critics, not to mention the wide array of views concerning the poem's inner unity and historical setting(s).[194] Therefore, the poem is dealt with only briefly. The recognition of features from the city-lament genre, however, might pave the way for a more holistic interpretation of this poem (at least of vv. 1-8a and 12-14).

In general the poem depicts the siege and destruction of Jerusalem. The first four verses permit a reading in *qînāh* meter[195] and are addressed to personified Jerusalem, "the Daughter of my people" (Isa 22:4).[196] Jerusalem's leadership flees (Isa 22:3) as in Lamentations (Lam 1:6b-c). "The destruction (*šōd*) of the Daughter of my people" (Isa 22:4) parallels "the ruin (*šeber*) of the Daughter of my people" (Lam 2:11b; 3:48; 4:10b). Predictably the prophet is moved by this destruction (Isa

---

[194] See Wildberger (*Jesaja 13-27*, 809-11, 812-13) for a convenient discussion of the opinions.

[195] Cf. *BHS*; Kaiser, *Isaiah 13-39*, 140; Wildberger, *Jesaja 13-27*, 811.

[196] Note the consistent use of 2fs pronominal suffixes throughout these verses. MT's *kullāk*, which caused the versions so many problems (see Wildberger, *Jesaja 13-27*, 807-8), is perhaps best explained as a stylistic feature, wherein a place name is followed by "all of it" or "all of you" (see Hillers, *Micah*, 38; Isa 14:31a quoted above). In this case the place name, Jerusalem, may be assumed from context.

22:4). Lamenting and mourning gestures are prominent (Isa 22:1; 12). Yahweh Sabaoth is the agent of destruction who does battle on the Day of Yahweh (Isa 22:5). He uses Elam and Kir as his instruments of destruction (Isa 22:6) and eventually withdraws his protection from Judah, leaving her open to enemy attack ("He [Yahweh] removed the covering of Judah," Isa 22:8a).[197]

ii. *Amos 5:1-3, 16-17, 18-21*   Hillers discusses Amos 5:1-3 (perhaps the earliest reflection of the city-lament genre in the Hebrew Bible) in some detail.[198] The nature of the personification of Israel in this chapter, however, is exceptional (cf. Jer 14:17). Normally when the city is personified, she is portrayed as mourning the destruction of the city. When the personified city's destruction is emphasized, it is done with imagery typically used to describe destroyed cities. In contrast to this pattern, here the destroyed city is personified as a dead person.[199] Compare *KTU* 1.5.VI.8-9, where Baal's fall to the ground unquestionably signals his death:

mġny. lbᶜl. npl. lars.	We reached Baal, he had fallen to the ground.
mt. aliyn. bᶜl	Aliyan Baal is dead,
hlq. zbl. bᶜl. ars	the Prince, Lord of Earth has perished!

The Maiden of Israel is not portrayed as grieving over her destroyed city, but rather she herself has fallen to the ground dead and is being lamented. This text provides the closest link to the genre of funeral dirges as studied by Jahnow.

However, the identification of Amos 5:1-3 as belonging to the city-lament genre is unmistakable. Like Ezekiel (Ezek 26:17; 27:1, 32; 32:16) Amos is to raise a lament over a political entity rather than an individual (Amos 5:1). Hillers calls attention especially to those features which are not so compatible with a personal funeral dirge, such as the

---

[197] Cf. Kaiser, *Isaiah 13-39*, 145; Clements, *Isaiah*, 182, 185.

[198] *Lamentations* (2d), 37-38; cf. Jahnow, 165.

[199] *Contra* John H. Hayes, *Amos: The Eighth-Century Prophet* (Nashville: Abingdon, 1988) 154.

use of *ʾadmātāh* designating Israel's political territory[200] and the continuation of the dirge (v. 3) in explicitly political or national terms. He also notes the presence of *qînāh* meter[201] and personified Israel (*bĕtûlat*)[202] and the significance of *nāpĕlāh* connoting "to fall in battle."[203] As the temple is construed as belonging to the Daughter of Zion in Lam 1:10b, so the land here is understood as personified Israel's (i.e. *her* land[204]). Hillers compares the short colon, *ʾên mĕqîmāh* "there is none to raise her up," with similar second cola in Lamentations (1:7c, 9b, 17a, 21a).[205]

Andersen and Freedman and Shalom Paul observe that vv. 16-17 continue the mourning imagery from vv. 1-2.[206] The motif of mourning in the city streets and squares has been met with previously (e.g. Isa 15:3; Jer 48:37-39). That these verses adjoin the Day of Yahweh passage in vv. 18-20 is perhaps not inadvertent.[207] Both lamentation and the Day of Yahweh constitute significant generic features of Lamentations. Moreover, the ominous note (cf. Exod 12:12) sounded in the final colon of v. 17 ("for I will pass in your midst, says Yahweh") feeds nicely into vv. 18-20. And the *hôy* particle in v. 18 picks up on the *hô hô* in v. 16.[208]

---

[200] Wolff, *Amos*, 236; Schmitt, "Virgin," 375.

[201] Cf. Jahnow, 167; Sellin, *Zwölf*, (1), 226; Robinson, 88; Weiser, *Propheten*, 157; Hayes, *Amos*, 187.

[202] Cf. Jahnow, 167. The personification is especially striking here, since elsewhere in the Hebrew Bible "Israel" is almost unexceptionally construed grammatically as masculine, see Schmitt, "Gender," 115-25.

[203] Wolff, *Amos*, 236; Andersen and Freedman, 474. It has also been seen that √*npl* is used typically to describe the fall of a city, e.g. Jer 51:8; Lambert's NB Tammuz lament, ln. 15. Cf. Shalom M. Paul, *Amos* (Hermeneia; Minneapolis: Fortress, 1991) 160, n. 10; Schmitt, "Virgin," 372-74. Thus, the term is appropriate both at the level of the literal subject, the city (see v. 3), and the level of the metaphorical predicate, the Maiden of Israel (see 2.7 above).

[204] See Hillers, *Lamentations* (2d), 37.

[205] See also Andersen and Freedman, 473; Paul, 160, n. 13.

[206] Andersen and Freedman, 513; Paul, 159, 178.

[207] Cf. Andersen and Freedman, 518.

[208] Cf. Andersen and Freedman, 515-16; Paul, 182.

In sum, Amos 5:1-3, 16-17, and perhaps even 18-21 contain significant city-lament features and motifs. Yet the passage's strong resemblance to the funeral dirge should not be overlooked or ignored. Jahnow suggests that Amos 5:1-3 represents a transformation of the funeral dirge.[209] To some extent she is probably correct. That is, it seems likely that city laments were created to some extent by analogy with laments for the dead. For example, in the Mesopotamian laments the frequent plaint, "Alas, my destroyed city! Alas, my destroyed house!" closely resembles the typical funeral plaint, "Oh, my wife!" or "Oh, my son!"[210] Moreover, there can be little doubt that the figure of the weeping goddess was patterned after a typical grieving mother. The image of the dead Maiden of Israel in Amos contributes yet more evidence towards this theory.

However, the basic argument of this study maintains that biblical texts like Amos 5:1-3 represent something more than just transformations of the funeral dirge. Rather, they are better characterized as belonging to a city-lament genre. That is, the characterization of these texts as merely transformations of funeral dirges fails to account for a variety of features that consistently appear in these texts, e.g. focus on the destruction of political entity, divine warrior imagery, personified city/country motif, divine abandonment and restoration themes, etc. Yet, when these texts are classified as city laments, the existence of these same features is completely understandable.

Thus, Amos 5:1-3 in fact may be a transformation of a funeral dirge. But if so, it is also something much more than just a transformation. It is a transformation that has evolved into a new genre. This supposition is consistent with what theorists know about how genres change and evolve. For example, Fowler notes that a simple change in function may ultimately lead to a loosening of the genre.[211] It is conceivable that such a change effected the funeral dirge when it was used to lament the collapse of a political entity. (The metaphorical conceptualization of the abstract death of a city, in terms of the

---

[209] Jahnow, 165.

[210] Cf. Jahnow, 11ff., 94ff.

[211] Fowler, 173-74.

experientially more familiar death of a person, would be very natural.[212])
This in turn would eventually lead to the development of a separate but
related city-lament genre. Therefore, Jahnow's transformation theory is
relevant developmentally, but her historical analysis does not hold. Fully
evolved city laments already existed in Mesopotamia during the second
millennia B.C.E.

c. **Local Modulation**

Isa 1:7-9 and 3:25-4:1 provide good examples of the local
extension of the city-lament genre in oracles about Jerusalem.

i. *Isa 1:7-9*   Isa 1:7-9 pictures a ruined country in which only a few
survivors remain.[213] At the center of this picture, is the Daughter of Zion
who has been left looking like a garden hut (1:8). Some commentators
have interpreted this image to mean that only Jerusalem among the cities
of Judah remains standing.[214] However, if the parallels to Lam 2:6 drawn
earlier are correct, then the image depicts Jerusalem's destruction. The
once fortified city has now been made into something akin to a frail
garden hut, useless and deteriorating after the harvest.[215] The remnant
idea, which itself presumes a military defeat, emerges fully only in v. 9.

The comparison with Sodom and Gomorrah (1:9) as a proverbial
way of underscoring the severity of the city's ruin could also reflect the
city-lament mode.

---

[212] Cf. Lakoff; Taylor.

[213] For *śārîd kimᶜāt*, see Wildberger, *Jesaja 1-12*, 19.

[214] E.g. Franz Delitzsch. *Biblischer Commentar über den Propheten Jesaia*
(Leipzig: Dörffling und Franke, 1879) 15-16; Duhm, 5; George B. Gray, *Isaiah I-
XXVII* (ICC 10a; 4th reprint; Edinburgh: T. & T. Clark, 1956) 12; Auvrey, 41;
Wildberger, *Jesaja 1-12*, 20; Clements, *Isaiah*, 30; Joseph Jensen, *Isaiah 1-39* (OTM
8; Wilmington: Michael Glazier, 1984) 42.

[215] Cf. Otto Kaiser, *Isaiah 1-12* (OTL; 2d ed.; trans. John Bowden; Philadelphia:
Westminster, 1983) 21-22; Oswalt, 91-92.

ii. *Isa 3:25-4:1*   Isa 3:26 reminds one of the imagery in Isa 47.[216] The personified city sits on the ground and mourns the death of her soldiers. Isa 3:25 is cast in *qînāh* meter.[217] The 2fs and 3fs suffixes and the feminine singular verb forms in Isa 3:25-26 demand the presence of the personified city.[218] The dead soldiers are considered to belong to the personified city. The city gates, like elsewhere in Lamentations and the Mesopotamian laments, are personified as mourning figures. The verses were appended at this point because the female imagery agrees with that of Isa 3:16-24.[219] Thus, Isa 3:25-4:1 clearly reflects the city-lament mode.

One can perhaps also suggest a similar interpretation of some of the images in Lam 1:8-10. Lam 1:8b refers to the Daughter of Zion's nakedness in a way similar to Isa 47:3. However, whether or not this reflects the motif of the plundering of the divine image, like in Isa 47, is difficult to say. Lamentations may refer elsewhere to the adultery metaphor (e.g. Lam 1:2), so it is tempting to see its reflection here as well.[220] Yet, as Kaiser observes, Lam 1:8b might refer to rape,[221] and thus the verse is also compatible with the plundering of the divine image motif discussed above. Moreover, note that in Lam 1:10a the enemy spreads their hands (*yādô pāraś ṣār*) over personified Zion's precious things (i.e. the temple treasures) just as they placed their hands on Inanna in *balag* 50. And in Lam 1:9b the Daughter of Zion falls down and is lamenting (1:9c) with no one to comfort her. The use of √*yrd* here is reminiscent of Isa 47:1 and *KTU* 1.5.VII.11-14.

Perhaps the poet intended the motif of public exposure to allude to both of the other motifs, as Roberts suggests for Nah 3:5 (see 3.1a.iii

---

[216] Cf. Hillers, "Roads," 127.

[217] Kaiser, *Isaiah 1-12*, 82.

[218] Gray, 75; Wildberger, *Jesaja 1-12*, 146; Clements, *Isaiah*, 52; Kaiser, *Isaiah 1-12*, 82-83; Watts, *Isaiah*, 46; Oswalt, 143.

[219] Wildberger, *Jesaja 1-12*, 146. More specifically, the seven women of Isa 4:1 pick up on the proud women of Isa 3:16-24, and the "daughters of Zion" (Isa 3:16, 17) may have attracted "the Daughter of Zion," the personified city implied by the feminine singular suffixes and verb forms in Isa 3:25-26.

[220] So Hillers, *Lamentations*, 23-24.

[221] *Isaiah 1-12*, 175.

and 3.1b.v above).[222] The plundering motif would call attention to the city's miserable state and how she had been publicly shamed,[223] while the harlot motif would highlight her own culpability. The personification of a country or city as a harlot is well established in the Hebrew Bible (e.g. Ezek 16, Hos 2). The prophets use this metaphor in a judgmental fashion, depicting the country or city in a negative light. Since harlotry was already associated with personified cities in the Israelite literary tradition, it would have been natural for the poets to use the harlot motif to further elaborate the depiction of the city in city laments. The transformation of topics or motifs from one genre into another genre is known as topical invention.[224] Isa 1:21 and Jer 13:20-27 are good examples of the harlot motif in city-lament modulated passages. Jer 4:30-31 juxtaposes Zion as harlot (v. 30) with Zion as mourner (v. 31). The first calls attention to Zion's culpability and the second, her tragic plight.

d. Restoration

Isa 1:21-26 contains a moderate amount of city-lament modulation. This oracle portends Jerusalem's destruction, yet it differs from the other oracles so far discussed in this section in that it also envisions the city's restoration. The other three passages discussed under this heading seem to pick up on the restoration theme sounded in Isa 1:21-26 and employ the city-lament mode in a hopeful manner. However, since oracles of hope abound in the prophetic books, the identification of the city-lament mode in these passages is not completely certain, though such an interpretation seems plausible enough in light of the significance of the restoration theme in the Mesopotamian laments.

---

[222] *Nahum*, 73.
[223] Cf. Cogan, 22-41.
[224] E.g. Fowler, 170-71.

i. *Isa 1:21-26* The inclusio formed by the mention of the "Faithful City" in vv. 21 and 26 determines the extent of this pericope.[225] The consistent reference to the "Faithful City" by feminine suffixes (3fs in 1:21; 2fs in 1:22 [twice], 25 [three times], 26 [three times]) and one feminine verb form (1:21) underscores the passage's coherence.

In general scholars recognize the lament character of this passage, noting especially the presence of the exclamatory particle ᵓēkāh, qînāh meter, and the contrast motif in Isa 1:21.[226] Additional factors signal Isaiah's use of the city-lament mode in this speech. First, Isa 1:21 reminds one very much of Lam 1:1[227]: both begin with the exclamatory particle ᵓēkāh, focus on the city of Jerusalem personified as a female (harlot and widow), and contrast Zion's glorious past with her woeful present.[228]

The titles "Faithful City" (*qiryāh* ne⁻ᵉmānāh) and "Righteous City" (ᶜîr ḥaṣṣedeq) applied to personified Jerusalem in Isa 1:21 and 26 are almost unique in the Hebrew Bible.[229] Within their Isaianic context they obviously contrast Israel's obedient past and future with its sinful present. Nevertheless, this seems to be a slight transformation of common epithets found throughout the Mesopotamian laments. In these laments the deity's shrine is referred to as the "Faithful House" (Sum. é-

---

[225] Cf. Duhm, 13; Gray, 32; Wildberger, *Jesaja 1-12*, 57; Clements, *Isaiah*, 35; Oswalt, 103; literature cited in John T. Willis ("Lament Reversed -- Isaiah 1,21ff.," *ZAW* 98 [1986] 238, n. 12).

[226] E.g. Delitzsch, *Jesaia*, 26; Duhm, 11; Jahnow, 254-55; Gray, 31; Wildberger, *Jesaja 1-12*, 58-59; Kaiser, *Isaiah 1-12*, 40; Watts, *Isaiah*, 16: Oswalt, 104: Willis, 240, n. 20.

[227] T. K. Cheyne, *The Prophecies of Isaiah* (2 vols. 3d rev. ed. London: Kegan Paul, 1884) I: 8; Hillers, *Lamentations*, 5; cf. Jer 50:23b; 51:41b.

[228] Many commentators omit MT's weᶜattāh mĕrassᵉhim as a gloss, e.g. Duhm, 11; Cheyne, *Book*, 111; Gray, 31; Wildberger, *Jesaja 1-12*, 56; Kaiser, *Isaiah 1-12*, 39. However, this phrase must be maintained in order to complete the contrast between the city's lamentable present and glorious past, cf. Waldemar Janzen, *Mourning Cry and War Oracle* (BZAW 125; Berlin: Walter de Gruyter, 1972) 58, n. 61. Thus, it would be better to retain MT as is, or understand mĕlē⁻ᵃti mišpāt and sedeq yālin bāh as variants which have been conflated, e.g. Paul Haupt (as cited in Gray [33]) omits mĕlē⁻ᵃti mišpāt; see Janzen's comments, *op. cit.*

[229] Cf. Wildberger, *Jesaja 1-12*, 58-60.

zi [Akk. *bītu kīnu*]; e.g. LU 119, 372; LSUr 73, 358; LE 7:21; LN 53, 60, 195; *balag*s 1:2-11, 29, 67-75; 3:2-3, 5, 7, 9, 16, 17; 4:141; 50:b+201-23; *eršemma* 106:21-22) and the city, as the "Faithful City" (Sum. urú-zi [Akk. *ālu kīnu*]; e.g. LU 42, 74; LN 12, 203; *balag*s 4:165; 6:32, b+137; 10:a+39; 42:48 [OB]; 45 [YBC 9862]:53). These epithets refer to the presumed innocence of the city or temple in the Mesopotamian laments. That is, they were correct in their cultic duties and moral behavior. The gods' decision to destroy the city and temple was not motivated by the their actions good or bad. As has been noted, on Israelite soil the responsibility for the city's destruction is blamed on the misdeeds of the city's population. One should especially note the striking resemblance between Isa 1:21a ("How she has become a harlot, the Faithful City!") and LN 12 ("The Faithful City, how it has been diminished!").[230]

A related title occurs in Zech 8:3. Zechariah writes that Yahweh's return will once again make Jerusalem a "Faithful City" (ᶜîr-hāᵓemet). One cannot rule out the possibility that the prophet was familiar with the city-lament genre, since the verse is a development of the divine abandonment and return of the gods themes. However, these themes also occur outside of the city laments.

Finally, the idea of the faithful or righteous city is possibly exploited one other time, in Isa 54. In this chapter Zion's restoration culminates in the re-establishment of the city's righteousness (*biṣdāqâ tikkônānî*, v. 14). This poem also makes use of features from the city-lament genre. Personified Zion was bereaved (v. 1) and widowed (v. 4), images commonly associated with a city's destruction within the genre (cf. Lam 1:1, 5; 2:22; Isa 23:4; 47:8-9). An angered Yahweh, like Enlil in the third *kirugu* of LN, abandoned Zion (v. 7; cf. LN 80-81) and turned his face away from her (v. 8; cf. LN 84). Yet in compassion (vv.

---

[230] Coincidently, the goddesses in the Mesopotamian laments are often described as being faithful. This shows up in a number of their epithets, e.g. Sum. egí-zi (*balag*s 5:f+242; 10:c+338; *eršemma*s 13:28; 79:4) and nu-nuz-zi (LU 289). The description of both city and city goddess as faithful corresponds quite well with the dual image of the personified city in the Hebrew Bible.

7-8; cf. LN 135, 152, 188) Yahweh promises to rebuild the city (vv. 11-12; cf. LN 65-74, 89, etc.) and re-establish her in righteousness (v. 14).

In Isa 1:22-23 the prophet utilizes the reversal motif, except here the imagery appears to depict Israel's sin rather than the chaos which results from the city's destruction.

R. J. Clifford and W. Janzen show that the *hôy*-oracle was at home in funeral laments,[231] and thus it is not surprising to find it in contexts with city-lament imagery. In the *hôy*-oracle which begins in Isa 1:24b, Yahweh, the divine warrior[232] and agent of destruction, tells (through the prophet) the "Faithful City"[233] of her impending destruction. Scholars tend to stress that the city is not destroyed but only corrupted; that Yahweh is only going to purge Jerusalem.[234] Yet one cannot doubt that the prophet intended to indicate Jerusalem's destruction. Isa 1:24-25 clearly portrays Yahweh fighting against Jerusalem. Yahweh's habitual action of fighting against his enemies is juxtaposed to what he intends to do against the "Faithful City." The message, however oblique, is clear: Yahweh will treat Israel as an enemy.

Finally, 1:26 announces Jerusalem's restoration. The theme of the city's restoration is characteristic of city laments, and thus cannot be used to infer that Isaiah really does not have the destruction of Jerusalem in mind here. The city laments bewail the city's destruction in one line and look forward to its restoration in the next. The very nature of the city laments presumes the existence of some remnant of the population who look forward to the city's eventual restoration.

---

[231] R. J. Clifford, "The Use of HÔY in the Prophets," *CBQ* 28 (1966) 459-64; Janzen. This is not to say that one must necessarily construe every *hôy*-oracle to reflect a funeral lament, see J. J. M. Roberts, "Form, Syntax, and Redaction in Isaiah 1:2-20," *Princeton Seminary Bulletin* n.s. 3/3 (1982) 297-98; Hillers, "*Hôy*," 187.

[232] Wildberger, *Jesaja 1-12*, 64.

[233] The *hôy*-oracle necessarily addresses the "Faithful City." Hillers argues that with a few exceptions a vocative element always follows the particle *hôy* ("*Hôy*"). The vocative element here is given by context. The direct address is picked up in vv. 25 and 26 with 2fs suffixes. These must refer to the "Faithful City." Since the "Faithful City" is in focus throughout these verse, it makes sense that she is addressed in v. 24b.

[234] E.g. Wildberger, *Jesaja 1-12*, 57; Clements, *Isaiah*, 36; Willis, 240.

The use of *qînāh* meter and the contrast motif and the personification of the "Faithful City" as a harlot signal the presence of the city-lament mode from the very beginning of this oracle. The agent of destruction and restoration features continue the extension of the mode throughout the oracle.

ii. *Mic 4:9-10*   The short oracle in Mic 4:9-10 takes themes from the city-lament genre and molds them into a salvation oracle. The Daughter of Zion cries and writhes in anguish because of the destruction of the city. She is then to be exiled to Babylon. The taunt in 4:9 asks why she is reacting as if her king is not in her. The identity of the king is disputed. Is it the human king[235] or Yahweh?[236] Either interpretation makes sense. Both would imply that the city had been destroyed. If Yahweh is designated as king here (as in Jer 8:19), then the divine abandonment theme is also present in this short oracle.

iii. *Isa 52:1-2* The theme of these verses is again Zion's restoration. The imagery is very suggestive. It appears to be a reversal of the imagery in Isa 47. The poet beckons Zion to awaken and put back on her queenly apparel (52:1), shake off the dust, loose the bonds from her neck, and be enthroned again (52:2):

> Awake, awake,
>> clothe yourself in splendor, O Zion!
> Put on your glorious robes,
>> O Jerusalem, the holy city!
> For they will never enter you again,
>> the uncircumcised and unclean.
> Shake off the dust,
>> Get back on the throne,[237] O Jerusalem!

---

[235] So Allen, 332-33; Mays, 105; Hillers, *Micah*, 59.

[236] So Rudolph, *Micha*, 86; Wolff, *Micah*, 139.

[237] Many would emend MT's *šĕbî* to read *šĕbiyyāh* as in 52:2b, so *BHS*; *NRSV*. However, the bicolon is cast in 2+3 meter (as is 52:1a), the second colon consisting of *qûmî šĕbî yĕrûšālāim*. Here *qûmî* is used as it often is as an aspectual verb indicating inceptive or ingressive action, lit. "begin to sit enthroned." The aspectual nuance is hard to capture in English, since English usually employs phrasal verbs to

Loose[238] the bonds from your neck,
O Captive, Daughter of Zion!

iv. *Zeph 3:14-20*   Zeph 3:14-20 portrays Yahweh's return to Jerusalem and the city's restoration. While the themes of restoration and return of the gods need not necessarily indicate the presence of the city-lament mode, the familiar personification of Jerusalem at least permits consideration of such an interpretation. The call to rejoice in 3:14 echoes a similar call addressed ironically to the Daughter of Edom in Lam 4:21. Presumably Edom would rejoice at Jerusalem's fall (cf. Obad 12), which implies Edom's salvation. The irony lies in the fact that Edom will not be saved; her punishment still awaits her, while Zion's was completed (4:22). In other words, this seems to be a backhanded way of sounding a faint note of hope for Zion.

In Zeph 3:14-20 the same presuppositions hold, minus the irony. Zion is to rejoice because Yahweh has turned away Zion's judgment and has returned to dwell within her (3:15). In this case, Yahweh's presence is salvific.[239] Yahweh as the divine warrior (3:17) will fight against Zion's enemies (3:19), instead of against Jerusalem. The conventional restoration motif (cf. Jer 46:26b [MT]; 48:47; 49:6 [MT]; 49:39) occurs

---

indicate the ingressive aspect of sitting, e.g. *sit up*, *sit down*. Hence, the circumlocution "get back on the throne." Two good Hebrew parallels are found in 2 Sam 19:9 (*wayyāqom hammelek wayyēšeb baššaᶜar* "So the king took his seat in the gateway," i.e. he sat down) and Gen 27:19 (*qûm-nāʾ šĕbāh* "Sit up!"). The use of finite (or serial) complementation (where both the aspectual and main verbs appear in identical finite forms) -- as opposed to non-finite complementation (where the main verb appears as an infinitive following the finite aspectual verb) -- is common in BH.

The verses' structure provides some confirmation of this interpretation. 52:1a is cast in 2+3 meter and the simple name Zion appears as the last element in the second colon. 52:1b consists of a bicolon with three words in the first colon and the equivalent of a full colon epithet in the second colon ("Jerusalem, the holy city"). The same structure emerges in 52:2. 52:2a is cast in 2+3 meter and the simple name Jerusalem appears as the last element in the second colon. 52:2b consists of a bicolon with three words in the first colon and a full colon epithet in the second colon ("Captive, Daughter of Zion").

[238] Reading a fs imperative with Q and some of the versions.
[239] Roberts, *Nahum*, 222.

in 3:20. Personified Jerusalem receives this same call to rejoice in Zech 2:14 and 9:9. In both passages the reason for the jubilation is Yahweh's return and the city's resulting restoration.

Note also that the charge to not let your hands grow weak in 3:16 is a reversal of the usual response to catastrophe.[240]

3. Psalms

a. Ps 137

Ps 137, one of the more distinctive psalms in the Psalter,[241] laments Jerusalem's destruction and inveighs against her enemies. The sincerity of this lament is reminiscent of Lamentations. The city-lament mode seems to have colored the psalm, plausibly accounting for its uniqueness. As Carroll Stuhlmueller remarks, the psalm is "closest of all to a funeral lament."[242] The *qînāh* meter is dominant (137:2, 5, 6a, b, 7b, 8, 9).[243] M. Buttenwieser compares the psalm's imagery to that found in some of the OAN.[244] The community laments Jerusalem's destruction (137:1). Ps 137:2-4 seem to be an elaboration of the motif of the removal of joyful sounds (see 2.2b above). The Edomites are accused of stripping Zion in 137:7 (cf. Isa 47:2-3; Lam 1:8; 4:21).[245] The Psalm concludes with curses against Edom (137:7) and Babylon (137:8-9; cf. Lam 1:22; 4:21-22).

---

[240] For the significance of this gesture, see Hillers, "Bad News," 88.

[241] Cf. Hans-Joachim Kraus, *Psalms 60-150* (trans. Hilton C. Oswald; Minneapolis: Augsburg, 1990) 501.

[242] "Psalms," in *Harper's Bible Commentary* (ed. James L. Mays; San Francisco: Harper & Row, 1988) 490; cf. Hermann Gunkel, *Die Psalmen* (5th ed.; 1892; Gottingen: Vandenhoeck & Ruprecht, 1968) 578.

[243] Franz Delitzsch, *The Psalms* (3 vols.; trans. David Eaton; London: Hodder and Stoughton, 1887) 330; Kraus, *Psalms*, 501.

[244] *The Psalms* (Chicago: University of Chicago, 1938) 218.

[245] Mitchell Dahood, *Psalms III: 101-150* (AB 17a; Garden City: Doubleday, 1970) 273.

b. **Communal Laments**

Attention has already been called to the formal resemblances between Lam 5 and the *balag*s (see 2.2d above). These resemblances extend to some of the communal laments of the Psalter as well. Note how Pss 44, 60, 74, 79, 80, and 83[246] contain the five elements outlined above:

a) all address Yahweh

b) they praise Yahweh (Pss 44:2-9; 74:12-17; 79:13; 80:2-3, 9-12, 19)

c) description of devastation (Pss 44:10-13, 20; 60:3-6; 74:4-9; 79:1-4; 80:6-7, 9-12, 14; 83:3-9)

d) lament (Pss 44:25; 60:11-12; 74:1, 10-11; 79:5, 10a; 80:5, 13)

e) plea (Pss 44:24, 27; 60:3, 7, 13; 74:2-3, 18-23; 79:6-9, 10b-12; 80:2-4, 8, 15-18, 20; 83:2, 10-19)

Much of the imagery in these psalms is compatible with imagery found in city laments. For example, note the following themes and motifs: divine abandonment (Pss 44:10 [*znh*]; 60:3 [*znh*]; 74:1 [*znh*], 11; 79:10), Yahweh's anger (Pss 60:3; 74:1; 79:5; 80:5), enemy (Pss 44:11; 74:3-4; 79:1, 10; 80:7; 83:3), destruction of the temple (Pss 74:4-9; 79:1), haunt of wild animals (Ps 44:20), taunt of the passers-by (Pss 44:14-15; 79:4; 80:7), lamentation (Ps 80:6), and prayer for restoration (Pss 60:3; 80:4, 8, 20). Notice especially the description of the destruction of the temple in Ps 74:4-9. It is comparable to the description of how Naramsin destroyed the Ekur in CA 94-148 (esp. 107-22). And the plea for Yahweh to inspect the temple's ruins (Ps 74:3) reminds one of the motif

---

[246] While these psalms contain much imagery that is compatible with the city-lament genre, they usually lack any of the genre's diagnostic features. Therefore, the communal laments included for review here are only those which explicitly complain about the destruction of the temple, city, or country. Moreover, the writer has done little more than sketch how these communal laments relate form critically to the *balag*s. A final evaluation of the *balag*s' significance for understanding biblical communal laments must await a more detailed investigation.

of the weeping goddess' wandering among the ruins of her shrine (e.g. *balag* 1:90-91).

However, these communal laments, like Lam 5, also differ from the other examples of the city-lament genre treated in this study. They lack some of the genre's diagnostic features, especially the motif of the personified city. Nonetheless, their formal similarity to the *balag*s compels this writer to include them.

4. Summary

This chapter has traced the city-lament mode in the Prophets and some of the Psalms. The city-lament mode occurs most frequently in the OAN, but it also appears in oracles about Israel and Judah in Isaiah, Jeremiah, Amos, and Micah. The extent of modulation varies from passage to passage. Some passages exhibit a wealth of city-lament features and their associated motifs, while others are affected by only a single motif. Thus, the city-lament genre's existence outside of Lamentations would seem to be established, since the existence of a mode "presupposes an earlier kind [i.e. genre] of which it is an extension."[247]

---

[247] Fowler, 167.

4

Conclusions

Lamentations contains nine of the major generic features commonly attributed to the Mesopotamian city laments, which fully justifies assigning the biblical book to a similar native Israelite city-lament genre, for which it is the prime evidence. Furthermore, various modal extensions of this genre occur frequently throughout the prophetic literature and even in some psalms. Therefore, one may plausibly conclude that knowledge of the city-lament genre is reflected in the Israelite literary record at least from the first half of the eighth century (Amos) to the middle of the sixth century (Second Isaiah), a period of approximately two hundred years. The majority of modal evidence, in fact, pre-dates Lamentations, the only full blown exemplar of the genre, thus implying the relatively early presence of the genre.

The working hypothesis that has guided this study suggested that the existence of a native city-lament genre in Israel, generically related to the Mesopotamian genre, best accounts for the nature of the biblical data. The hypothesis has withstood the test of this study and remains attractive. First, it seems unlikely that a theory of dependence on Mesopotamian sources alone can adequately account for the fairly widespread occurrence of the genre in the Hebrew Bible. One would have to make the improbable supposition that several different writers (i.e. poets and prophets) had access to and chose to borrow from one or more of the Mesopotamian laments over a period of at least two hundred years.

Second, the theory of a native Israelite city-lament genre can better explain a variety of phenomena unique to the Israelite genre. Israelite and/or Syro-Palestinian motifs and imagery appear throughout the biblical genre. The divine warrior imagery, the Day of Yahweh, the conception of Israel's sin as breach of covenant, and the employment of *qînāh* meter, Semitic and West Semitic divine epithets for the personified cities, the taunt of the passers-by, and the Sodom and Gomorrah motif, are only the most prominent of such concepts used in the biblical genre. Concepts like these are integral to the genre and indicate that at least at some point prior to the eighth century, the city-lament genre was internalized in the Israelite literary tradition.

Moreover, the Israelite genre assigns responsibility for destruction differently than does the Mesopotamian. Also the fact that the Mesopotamian laments use concepts (e.g. plurality of deities), motifs, and devices (e.g. *kirugu*s [2.2e], Emesal [2.2e], lists [2.2f]) which are uniquely Mesopotamian in nature further underscores the fact that the Israelite and Mesopotamian genres are distinct.

The remarkable similarities between the two generic repertoires (e.g. subject and mood [2.1], contrast and reversal motifs [2.2b], divine abandonment [2.3], certain destruction motifs [2.6], lamentation [2.8], and restoration [2.9]) can be explained as reflecting the Israelite and Mesopotamian city laments' wider generic relationship. Given the geographical proximity of and cultural continuity between Israel and Mesopotamia, such a kinship is entirely likely and would be marked by certain shared family resemblances of the kind enumerated above.

Nonetheless, several features make it likely that the two genres had some type of closer past connection: 1) the close parallels that have been cited throughout this study (e.g. haunt of wild animals [2.6a], songs turned into lament [2.2b], wide open gates [2.6a; 3.1b.v], plundering of sanctuary and turning it into a garden hut [2.6b; 3.2c.i], famine inside and sword outside [2.6c], piles of corpses [2.6c], geographical motif [3.1a.i-ii; 3.2a.i], father does not turn back for children [3.1c.iv]); 2) the personification of cities and countries, which is almost certainly a partial adaptation of the weeping goddess motif; and 3) some of the structural affinities noted in Chapter Two (e.g. authorial points of view [2.2a], focus [2.2c], the formal resemblances between the *balag*s and communal laments [2.2d]). The nature of this connection, when it occurred, how it came about, etc., unfortunately, is difficult (if not impossible) to determine. It seems probable that the direction of the influence is from Mesopotamian to Israel, but even this is not completely certain.

The suggestion that periods of exile, whether in Assyria or Babylonia, provided the best opportunities for the Israelites to come into contact with the Mesopotamian genre will doubtless remain attractive, since it points to known instances where Israelites would have been exposed to Mesopotamian culture. However, little that is concrete is known about life in exile. Thus, the question of the Mesopotamian and Israelite genre's closer connection must remain open and other alternatives explored.

Interest in Mesopotamian culture on the part of Israel need not be restricted solely to known periods of Israelite presence in Mesopotamian. There is no doubt that a certain amount of trading took place periodically between Israel and Mesopotamian. This would provide a natural avenue for the oral transmission of non-material culture such as literary genres and cultic practices. Assyrian and Babylonian domination of Palestine would also bring with it exposure to Mesopotamian culture. Moreover, one could reasonably expect Israel to be well informed about her important neighbor to the east and even emulate certain aspects of Mesopotamian culture.[1] Thus, one can imagine a variety of ways in which specific literary parallels, etc. may have passed from Mesopotamia to Israel without leaving any trace in the material record.

While so far unattested, actual exemplars of the Mesopotamian city-lament genre may have even made their way to Palestine, thus providing a possible literary vehicle for the type of influence noted above. Although the number of cuneiform artifacts found in Palestine remains relatively small (ca. fifty-one), their kinds suggest the likelihood of some type of cuneiform literacy in Palestine during the early and late second millennium, and perhaps in the first millennium as well. Thus, the possibility that Mesopotamian city laments existed in Palestine cannot be discounted, especially given the small percentage of texts that have survived from antiquity.

To summarize, the main conclusions of this study are as follows: 1) the Hebrew Bible contains evidence of a city-lament genre comparable to the one in Mesopotamia; 2) the biblical genre appears to be native

---

[1] See Hillers, *Lamentations* (2d), 35-36.

to Israel and generically related to the Mesopotamian genre; and 3) some evidence suggests that the two genres had some type of closer contact.

The Israelite genre as sketched in this study can stand on its own. That is, the genre coheres by itself, the connection to the Mesopotamian genre notwithstanding. Obviously one would have had some difficulty in coming up with the general outline of the genre without reference to the Mesopotamian evidence. But after a survey of the biblical texts which it is suggested constitute the city-lament genre, it is clear that they form a cohesive group in themselves.

This study has further suggested two interrelated ways of understanding how funeral laments and city laments may be connected, thus accounting for some of their resemblances. In the first chapter (see 1.6) it was suggested that they could reflect two subgenres of a more general lament genre, such as is found in the Greek literary tradition. More specifically, in Chapter Three, it was noted that city laments perhaps reflect partial transformations of funeral laments. That is, the former was partially conceptualized in terms of the latter. Whether the city-lament genre originated in Mesopotamia would seem to be a moot question. That is, the Mesopotamian laments are clearly the oldest and best attested city laments, and it is likely that some generic influences may have radiated out from Mesopotamia. Nevertheless, this does not preclude the generic development of city laments from funeral laments from having occurred in Israel as well.

Although the city-lament mode appears in some psalms and oracles about Israel and Judah, it has been found most frequently in the OAN. One naturally wonders why this should be. Although a final answer is not yet at hand, one suggestion deserves consideration. Jahnow and Janzen observe that the movement from lament to invective occurs within funeral dirges.[2] Jahnow presents examples where the lament for a murder victim turns into a curse against the murderer. Janzen cites Danil's lament over Aqht and his subsequent curse of the place(s) where

---

[2] Jahnow, 88-90; Janzen, 27-34.

Aqht lived (*KTU* 1.19) as a good Near Eastern example of the phenomenon.[3]

This phenomenon occurs at least twice in biblical texts associated with the city-lament genre. The lament over Jerusalem in Lamentations twice turns into words of vengeance against the city's enemies (Lam 1:22 and 4:21-22).[4] Ps 137 both laments Jerusalem and curses her enemies (see 3.3a above). As in the funeral dirges, the objects of the lament and curse in these texts are different. In the OAN which contain city-lament features and motifs, the pattern is slightly changed. These oracles seem to lament and curse the same object. It is as if the laments themselves are lifted up as curses. Hence, they are usually referred to as taunts or mock dirges. In this way they are more analogous to CA, which contains laments for the same object which it curses, Agade. This use of the city-lament genre to rebuke or mock nations perceived by Israel to be responsible for Jerusalem's destruction could be explained as a further extension of the lament-to-invective movement found in funeral dirges and some city laments. Partial support for this theory is found in some oracles, e.g. Jer 50-51. In this oracle, which has a relatively high degree of city-lament modulation (see 3.1a.iv above), Babylon's crimes against Israel seem to have motivated the oracle's delivery. Yet, the oracle does not lament Jerusalem's destruction. Rather, it uses city-lament features to mock Babylon's downfall; lament and curse have seemingly become one.

However, this theory remains only suggestive. In many of the other OAN featuring the city-lament mode, the rationale for the oracles is unexpressed. Furthermore, it is clear that at present one cannot account for all the OAN by presuming that they developed in relation to the city-lament genre. Some of the OAN do not contain any diagnostic city-lament features, yet they are nonetheless directed against foreign nations presumably for crimes committed against Israel. Thus,

---

[3] Janzen, 28; cf. Enkidu's lament over his impending death and his curse of the hunter and harlot, *ANET*[3] 86, 504.

[4] Cf. Janzen, 32.

until a more satisfying explanation of the OAN themselves emerges,[5] a reason for the predominance of city-lament features and motifs in the OAN will remain somewhat obscure.

In closing, some observations concerning the possible precursors of the biblical city laments may be offered. The Mesopotamian laments were commonly used in cultic ceremonies at the razing and restoration of old sanctuaries. On the basis of Jer 41:5 and Zech 7:3-5 and 8:19, scholars have called attention to the possible liturgical use of Lamentations.[6] However, the evidence remains inconclusive. It is also unlikely that the use of the city-lament mode in the Hebrew Bible reflects actual cultic compositions used to lament fallen cities. Moreover, the nature of the Israelite cult and the rituals associated with it is a widely debated topic upon which there is little consensus among biblical scholars. Thus, it would be less than prudent to assume a cultic setting for the biblical city laments in the absence of hard data. This apparent difference between the biblical and Mesopotamian genres is not problematic theoretically. The idea that genres must reflect a single social setting is no longer tenable. Genres may arise from occasions of the mind just as easily as they may reflect the actual social settings with which they are associated.[7] In other words, the ancient poets were entirely capable of imaginatively creating situations for which the city-lament genre would be appropriate or writing about actual destructions without necessarily having any connection to the cult.

Nonetheless, the cultic use of the Mesopotamian laments increases the likelihood that actual liturgical "laments over destroyed sanctuaries" did exist in Israel. Note that in Ezra 3:12-13 weeping is associated with Zerubbabel's rebuilding of the temple. Thus, one may imagine the existence of cultic compositions in ancient Israel that were

---

[5] So far this remains elusive, see John H. Hayes, "The Usage of Oracles Against Foreign Nations in Ancient Israel," *JBL* 87 (1968) 81-92; Ronald E. Clements, *Prophecy and Tradition* (Oxford: Basil Blackwell 1975); Duane L. Christensen, *Transformation of the War Oracle in Old Testament Prophecy: Studies in the Oracles Against the Nations* (HDR 3; Missoula: Scholars, 1975).

[6] E.g. Kraus, *Klagelieder*, 12-13; Hillers, *Lamentations*, xl-xli; Westermann, *Klagelieder*, 61-63.

[7] See Longman, *Fictional Akkadian*, 17-18.

somewhat more analogous to the *balag*s. These more liturgical city laments no doubt would be related to the biblical city laments, but they nevertheless need not correspond completely to them. This supposition accords well with theorists' knowledge that many literary genres coincide with related, non-literary speech acts.[8]

---

[8] Todorov, *Genres*, 20-26; cf. Fowler, 149-69.

Appendix 1
Correspondences Between $4R^2$ 53 and *CLAM*

---

[1] According to the NA catalogue, $4R^2$ 53 (= K_1 in Cohen, *Sumerian Hymnology*, 7; see also 42-47 for Cohen's edition of the catalogue).

[2] According to *CLAM*.

balag 31	a-gal-gal buru$_{14}$ su-su	p. 500
balag 33	^{d}Utu-gin$_7$ è-ta *ahû*	p. 519
balag 35	am-e amaš-a-na *ahû*	p. 523
balag 39	dingir pa-è-a	p. 731
balag 40	áb-gin$_7$ gù-dé-dé	p. 533
balag 42	úru àm-me-ir-ra-bi	p. 536
balag 43	im-ma-al gù-dé-dé	p. 604
balag 44	...é-mu ...	p. 637
balag 45	a urú-mu im-me	p. 642
balag 48	urú-hul-e-ke$_4$	p. 650
balag 49	eden-na ú-sag-gá-ke$_4$	p. 668
balag 50	a-še-er gi$_6$-ta	p. 704
balag 51	guruš mu-lu-ér-ra	p. 726
balag 57	é-e še àm-ša$_4$	Krecher, *Kultlyrik*
balag 58[3]	lugal dìm-me-er-an-ki-a	p. 728

---

[3] This *balag* is not included in the catalogue. For the purposes of this study it has been numbered consequtively after the last *balag* in the catalogue.

Appendix 2
A Summary of City-lament Features
in the Mesopotamian and Israelite Genres

This appendix conveniently brings together in one place a compilation of the major city-lament features and where they occur in the Mesopotamian and Israelite genres. However, it is not meant to substitute for the more detailed genre study carried out in the body of this work. Rather, it is intended to serve for reference purposes only. Moreover, the appendix is not completely exhaustive in its assemblage of generic features (e.g. no attempt has been made to document every shift in authorial point of view). It focuses only on the most notable city-lament features.

Bold faced type signifies features that are specifically or primarily characteristic of the Mesopotamian genre
Italicized type signifies features that are specifically or primarily characteristic of the Israelite genre

Feature	Mesopotamian Laments	Hebrew Bible
1. SUBJECT AND MOOD*		
2. STRUCTURE AND POETIC TECHNIQUE		
a. Authorial Point of View		
Narrator	throughout the laments	throughout Lam 1-5 Isa 15:1-4, 6-8; 16:8

Poet as internal observer	e.g. *kirugu* 8 of LU; 5 of LN; 7 of LE (esp. lns. 1-2); *balag*s 4:1-14, 108-27, 171-76; 5:f+225-65, 266-77; 6:30-95; 7:b+73-85; 10:a+45-46, 49-51; 12:62-74 (FM); 25:f+109-34; 42:c+280-81 (FM)	Lam 2:11, 13-19 Isa 15:5; 16:9-11 Jer 8:18-23 Jer 22:4
City Goddess / Personified City	e.g. LU, *kirugu* 4, esp. lns. 145-46, 155-56; *balag*s 1:60-63; 7:1-25; 8:b+58-82 [OB]; 26:38-59; 43:g+335-61; 39:a+71-89; *eršemma*s 79:29-32; 32:36-48; 171:30-38	Lam 1:11c-22; 2:20-22 Jer 4:19-21; 10:19-21
Divine Agent	e.g. LSUr 360-70, 460-69; LW 3:2ff.; *balag*s 3:f+187-89; 12:d+117-30 [OB]; VAS 2 16 rev. col. v:1-15; 29:d+153-63; 31:a+136-61; *eršemma* 171:40-45; 185:33-36	Isa 15:9
Community	e.g. LSUr 227-42, 396-402; *balag*s 5; 6; 16 (FM); 12:e+161-71 (OB), 15:a+177-87	Lam 3:42-51; 4:17-20; 5 Pss 44, 60, 74, 79, 80, and 83

b. Contrast and Reversal

Contrast motif	e.g. LU 116-17, 122-23, 133; LSUr 52, 259, 304, 312, 313, 315, 442; LE 1:16-17; LW 5:16; LN 31, 32-33, 103; CA1-54, 210-81, 249	Lam 1:1; 2:1b, 6b, 15; 4:1-10, 5, 20 Isa 47:1-2, 5 Isa 23:7, 8, 12 Zeph 2:15 Ezek 27:1-11, 26-36 Isa 1:21
Reversal motif	e.g. LU 233-35, 359-60, 361-66, 367-68; LSUr 12-16, 42-46, 95-96, 293, 335-37, 351, 436-37; LW 2:14'-16'; LN 42, 69, 107, 118-21, 212; CA 162, 166-67, 210-81, 216-18, 264-65; *balag*s 5:97-101; 6:31-33, b+133-38; 10:a+112-21; 13:f+203-15; 42:27 (OB); 43:a+44-45, c+212-23	Lam 1:4a-b; 5:8-14, 8, 15b Isa 16:10 Isa 1:22-23

c. Focus

Destructive power	e.g. "*balag*s of Enlil;" *kirugu* 4 of LU; LSUr 22-26, 58-64, 72-80, 164-66; the monster in LW; LN 79-96; CA 149ff., 210ff.	Lam 2:1-9a Jer 50:1-51:58
Destruction wrought	e.g. "*balag*s of Inanna;" LU 208-51;	Lam 1:1-11b, 11c-22 Jer 48:1-47

LSUr 340-56; LN
53-78, 118-40

d. External and Met-
rical Structure

qînāh meter

throughout Lam 1-5
Isa 15:2a-b, 3a
[MT], 3b, 4b, 5a, 6a,
9b; 16:6a, 7a, 8a, 9a,
c, 10b, 11
Isa 47:1a-c, 2a-b,
5a-b, 6a, 9a-b
Jer 50:11a, 12a, 22,
23, 27b, 28a, 31b,
41, 42c; 51:1b, 2b,
4, 5b, 8, 13a, 35,
37a, 41, 44b
Isa 23:1b, 2a, 2γ-
3α, 4δ-ε, 10, 11a-b
Zeph 2:13-15
Isa 13:4, 5, 8a, b;
9a; 11a; 19; 21b
Ezek 26:17-18
Isa 14:31a
Mic 1:1:11b, 12a, b,
13a, 14b, 15a, 16b
Jer 22:1-4
Amos 5:2-3
Isa 3:25
Isa 1:21
Ps 137:2, 5, 6a, b,
7b, 8, 9

e. Lists

e.g. LU, *kirugu* 1;
LSUr, *kirugu* 2
kirugu 6 of LE; LN,
*kirugu*s 1, 2, 8; CA
264-71;

Geographical motif	e.g. LSUr 115-284, 371-76, 377-407a; LE 6:2'-24'; LW 4:22-5:22; CA 149-57, 158-92, 210-81	Isa 15:1, 2, 4, 5, 6, 8, 9; 16:7, 8, 9, 11 Jer 48:1-10, 29-47 Mic 1:10-16
3. DIVINE ABANDONMENT	e.g. LU 1-39, 237-38, 373-84; LSUr 58-64, 115-284. 370, 373-76,475-77a; LE 1:11-15, 5:1-2, 6:2'-27', 7:1-83a; LW 2:21'-26'; LN 80-81. 89. 208-9, 214; CA 60-65, 67-76. 209; *balag*s 4:100-27; 5:f+266-77; 6:84-95, b+179-92;16:c+158-69 (FM); *eršemma* 166.1:16-17	Lam 1:1a; 2:1c, 3b, 6c, 7a, 8a; 5:20, 22a Jer 48:7 Isa 46:1-2 Jer 50:2; 51:44 Jer 46:15 Jer 49:3 Jer 49:25 Jer 8:19 Isa 22:8a Pss 44:10; 60:30; 74:1, 11; 79:10
Spoliation of the Divine Image	e.g. LU 275-81; LSUr 408-10; CA 131-33, 134-45; *balag* 10: a+196-203; 50:b+155-61;	Isa 47:2-3
4. ASSIGNMENT OF RESPONSIBILITY		
No fault, divine capriciousness, decision of divine assembly	e.g. LU, *kirugu* 4; LSUr 22-26, 55-57, 366-69; LW 1:1-13;	
Sin	CA 151, 212-14 (Naramsin's sacrilege)	Lam 1:5b, 8a, 14a, 18a, 20b, 22b;

2:14a; 3:42; 4:13;
5:7, 16
Jer 50:15, 18, 24,
27, 28, 29, 31; 51:6,
11, 24, 44, 47, 51,
52, 56
Jer 4:14, 17-18, 22;
6:6-7; 8:14; 10:21

5. DIVINE AGENT

Responsibility

Enlil: e.g. LU 203,
257-60; LSUr 72,
175-77, 261, 296-99;
LN 89-96; *balag*s
4:b+253-56; 5:59-60;
6 : 1 9 - 2 3 ,   3 0 ;
5 0 : b + 1 7 7 - 8 0 ;
5 : b + 1 5 5 - 6 2 ;
1 0 : a + 3 0 - 3 6 ;
43:c+224, d+269-77;
50:b+181-84, 224-28
Other deities: *balag*
3:c+89-109;   25:1-
a+26;   26:61-97;
29:c+43-64, 65-81;
S B H   7 : 3 7 - 5 7 ;
3 1 : a + 5 0 - 6 7 ;
*eršemma*s 23.1; 168;
184

Yahweh: Lam 1:5b,
12c, 13, 14c, 15,
21b; 2:1-9a, 17, 21c
Jer 48:12, 33 [MT],
35, 38, 44
Isa 47:6
Jer 50:32; 51:45
Zeph 2:13
Jer 49:5
Jer 6:8; 8:14; 9:10;
10:18

Storm

e.g. LU 171-204,
173, 175-76, 391-
415; LE 1:5-10, 19-
24; LW 3:2-3; LN
96-107; *balag*s 5:1-
12; 9:c+156, 162;
11:a+93-97, 109-19,
12:b+93-101 [OB],

	a+99-108 [FM]; 13:a+28-45; 43:1-a+57	
Pickaxe	e.g. LU 245, 258, 272, 340; LSUr 42, 80b, 264, 346; LN 98; CA 125	
Enemy Invasion	e.g. LU 219-25, 244; LSUr 33, 75, 146, 166, 230, 254, 257, 261, 381-88; LE 4:10; LW 4:11; 5:11-19; LN 64, 95, 136, 155, 159, 169, 266, 302; CA 155, 164	Lam 1:5, 7, 10, 14, 16, 17, 21; 2:7, 17, 22; 4:12 Isa 15:9 Jer 48:8, 18, 32 Isa 47:6b Jer 50:3, 9, 14, 21-22, 26-29, 41-42; 51:1-2, 11-12, 14, 27-28 Isa 23:13 Isa 13:17 Jer 46:20-23 Nah 2:4-14 Jer 4:6b, 7, 13, 16-17, 29; 6:1-8, 22-23; 8:16, 17 Isa 22:6 Pss 44:11; 74:3-4; 79:1, 10; 80:7; 83:3
Divine Warrior		Lam 2:1-9a, 1a, 3b, 3c, 4a, 4b, 4c, 5a Jer 50:25; 51:25 Isa 23:11a Zeph 2:13 Isa 13:1-13 Jer 46:3-12 Mic 1:2-7 Isa 22:5

Isa 1:24
Zeph 3:14-20

Day of Yahweh   Lam   1:12c;   2:1c,
                                                   21c, 22b
                                                   Isa 1-13
                                                   Jer 46:10
                                                   Isa 22:5
                                                   Amos 5:18-20

Divine Word/Plan   e.g. LU 150-51, 160-   Lam   1:21c;   2:8a,
                          61, 168-69; LSUr   17a;
                          57, 163-64, 365; CA   Jer 50:45; 51:11-12,
                          99; LW 3:27, 12:38;   29
                          *balag*s 4:b+235-36;   Isa 23:8, 9
                          5:1-52, 58-59, 72-   Jer 49:20
                          73, 94, b+142-53;   Jer 4:28
                          6:5-6; 8:1-12 (FM),
                          a+39-57 (OB); 9:1-
                          17,   c+137-53;
                          10:b+237-38;
                          11:a+79-80; 12:1-13,
                          19-28   (OB);
                          13:a+13-14, 28-45;
                          29:c+43-64;
                          31:a+50-67;
                          eršemma 160:4-5

Divine Look   e.g.   LU   431-32;   Lam   1:9c,   11c;
                          LSUr 22, 23; LE   2:20a; 3:50; 5:1;
                          1:26; 6:4; LW 1:19;
                          12:31; LN 71, 84,
                          233, 269; CA 1,
                          152; *balag*s 5:108-
                          19,   120;   6:25,
                          b+121-32, 193-209;
                          10:a+52-67;
                          13:c+119-22, CT 42
                          26: 1-2; 16:a+67-71

(OB), c+196-99
(FM); 42:24 (OB);
eršemma 1.1:1ff.

6. Destruction

a. City and Environs	e.g. LU 209, 246, 261-64, 345; LSUr 40; 346-47; LW 4:25; LN 97; *balag* 4:a+210	
Haunt of wild animals	e.g. LSUr 143-46, 222, 346-49; CA 257; LE 4:4-8; LN 100, 103; *balag*s 4:a+210, 223; 5:d+179, 194; 10:a+22-27, 31, 122-25; 13:f+212-15	Lam 5:18 Jer 50:12, 13, 39-40; 51:37, 42-43 Isa 23:13 Zeph 2:14 Isa 13:20-22 Jer 9:10 Ps 44:20
Sodom and Gomorrah		Lam 4:6 Jer 50:40 Isa 13:19 Isa 1:9; Jer 49:18; Isa 1:9
Taunt of the passer-by		Lam 1:7c; 2:15, 16 Jer 48:39 Jer 50:13; 51:37 Zeph 2:15d Ezek 27:35-36 Pss 44:14-15; 79:4; 80:7
City gates, walls, and buildings	e.g. LU 212, 261-64; LSUr 292, 404; LE 2:4; LW 5:11-16; CA 168; *eršemma*s	Lam 1:4b; 2:2a-b, 5b, 8a, 9a Jer 50:15; 51:30, 44, 58

	1 6 3 . 1 : 1 3 ; 163.2:a+14	Nah 2:7; 3:13
Disruption of agriculture and alteration of water supply	e.g. LU 271, 273; LSUr 9, 11; CA 68, 69, 172, 174;	Isa 15:6; 16:8-11
Unsafe roads	e.g. LU 367-68; LSUr 38-39, 94; CA 163-4, 166-67; *balag* 42:46-48 (OB)	Jer 6:25
b. Sanctuary	e.g. LU 116-33, 276-81; LSUr 407b-48; LE 2:12-3:7; LN 53-78; CA 100-48; *balags* 3:1-28; 4:137-70; 5:e+202-12; 10:a+1-2; 50:b+155-61	Lam 1:10b Jer 4:20; 10:20 Pss 74:4-9; 79:1
Plundering of temple treasures	e.g. LU 133, 239, 275-81; LSUr 169-70; LW 3:29; LN 63, 276-77; CA 136-45; *balags* 10:a+196-203; 26:57; 27:57; 50:b+226-27	Lam 1:10a;
Garden hut motif	e.g. LU 122-23, 125-29; *balags* 6:20; CT 42 26:13	Lam 2:6a; Isa 1:8
c. Persons		
Piles of corpses	e.g. LU 213-16; LE 2:5; LW 2a:6; LN 66; *balags* 2:27-31;	Lam 1:15a Jer 50:26, 30: 51:4, 47

	43:a+36; *eršemma* 35.2:27-31	Nah 3:3 Jer 49:26
Famine	e.g. LSUr 303-8, 389, 399-401; CA 249-53; *balag*s 8:36- 37 (FM); 13:b+64- 65; 43:a+42-43, c+214-15	Lam 1:20c; 4:5, 9a; Jer 14:18
Exile	e.g. LU 283, 285; LSUr 34-37; LW 2a:3; LN 44, 21-23, 219	Lam 1:5c, 18c; 2:9b; 4:20; Isa 13:14
d. Social, Religious, and Political Cus- toms		
Parents do not turn back for their chil- dren	e.g. LU 233, 234; LSUr 96; LN 212; *balag*s 5:99; 6:32	Jer 47:3
Religious Upheaval	e.g. LU 70, 117, 192, 213-16, 322; LSUr 31, 102, 184, 192, 205, 250, 343- 45; LE 1:16; 3:9-14; LN 112, 169-71, 282-85, 302-5; *balag*s 1:81-89; 3:a+51-54; 4:a+198- 232; 5:d+165-201; 6:b+214-246; PBS 10/2 no. 12 + VAS 2 12:obv. col. ii 1- 31; 50:a+81-86; *eršemma*s 106; 159	Lam 1:4a-b, 10; 2:6- 7, 9c, 14;

7. WEEPING GOD-
DESS / PERSONIFIED
CITY

Weeping and Mourning Gestures	e.g. LU 80-85, 108-9, 137-72, 154, 247, 299-301; LSUr 115-284; LE 5:3-11; *kirugu* 4 of LN; *balag*s 1:46-63; 2:b+61-75; 3:18, c+65-74; 4:177-95, b+257-60; 7:b+160-68; 20:g+111-20; 42:c+362; 43:a+62-94, 58-119, c+239-51, g+338ff; 48:1-21 (FM); 50:a+42-86, b+186-232, 233-43; *eršemma*s 32; 79, esp. lns. 25-35; 106; 159; 166.1 and 2; 10	Lam 1:2a, 4c, 8c, 16a, 17a, 21a,; 2:18-19 Isa 15:2a, b, 4; 16:7 Jer 48:18, 19 Isa 47:1-3a, 5 Jer 50:12 Isa 23:4 Jer 49:3 Jer 46:11-12 Mic 1:10, 11, 12, 16 Jer 4:31; 6:26; 31:15 Isa 3:26
Possessor	e.g. LU 133, 275-81; LSUr 169-70, 273-74; *balag*s 1:60, 75-89; 10:a+196-203; 42:122 (OB); 50:a+54-71; *eršemma*s 166.1 and 2; 171:7-8	Lam 1:10a-b; Jer 4:20; 10:20 Amos 5:2
Mother and Widow Imagery	e.g. LU 28, 103, 283, 341, 357, 365-66, 369-70, 378; LSUr 117, 137, 141; LE 1:15; *balag*s 1:76-77; 5 {N,O,P}:168; 42:9-	Lam 1:4b-c, 5c, 11a, 15, 16c; 2:9b-c, 10a, 14,19c, 21b, 22c; 4:13; Isa 47:8-9 Isa 23:4

	11, 68, 100 (OB); 43:c+234-38, 239, d+270-76; 48:b+37, 39-40, 44 (FM); 49:b+48-49 (OB); 50:b+129-31, 224-25, 262; 57.8:43, 46	Jer 31:15 Jer 50:12; 51:5
Exile	e.g. LU 294, 306-8; LSUr 150, 273-74; *balag*s 27:58; 50:b+-252-57; 57.8:37-54; *eršemma* 32:49-54; 159:26-28; 171:51-55	Lam 1:1c, 3a-b Isa 47:2 Isa 23:12b Jer 46:19 Nah 2:8; 3:5, 10 Mic 4:10

Divine Epithets

bĕtûlat GN		Jer 31:4, 21 Amos 5:2
bĕtûlat bat GN		Lam 1:15c; 2:13b Isa 47:1a Isa 23:12 Jer 46:11
yōšebet GN/*b*-GN		Lam 4:21 Jer 48:19 Jer 51:35 Nah 3:8 Mic 1:11, 12, 13, 15 Jer 22:23
yōšebet bat GN		Jer 48:18 Jer 46:19
rabbātî, śārātî		Lam 1:1;
bat ᶜammî		Lam 2:11; 3:48; 4:3,

		6, 10; Jer 4:11; 6:26; 8:11, 19, 21, 22, 23; 14:17 Isa 22:4
bat GN		Lam 1:6, 15; 2:1, 2, 4, 8, 10, 13, 15, 18; 4:21, 22 Isa 47:1b, 5a Jer 50:42; 51:33 Isa 23:10 Jer 46:24 Mic 1:13 Jer 4:31; 6:2, 23 Isa 1:8; 22:4; 52:2; Mic 4:10; Zeph 3:14; Ps 137:8
The Glorious City		Lam 2:1b, 15c Jer 48:2 Isa 23:7 Zeph 2:15 Isa 13:19 Ezek 26:17; 27:3 Nah 2:8a Jer 49:25 Isa 22:2
Faithful City	e.g. LU 42, 74; LN 12, 203; *balag*s 4:165; 6:32, b+137; 10:a+39; 42:48 (OB); 45 (YBC 9862):53	Isa 1:21, 26 Zech 8:3 Isa 54:14
Personification of gates, roads, walls, temple, etc.	e.g. LU 40-41, 48- 62, 269-72; LSUr 380; LW 1:18-19; 4:29; LN 53-78,	Lam 1:4a-b; 2:8c, 18a Isa 23:1, 14 Isa 14:31a

	141; CA 227; *balag*s 2:1-32; 3:21-28; *eršemma* 35.2:1-14	Isa 3:26
8. LAMENTATION	e.g. LU 231-34, 374; LSUr 361-62, 479- 81, 398, 451; LE 6:27'; LN 30, 31, 36, 37, 41, 43, 46, 53- 78, 80; CA 196-209; *balag*s; 3:13-28; 4:137-70, 195, a+207-32; 5:e+202- 12; 6:24-29, a+107- 19; 8:b+77-82 (OB); 10:a+10-21, a+113- 16; 16:a+2-8, 33-36 (OB), a+28-30, 99- 111 (FM); 23:a+36- 4; *eršemma*s 1.1:25- 29; 1.2:38-42; 29:20; 160:36; 163.1:19	Lam 1:1, 4, 11a; 2:1, 5c, 10, 11; 3:48-51; 4:1; 5:15, 17 Isa 15:2-3; 16:7 Jer 48:1, 2, 4, 5, 17b-20a, 18, 20, 31- 32, 37-39, 46 Jer 50:23; 51:8, 41 Isa 23:1, 2, 6, 14 Zeph 2:13-15, 2:15aβ-b Jer 49:3 Ezek 26:15-18; 27:28-32 Nah 2:12-13; 3:1-7 Jer 4:8; 9:9 (LXX); 9:16-21 Isa 22:1, 12 Amos 5:16-17 Isa 1:21 Ps 137:1 Ps 80:6
9. RESTORATION AND RETURN		
Restoration of the City	e.g. LU 423, 435; LSUr 352-56, 460- 74, 493-518; LE 8:1; LN *kirugu*s 6, 8-11; *balag*s 3:e+141-49; 5:f+279; 7:b+84-85; 8:c+89-e+137 (OB); VAS 2 16 rev. col.	Lam 4:22 Jer 48:47 Jer 50:4-5, 19; 51:5, 45 Isa 13:6 Jer 46:26b (MT) Jer 49:6 (MT) Jer 49:39

	vi:6-18; 10:c+384; 12:e+292 (OB); 29:f+248; 48:e+172 (FM)	Jer 31:4-5, 21-22 Isa 1:26 Mic 4:10 Isa 52:1-2 Zeph 3:14-20
Return of the Gods	e.g. LU 331-84; LSUr 475-77a; LE 7:1-24; LN 207-14; *balag*s 6:c+247-57; 8:e+137 (OB)	Zeph 3:14-20
Prayer for Restoration	e.g. LU 419-30; LSUr 352-56; LE 8:1; LW *kirugu* 12; LN 307; *balag*s 3:e+141-49; 5:f+225-65; 6:43-83; 8:c+89-e+137 (OB); 12:e+161-280 (OB); 15:a+177ff.; 16:b+112-25 (FM); SBH 7:58-98	Lam 5:22 Pss 60:3; 80:4, 8, 20

*   All of the texts in this study by definition have as their subject matter the destruction of the city and/or country.

Bibliography

Abrams, M. H.
    1988   *A Glossary of Literary Terms*. 5th ed. New York: Holt, Rinehart and Winston.

Albrektson, Bertil
    1963   *Studies in the Text and Theology of the Book of Lamentations*. Lund: CWK Gleerup.
    1967   *History and the Gods*. Lund: CWK Gleerup.

Alexiou, Margaret
    1974   *The Ritual Lament in Greek Tradition*. Cambridge: Cambridge University.

Allen, Leslie C.
    1976   *The Books of Joel, Obadiah, Jonah and Micah*. NIC. Grand Rapids: Wm. B. Eerdmans.

Alster, Bendt
    1983   "The Mythology of Mourning." *ASJ* 5: 1-16.
    1985   Review of *The Curse of Agade* by Jerrold S. Cooper. *WO* 16: 159-62.

Alter, Robert
    1981   *The Art of Biblical Narrative*. New York: Basic Books.
    1985   *The Art of Biblical Poetry*. New York: Basic Books.

Andersen, Francis I., and David Noel Freedman
    1989   *Amos*. AB 24a. Garden City: Doubleday.

Auvrey, Paul
    1972   *Isaïe 1-39*. Paris: Librairie Lecoffre.

Avi Yonah, Michael, and Israel Shatzman
    1975   *Illustrated Encyclopaedia of the Classical World*. New York: Harper & Row.

Barré, Michael L.
    1983   *The God-List in the Treaty between Hannibal and Philip V of Macedonia: A Study in Light of the*

Ancient Near Eastern Treaty Tradition. Baltimore: Johns Hopkins University.

Barstad, Hans M.
1984   *The Religious Polemics of Amos.* Leiden: E. J. Brill.

Barton, John
1984   *Reading the Old Testament.* Philadelphia: Westminster.

Bechtel, Lyn M.
1991   "Shame as a Sanction of Social Control in Biblical Israel: Judicial, Political, and Social Shaming." *JSOT* 49: 47-76.

Berlin, Adele
1983   *Poetic and Interpretation of Biblical Narrative.* Sheffield: Almond.

Bertholet, Alfred
1936   *Hesekiel.* HAT 13. Tübingen: J. C. B. Mohr.

Biddle, Mark E.
1991   "The Figure of Lady Jerusalem: Identification, Deification and Personification of Cities in the Ancient Near East." Pp. 173-94 in *The Biblical Canon in Comparative Perspective.* Eds. K. L. Younger, Jr., W. W. Hallo, and B. F. Batto. Lewiston: Edwin Mellen.

Black, Jeremy A.
1985   "A-še-er Gi$_6$-ta, a Balag of Inana." *ASJ* 7: 11-87.

Block, Daniel I.
1988   *The Gods of the Nations.* ETS Monograph Series 2. Jackson: Evangelical Theological Society.

Bright, John
1965   *Jeremiah.* AB 21. Garden City: Doubleday.

Budde, Karl
1882   "Das hebräische Klagelied." *ZAW* 2: 1-52.

Buttenwieser, Moses
1938   *The Psalms.* Chicago: University of Chicago.

Callaway, Mary
1986   *Sing, O Barren One: A Study in Comparative Midrash.* SBLDS 91. Atlanta: Scholars.

Camp, Claudia, V.
1985   *Wisdom and the Feminine in the Book of Proverbs.* Bible and Literature Series 11. Sheffield: Almond.

Cagni, Luigi

1969   *L'Epopea di Erra.* Studi Semitici 34. Rome: Universita di Roma.

1977   *The Poem of Erra.* SANE 1/3. Malibu: Undena.

Carroll, Robert P.

1986   *Jeremiah.* OTL. Philadelphia: Westminster.

Cathcart, Kevin J.

1973   *Nahum in the Light of Northwest Semitic.* BibOr 26. Rome: Pontifical Biblical Institute.

Cheyne, T. K.

1884   *The Prophecies of Isaiah.* 2 vols. 3d rev. ed. London: Kegan Paul.

1899   *The Book of the Prophet Isaiah.* Leipzig: J. C. Hinrichs'sche.

Christensen, Duane L.

1975   *Transformation of the War Oracle in Old Testament Prophecy: Studies in the Oracles Against the Nations.* HDR 3. Missoula: Scholars.

Clements, Ronald E.

1975   *Prophecy and Tradition.* Oxford: Basil Blackwell.

1980   *Isaiah 1-39.* Grand Rapids: Wm. B. Eerdmans.

Clifford, Richard J.

1966   "The Use of HÔY in the Prophets." *CBQ* 28: 459-64.

1974   Review of *Mourning Cry and Woe Oracle* by Waldemar Janzen. *Biblica* 55: 98-100.

Cogan, Morton

1974   *Imperialism and Religion: Assyria, Judah and Israel in the Eighth and Seventh Centuries B.C.E.* Missoula: Scholars.

Cohen, Chayim,

1973   "The 'Widowed' City." *JANES* 5: 75-81.

Cohen, Mark E.

1970   *An Analysis of the Balag-Compositions to the God Enlil Copied in Babylon During the Seleucid Period.* Ann Arbor: University Microfilms.

1974   balag-*Compositions: Sumerian Lamentation Liturgies of the Second and First Millennium B. C.. SANE* 1/2. Malibu: Undena.

1981   *Sumerian Hymnology: The Eršemma.* HUCAS 2. Cincinnati: KTAV.

1988   *The Canonical Lamentations of Ancient Mesopotamia.* 2 vols. Potomac: Capital Decisions Limited. *(CLAM)*

Colie, Rosalie L.
1973   *The Resources of Kind: Genre Theory in the Renaissance.* Ed. Barbara K. Lewalski. Berkeley: University of California.

Cooke, G. A.
1937   *The Book of Ezekiel.* ICC. New York: Charles Scribner's Sons.

Cooper, Jerrold S.
1971   "New Cuneiform Parallels to the Song of Songs." *JBL* 90: 157-62.

1983   *The Curse of Agade.* Baltimore: Johns Hopkins University.

Cornill, D. C. H.
1905   *Das Buch Jeremia.* Leipzig: Tauchnitz.

Coxon, Peter W.
1986   "The 'List' Genre and Narrative Style in the Court Tales of Daniel." *JSOT* 35: 95-121.

Cross, Frank Moore
1973   *Canaanite Myth and Hebrew Epic.* Cambridge: Harvard University.

Dahood, Mitchell
1959   "The Value of Ugaritic for Textual Criticism." *Biblica* 40: 164-68.

1960   "Textual Problems in Isaia." *CBQ* 22: 400-9.

1970   *Psalms III: 101-150.* AB 17a. Garden City: Doubleday.

Delitzsch, Franz
1879   *Biblischer Commentar über den Propheten Jesaia.* Leipzig: Dörffling und Franke.

1887   *The Psalms.* 3 vols. Trans. David Eaton. London: Hodder and Stoughton.

Dobbs-Allsopp, F. W. (Chip)
1992   "*bat* GN in the Hebrew Bible." A paper presented to the Hebrew Scriptures and Cognate Literature section at the Annual Meeting of the SBL (Nov 21; San Francisco).

Dubrow, Heather

1982   *Genre*. London: Methuen.

Duhm, D. Bernh.

1892   *Das Buch Jesaia*. AT. Göttingen: Vandenhoeck & Ruprecht.

Eichrodt, Walther

1970   *Ezekiel*. OTL. Trans. C. Quinn. Philadelphia: Westminster.

Eissfeldt, Otto

1976   *The Old Testament: An Introduction*. Trans. P. R. Ackroyd. New York: Harper & Row.

Elliger, Karl

1951   *Das Buch der zwölf Kleinen Propheten 2*. ATD 25. Göttingen: Vandenhoeck & Ruprecht.

Everson, A. J.

1974   "The Days of Yahweh." *JBL* 93: 329-37.

Fitzgerald, Aloysius

1972   "The Mythological Background for the Presentation of Jerusalem as a Queen and False Worship as Adultery in the OT." *CBQ* 34: 403-16.

1975   "*BTWLT* and *BT* as Titles for Capital Cities." *CBQ* 37: 167-83.

Fohrer, Georg

1955   *Ezechiel*. HAT 13. Tübingen: J. C. B. Mohr.

Follis, Elaine R.

1987   "The Holy City as Daughter." Pp. 173-84 in *Directions in Biblical Hebrew Poetry*. Ed. Elaine R. Follis. *JSOT* Supplement 40. Sheffield: *JSOT*.

Fowler, Alastair

1982   *Kinds of Literature: An Introduction to the Theory of Genres and Modes*. Cambridge: Harvard University.

Frymer-Kensky, Tikva

1992   *In the Wake of the Goddesses*. New York: Free.

Gadd, C. J.

1963   "The Second Lamentation for Ur." Pp. 59-71 in *Hebrew and Semitic Studies Presented to Godfrey Rolles Driver*. Eds. D. W. Thomas and W. D. McHardy. Oxford: Clarendon.

Gesenius, Wilhelm

1910   *Gesenius' Hebrew Grammar.* 2d Eng. ed. Ed. Emil Kautzsch. Trans. A. E. Cowly. Oxford: Clarendon. (GKC)

Gerstenberger, E.
1962   "The Woe-Oracles of the Prophets." *JBL* 81: 249-63.

Giesebrecht, F.
1907   *Das Buch Jeremia.* HAT 2/1. Göttingen: Vandenhoeck & Ruprecht.

Gordis, R.
1974   *The Song of Songs and Lamentations.* 3d ed. New York.

Gottwald, Norman K.
1954   *Studies in the Book of Lamentations.* London: SCM.
1985   *The Hebrew Bible -- A Socio-Literary Introduction.* Philadelphia: Fortress.
1988   "Lamentations." Pp. 646-51 in *Harper's Bible Commentary.* Ed. James L. Mays. San Francisco: Harper & Row.

Gray, George B.
1956   *Isaiah I-XXVII.* ICC 10a. 4th reprint. Edinburgh: T. & T. Clark.

Green, Margaret W.
1975   "Eridu in Sumerian Literature." Ph. D. dissertation, University of Chicago.
1978   "The Eridu Lament." *JCS* 30: 127-67.
1984   "The Uruk Lament." *JAOS* 104: 253-79.

Greenberg, Moshe
1983   *Ezekiel 1-20.* AB 22. Garden City: Doubleday.

Grice, H. P.
1975   "Logic and Conversation." Pp. 41-58 in *Syntax and Semantics: Speech Acts.* Vol. 3. Eds. P. Cole and J. L. Morgan. New York: Academic Books.

Grimal, Pierre
1986   *The Dictionary of Classical Mythology.* Trans. A. R. Maxwell-Hyslop. New York: Blackwell.

Grossberg, Daniel
1989   *Centripetal and Centrifugal Structures in Biblical Poetry.* SBL Monograph Series no. 39. Atlanta: Scholars.

Gunkel, Hermann
1968   *Die Psalmen*. 5th ed. 1892. Gottingen: Vandenhoeck & Ruprecht.

Gwaltney, W. C., Jr.
1983   "The Biblical Book of Lamentations in the Context of Near Eastern Lament Literature." Pp. 191-211 in *Scripture in Context II: More Essays on the Comparative Method*. Eds. W. W. Hallo, J. C. Moyer, and L. G. Perdue. Winona Lake: Eisenbrauns.

Hallo, William W.
1968   "Individual Prayer in Sumerian: The Continuity of a Tradition." *JAOS* 88: 71-89.

1977   "New Moons and Sabbaths: A Case Study in the Contrastive Approach." *HUCA* 48: 1-18.

1980   "Biblical History in Its Near Eastern Setting: The Contextual Approach." Pp. 1-26 in *Scripture in Context: Essays on the Comparative Method*. Eds. C. D. Evans, W. W. Hallo, and J. B. White. Pittsburgh: Pickwick.

1990   "Compare and Contrast: The Contextual Approach to Biblical Literature." Pp. 1-30 in *The Bible in the Light of Cuneiform Literature*. Eds. W. W. Hallo, B. W. Jones, and G. L. Mattingly. Lewiston: Edwin Mellen.

Harrington, Daniel
1981   *Interpreting the Old Testament*. Wilmington: Michael Glazier.

Hayes, John H.
1968   "The Usage Against Foreign Nations in Ancient Israel." *JBL* 87: 81-92.

1988   *Amos: The Eighth-Century Prophet*. Nashville: Abingdon.

Heimpel, Wolfgang
1986   "The Sun at Night and the Doors of Heaven." *JCS* 38: 127-51.

Herandi, Paul
1972   *Beyond Genre*. Ithaca: Cornell University.

Herrmann, D. Johannes
1924   *Ezechiel*. KAT 11. Leipzig: A. Deicherische.

Hillers, Delbert R.

190   BIBLIOGRAPHY

1964   *Treaty-Curses and the Old Testament Prophets*. BibOr 16. Rome: Pontifical Biblical Institute.

1965   "A Convention in Hebrew Literature, the Reaction to Bad News." *ZAW* 77: 86-90.

1971   "'The Roads to Zion Mourn' (Lam 1:4)." *Perspective* 12: 121-33.

1972   *Lamentations*. AB 7a. Garden City: Doubleday.

1983   "*Hôy* and *Hôy*-Oracles: A Neglected Syntactic Aspect." Pp. 185-88 in *The Word of the Lord Shall Go Forth*. Eds. C. L. Meyers and M. O'Connor. Winona Lake: Eisenbrauns.

1984   *Micah*. Hermeneia. Philadelphia: Fortress.

1992   *Lamentations*. AB 7a. 2d rev. ed. Garden City: Doubleday.

Hirsch, E. D., Jr.

1967   *Validity in Interpretation*. New Haven: Yale University.

Holladay, William L.

1976   *The Architecture of Jeremiah 1-20*. Lewisburg: Bucknell University.

1986   *Jeremiah 1*. Hermeneia. Philadelphia: Fortress.

1989   *Jeremiah 2*. Hermeneia. Philadelphia: Fortress.

Hörig, Monika

1979   *Dea Syria*. AOAT 208. Neukirchen-Vluyn: Neukirchener.

Horst, Friedrich

1938   *Die Zwölf kleinen Propheten: Nahum bis Maleachi*. Tübingen: J. C. B. Mohr.

Huehnergard, John

1983   "Asseverative **la* and Hypothetical **lu/law* in Semitic." *JAOS* 103: 569-93.

Jacobsen, Thorkild

1941   Review of *Lamentation over the Destruction of Ur* by Samuel Noah Kramer. *AJSL* 58: 219-24.

1946   Review of *The Sumerians* by Samuel Noah Kramer. *JNES* 1: 147ff.

1970   *Toward the Image of Tammuz*. HSS 21. Ed. W. L. Moran. Cambridge: Harvard University.

1976   *Treasures of Darkness*. New Haven: Yale University.

1987   *The Harps That Once...*. New Haven: Yale University.

Jahnow, Hedwig
1923   *Das hebräische Leichenlied im Rahmen der Völkerdichtung*. BZAW 36. Giessen: A. Topelmann.

Janzen, Waldemar
1972   *Mourning Cry and War Oracle*. BZAW 125. Berlin: Walter de Gruyter.

Jensen, Joseph
1984   *Isaiah 1-39*. OTM 8. Wilmington: Michael Glazier.

Johnson, Bo
1985   "Form and Message in Lamentations." *ZAW* 97: 58-73.

Kaiser, Barbara Bakke
1987   "Poet as 'Female Impersonator': The Image of Daughter Zion as Speaker in Biblical Poems of Suffering." *Journal of Religion* 67: 164-82.

Kaiser, Otto
1974   *Isaiah 13-39*. OTL. Trans. R. A. Wilson. Philadelphia: Westminster.

1983   *Isaiah 1-12*. OTL. 2d ed. Trans. John Bowden. Philadelphia: Westminster.

Kang, Sa-Moon
1989   *Divine War in the Old Testament and in the Ancient Near East*. BZAW 177. Berlin: Walter de Gruyter.

Kramer, Samuel Noah
1940   *Lamentation over the Destruction of Ur*. AS 12. Chicago: University of Chicago.

1959   "Sumerian Literature and the Bible." *Analecta Biblica* 12: 185-204.

1960   *Two Elegies on a Pushkin Museum Tablet: A New Sumerian Literary Genre*. Moscow: Oriental Literature Publishing House.

1963   *The Sumerians: Their History, Culture, and Character*. Chicago: University of Chicago.

1967   "The Death of Ur-Nammu and his Descent to the Netherworld." *JCS* 21: 104-22.

1969a   "Lamentation over the Destruction of Ur." Pp. 455-63 in *ANET*[3].

1969b   "Lamentation over the Destruction over Sumer and Ur." Pp. 611-19 in *ANET*[3].

1969c   "Lamentation over the Destruction of Nippur." *EI* 9:
               89-93.
1972   *Sumerian Mythology*. Rev. ed. Reprint. 1961. Philadel-
               phia: University of Pennsylvania.
1982a   "BM 98396: A Sumerian Prototype of the Mater-
               Dolorosa." *EI* 16: 141*-146*.
1982b   "Lisin, the Weeping Mother Goddess: A New
               Sumerian Lament." Pp. 133-44 in *Zikir Sumim:
               Assyriological Studies Presented to F. R. Kraus*. Eds.
               G. van Driel, Th. J. H. Krispun, M. Stol, and K. R.
               Veenhof. Leiden: E. J. Brill.
1983   "The Weeping Goddess: Sumerian Prototypes of the
               Mater Dolorosa." *BA* 46: 69-80.
1991   "Lamentation over the Destruction of Nippur." *ASJ* 13:
               1-26.

Kraus, Hans-Joachim
1968   *Klagelieder* (Threni). BKAT. 3d ed. Neukirchen-
               Vluyn: Neukirchener.
1990   *Psalms 60-150*. Trans. Hilton C. Oswald. Minneapolis:
               Augsburg.

Krecher, Joachim
1966   *Sumerische Kultlyrik*. Wiesbaden: Otto Harrassowitz.
1984   "Klagelied." *RlA* 6: 1-6.

Kugel, James L.
1981   *The Idea of Biblical Poetry*. New Haven: Yale Univer-
               sity.

Kutscher, Raphael
1975   *Oh Angry Sea (a-ab-ba hu-luh-ha): The History of a
               Sumerian Congregational Lament*. YNER 6. New
               Haven: Yale University.

Lakoff, George
1987   *Women, Fire, and Dangerous Things*. Chicago:
               University of Chicago.

Lambert, W. G.
1965   "A New Look at the Babylonian Background of
               Genesis." *JTS* n.s. 16: 287-300.
1975   "The Historical Development of the Mesopotamian
               Pantheon: A Study in Sophisticated Polytheism." In

Unity and Diversity. Eds. H. Goedicke and J. J. M. Roberts. Baltimore: Johns Hopkins University.

1984   "A Neo-Babylonian Tammuz Lament." Pp. 211-15 in *Studies in Literature from the Ancient Near East... Dedicated to Samuel Noah Kramer.* Ed. Jack M. Sasson. New Haven: American Oriental Society.

Lanahan, William F.

1974   "The Speaking Voice in the Book of Lamentations." *JBL* 93: 41-49.

Loewenstamm, Samuel E.

1982   "Did the Goddess Anat Wear Side-Whiskers and a Beard?" *UF* 14: 119-23.

Long, Burke O.

1966   "The Divine Funeral Lament." *JBL* 75: 85-86.

Longman, Tremper, III

1985   "Form Criticism, Recent Developments in Genre Theory, and the Evangelical." *WTJ* 47: 46-67.

1987   *Literary Approaches to Biblical Interpretation.* Grand Rapids: Academic Books.

1991   *Fictional Akkadian Autobiography: A Generic and Comparative Study.* Winona Lake: Eisenbrauns.

Loretz, Oswald

1986   *Regenritual und Jahwetag im Joelbuch.* UBL 4. Ugaritisch-Biblische Literatur.

McCarter, P. Kyle, Jr.

1987   "Aspects of the Religion of the Israelite Monarchy: Biblical and Epigraphic Data." Pp. 137-55 in *Ancient Israelite Religion.* Eds. P. D. Miller, Jr., P. D. Hanson, and S. D. McBride. Philadelphia: Fortress.

McDaniel, Thomas F.

1968a   "The Alleged Sumerian Influence upon Lamentations." *VT* 18: 198-209.

1968b   "Philological Studies in Lamentations, I." *Biblica* 49: 27-53.

1968c   "Philological Studies in Lamentations, II." *Biblica* 49: 199-220.

McKane, William

1986   *Jeremiah.* ICC 11/1. Edinburgh: T. & T. Clark.

McKenzie, John L.

1968   *Second Isaiah.* AB 20. Garden City: Doubleday.

Machinist, Peter

1976   "Literature as Politics: The Tukulti-Ninurta Epic and the Bible." *CBQ* 38: 455-82.

Magoulias, Harry J., trans.

1975   *Decline and Fall of Byzantium to the Ottoman Turks.* Detroit: Wayne State University.

1984   *O City of Byzantium, Annals of Niketas Choniatës.* Detroit: Wayne State University.

Mann, Thomas W.

1977   *Divine Presence and Guidance in Israelite Traditions: The Typology of Exaltation.* Baltimore: Johns Hopkins University.

Mays, James L.

1976   *Micah.* OTL. Philadelphia: Westminster.

Michalowski, Piotr

1983   "History as Charter: Some Observations on the Sumerian King List." *JAOS* 103: 237-48.

1989   *The Lamentation over the Destruction of Sumer and Ur.* Winona Lake: Eisenbrauns.

1991   "Sailing to Babylon, Reading the Dark Side of the Moon" (to be published in the proceedings of the 1991 William Foxwell Albright Centennial Conference).

Miller, Patrick D., Jr.

1967   "El the Warrior." *HTR* 60: 411-31.

1968   "The Divine Council and the Prophetic Call to War." *VT* 18: 100-7.

1973   *The Divine Warrior in Early Israel.* Cambridge: Harvard University.

1986   "The Absence of the Goddess in Israelite Religion." *HAR* 10: 239-48.

Miller, Patrick D., Jr., and J. J. M. Roberts

1977   *The Hand of the Lord: A Reassessment of the 'Ark Narrative' of 1 Samuel.* Baltimore: Johns Hopkins University.

Müller, Hans-Peter

1978   "Gilgameschs Trauergesang um Enkidu und die Gattung der Totenklage." *ZA* 68: 233-50.

Nilsson, Martin P.

1945   *A History of Greek Religion.* 2d ed. Oxford: Clarendon.

North, Christopher R.
1964   *The Second Isaiah.* Oxford: Clarendon.

Nötscher, F.
1927   *Enlil in Sumer und Akkad.* Hannover: H. Lafaire.
1938   "Enlil." *RlA* 2: 382-87.

O'Connor, Michael
1980   *Hebrew Verse Structure.* Winona Lake: Eisenbrauns.

Oppenheim, A. Leo
1977   *Ancient Mesopotamia.* Rev. ed. Chicago: University of Chicago.

Oswalt, John
1986   *The Book of Isaiah: Chapters 1-39.* Grand Rapids: Wm. B. Eerdmans.

Overholt, Thomas W.
1988   "Jeremiah." Pp. 597-645 in *Harper's Bible Commentary.* Ed. James L. Mays. San Francisco: Harper & Row.

Parker, Simon
1979   "Some Methodological Principles in Ugaritic Philology." *MAARAV* 2/1: 7-41.

1989   *The Pre-Biblical Narrative Tradition.* SBLSBS 24. Atlanta: Scholars.

Paul, Shalom M.
1991   *Amos.* Hermeneia. Minneapolis: Fortress.

Pope, Marvin H.
1977   *Song of Songs.* AB 7c. Garden City: Doubleday.

Pritchard, James B., ed.
1969   *Ancient Near Eastern Texts Relating to the Old Testament.* 3d ed. Princeton: Princeton University. (*ANET*)

Provan, Iain
1991   *Lamentations.* NCBC. Grand Rapids: Wm. B. Eerdmans.

von Rad, Gerhard
1959   "The Origin of the Concept of the Day of Yahweh." *JSS* 4: 97-108.

Rawlinson, Sir Henry

1861-
1909			*The Cuneiform Inscriptions of Western Asia*. 2d ed. 5
			vols. London: British Museum.

Reiner, Erica
1974			"A Sumero-Akkadian Hymn of Nanâ." *JNES* 33: 221-
			36.

Renaud, R.
1987			*Michée, Sophonie, Nahum*. Paris: Librairie Lecoffre.

Roberts, J. J. M.
1976			"Myth versus History." *CBQ* 38: 1-13.
1977			"Nebuchadnezzar I's Elamite Crisis in Theological
			Prespective." Pp. 183-87 in *Essays on the Ancient
			Near East in Memory of Jacob Joel Finkelstein*. Ed.
			M. de J. Ellis. Hamden: Archon Books.
1982			"Form, Syntax, and Redaction in Isaiah 1:2-20."
			Princeton Seminary Bulletin n.s. 3/3: 293-306.
1985			"The Ancient Near Eastern Environment." Pp. 75-121
			in *The Hebrew Bible and Its Modern Interpreters*. Eds.
			D. A. Knight and G. M. Tucker. Chico: Scholars.
1988			"The Bible and the Literature of Antiquity: The
			Ancient Near East." Pp. 33-41 in *Harper's Bible
			Commentary*. Ed. James L. Mays. San Francisco:
			Harper & Row.
1991			*Nahum, Habakkuk, and Zephaniah*. OTL. Louisville:
			Westminster/John Knox.

Robinson, Theodore H.
1938			*Die Zwölf kleinen Propheten: Hosea bis Micha*.
			Tübingen: J. C. B. Mohr.

Rosmarin, Adena
1985			*The Power of Genre*. Minneapolis: University of
			Minnesota.

Rudolph, Wilhelm
1962			*Das Buch Ruth, Das Hobe Leid, Die Klagelieder*.
			KAT 17. 2d ed. Gütersloh: Mohn.
1968			*Jeremia*. HAT 12. 3d ed. Tübingen: Mohr.
1975			*Micha, Nahum, Habakuk, Zephanja*. KAT 13.
			Gütersloher: Mohn.

Saggs, H. W. F.

1978   *The Encounter with the Divine in Mesopotamia and Israel.* London: Athlone.

Salters, Robert B.
1986   "Lamentations 1.3: Light from the History of Exegesis." Pp. 74-89 in *A Word in Season.* Eds. J. D. Martin and P. R. Davies. *JSOT* Supplement 42. Sheffield: *JSOT.*

Sasson, Jack M.
1990   *Jonah.* AB 24b. Garden City: Doubleday.

Sawyer, John F. A.
1989   "Daughter of Zion and the Servant of the Lord in Isaiah: A Comparison." *JSOT* 44: 89-107.

Schmitt, John J.
1983   "The Gender of Ancient Israel." *JSOT* 26: 115-25.
1985   "The Motherhood of God and Zion as Mother." *RB* 92/4: 557-69.
1991   "The Virgin of Israel: Referent and Use of the Phrase in Amos and Jeremiah." *GBQ* 53: 365-87.

Sellin, D. Ernst
1929   *Das Zwölfprophetenbuch.* KAT 12/1. Leipzig: A. Deichertsche.
1930   *Das Zwölfprophetenbuch.* KAT 12/2. Leipzig: A. Deichertsche.

Seow, C. L.
1985   "A Textual Note on Lamentations 1:20." *CBQ* 47: 416-19.

Shawcross, John R.
1985   "Literary Revisionism and a Case for Genre." *Genre* 18: 413-34.

Smith, J. M. P. *et al*
1911   *Micah, Zephaniah, Nahum, Habakkuk, Obadiah and Joel.* ICC 14. New York: Charles Scribner's Sons.

Smith, Mark S.
1985   "Baal in the Land of Death." *UF* 17: 311-14.
1987a   "Jeremiah IX 9-- A Divine Lament." *VT* 37: 97-99.
1987b   "Death in Jeremiah, IX, 20." *UF* 19: 289-93.

Smith, Sidney
1944   *Isaiah Chapters XL--LV: Literary Criticism and History.* London: Oxford.

Steck, O. H.
    1989   "Zion als Gelande und Gestalt." *ZTK* 86/3: 261-81.
Stinespring, W. F.
    1965   "No Daughter of Zion, A Study of the Appositional
                    Genitive in Hebrew Grammar." *Encounter* 26: 133-41.
    1976   "Zion, Daughter of." P. 985 in *The Interpreter's
                    Dictionary of the Bible: Supplementary Volume*. Ed.
                    K. Crim. Nashville: Abingdon.
Stuart, Douglas K.
    1976   *Studies in Early Hebrew Meter*. HSM 13. Cambridge:
                    Havard Semitic Museum.
Stuhlmueller, Carroll
    1988   "Psalms." Pp. 433-94 in *Harper's Bible Commentary*.
                    Ed. James L. Mays. San Francisco: Harper & Row.
Tallgvist, K. L.
    1938   *Akkadische Götterepitheta. StOr* 7. Helsinki: Academic
                    Bookshop.
Talmon, Shemaryahu
    1978   "The 'Comparative Method' in Biblical Interpretation -
                    - Principles and Problems." Pp. 320-56 in *Göttigen
                    Congres Volume*. Supplements to *VT* no. 29. Leiden:
                    E. J. Brill.
Taylor, John R.
    1989   *Linguistic Categorization: Prototypes in Linguistic
                    Theory*. Oxford: Clarendon.
Tigay, Jeffrey H.
    1976   Review of *Lamentations* by Delbert R. Hillers. *JNES*
                    35: 140-43.
Todorov, Tzvetan
    1975   *The Fantastic: A Structural Approach to a Literary
                    Genre*. Ithaca: Cornell University.
    1990   *Genres in Discourse*. Cambridge: Cambridge University.
Toy, C. H.
    1899   *The Book of the Prophet Ezekiel*. Leipzig: J. C.
                    Hinrichs'sche.
Vanstiphout, H. L. J.
    1980   "The Death of an Era: The Great Mortality in the
                    Sumerian City Laments." Pp. 83-89 in *Death in Meso-*

potamian. XXVI Recontre assyriologique internationale. Ed. Bendt Alster. Copenhagen: Akademisk Forlag.

1983   "Een sumerische Stadtsklacht uit de oudbabylonische Periode: Turmenuna of de Nippurklacht." Pp. 330-41 in *Schrijvend Verleden*. Ed. K. R. Veenhof. Leiden: Ex Oriente Lux.

1986   "Some Thoughts on Genre in Mesopotamian Literature." Pp. 1-11 in *Keilschriftliche Literaturen. Ausgewählte Vorträge der XXXII. Rencontre Assyriologique Internationale. Münster, 8.-12.7.1985.* Eds. K. Hecker and W. Sommerfeld. Berlin: D. Reimer.

Van Zyl, A. H.
1960   *The Moabites*. Leiden: E. J. Brill.

Volk, K.
1989   *Die Balag-Komposition ÚRU ÀM-MA-IR-RA-BI.* Stuttgart: Franz Steiner.

Volz, D. Paul
1928   *Der Prophet Jeremia*. KAT 10. 2d ed. Leipzig: A. Deichertsche.

Waltke, Bruce K., and M. O'Connor
1990   *An Introduction to Biblical Hebrew Syntax*. Winona Lake: Eisenbrauns. (WOC)

Walton, John H.
1989   *Ancient Israelite Literature in its Cultural Context*. Grand Rapids: Zondervan.

Watson, W. G. E.
1984   *Classical Hebrew Poetry*. JSOT Supplement Series 26. Sheffield: JSOT.

Watts, John D. W.
1975   *The Books of Joel, Obadiah, Jonah, Nahum, Habakkuk and Zephaniah*. Cambridge: Cambridge University.

1985   *Isaiah 1-33*. WBC 24. Waco: Word Books.

Weippert, Manfred
1972   "'Heiliger Krieg' in Israel und Assyria." *ZAW* 460-93.

Weiser, Artur
1952   *Der Prophet Jeremia 1-25:13*. ATD 20. Göttingen: Vandenhoeck & Ruprecht.

1955   *Der Prophet Jeremia 25:14-52:34.* ATD 21. Göttingen: Vandenhoeck & Ruprecht.

1962   *Klagelieder.* ATD 16. Göttingen: Vandenhoeck & Ruprecht.

1962   *The Psalms.* OTL. Trans. H. Hartwell. Philadelphia: Westminster.

1985   *Die Propheten Hosea, Joel, Amos, Obadja, Jona, Micha.* ATD 24. Göttingen: Vandenhoeck & Ruprecht.

Weisstein, Ulrich

1973   *Comparative Literature and Literary Theory.* Bloomington: Indiana University.

Wellek, René, and Austen Warren

1956   *Theory of Literature.* 3d ed. New York: Harcourt, Brace, & World.

Westermann, Claus

1969   *Isaiah 40-66.* OTL. Trans. D. M. G. Stalker. Philadelphia: Westminster.

1990   *Die Klagelieder.* Neukirchen-Vluyn: Neukirchener.

Whitaker, Richard E.

1969   "A Formulaic Analysis of Ugaritic Poetry." An unpublished Ph. D. dissertation from Harvard University.

1972   *A Concordance of the Ugaritic Literature.* Cambridge: Harvard University.

Wildberger, Hans

1972   *Jesaja 1-12.* BKAT 10. Neukirchen-Vluyn: Neukirchener.

1978   *Jesaja 13-27.* BKAT 10. Neukirchen-Vluyn: Neukirchener.

1982   *Jesaja 28-39.* BKAT 10. Neukirchen-Vluyn: Neukirchener.

Willis, John T.

1986   "Lament Reversed -- Isaiah 1,21ff.." *ZAW* 98: 236-48.

Wilshire, Leland E.

1990   "Jerusalem as the 'Servant City' in Isaiah 40-66: Reflections in the Light of Further Study of the Cuneiform Tradition." Pp. 231-55 in *The Bible in the Light of Cuneiform Literature.* Eds. W. W. Hallo, B. W. Jones, and G. L. Mattingly. Lewiston: Edwin Mellen.

Winter, Urs
    1983   *Frau und Göttin*. OBO 53. Göttingen.

Wittgenstein, Ludwig
    1953   *Philosophical Investigations*. Trans. G. E. M. Anscombe. New York: Macmillan.

Wolff, Hans Walter
    1977   *Joel and Amos*. Hermeneia. Trans. Waldemar Janzen, S. Dean McBride, Jr., and Charles A. Muenchow. Philadelphia: Fortress.
    1990   *Micah*. Trans. Gary Stansell. Minneapolis: Augsburg.

Wright, G. Ernest
    1965   "The Nations in Hebrew Prophecy." *Encounter* 26: 225-37.

Yee, Gale A.
    1988   "The Anatomy of Biblical Parody: The Dirge Form in 2 Samuel 1 and Isaiah 14." *CBQ* 50: 565-86.

Zimmerli, Walther
    1979   *Ezekiel 1*. Hermeneia. Trans. Ronald E. Clements. Philadelphia: Fortress.
    1983   *Ezekiel 2*. Hermeneia. Trans. James D. Martin. Philadelphia: Fortress.

Index of Textual Citations

Hebrew Bible

Lamentations

Miscellaneous

Index of Authors

Finito di stampare il 29 gennaio 1993
Tipografia Poliglotta della Pontificia Università Gregoriana
Piazza della Pilotta, 4 – 00187 Roma